D1107499

# Grammar of
# The Art of Dancing

*Friedrich Albert Zorn.*

# GRAMMAR

OF THE

# ART OF DANCING

## THEORETICAL
### AND
## PRACTICAL

Lessons in the Arts of Dancing and
Dance Writing (Choregraphy)

With Drawings, Musical Examples, Choregraphic Symbols
and Special Music Scores

Translated from the
German of

## FRIEDRICH ALBERT ZORN

**Teacher of Dancing at the Imperial Russian
Richelieu-Gymnasium, Odessa,
and Member of the German
Academy of the Art
of Teaching
Dancing**

Edited by ALFONSO JOSEPHS SHEAFE
**Master of Dancing, Member A. N. A. M. of D.**

BURT FRANKLIN
New York, N. Y.

Published by BURT FRANKLIN
235 East 44th St., New York, N.Y. 10017
Originally Published: 1905
Reprinted: 1970
Printed in the U.S.A.

S.B.N. 39239
Library of Congress Card Catalog No.: 78-125637
Burt Franklin: Research and Source Works Series 543

*To the*
*American National Association of Masters of Dancing*
*of the United States and Canada*
*this work is*
*respectfully dedicated*

# Foreword

ORN'S GRAMMAR *is too well known to friends of the art which it describes to need any introduction; still an explanation of the particular differences between this and other editions and the reasons therefor may not be out of place.*

*The work was originally published under the direct patronage of the German Academy of the Art of Teaching Dancing, in Berlin, and the reader will find a very clear and concise history of the conception and execution of it in the Author's Preface which follows. The plan upon which the work has been written is made plain by the text itself.*

*The original edition was in three parts, consisting of the Grammar, which contained the text, the Atlas, which contained the illustrations, scores and choregraphy, and the "Notenheft," which contained the full score of the musical examples, arranged for violin and piano.*

*The arrangement of this translation is unique. It differs from the German edition in the fact that the Atlas has been incorporated in the text, by distributing the various cuts, diagrams, scores and choregraphic symbols at their proper places.*

*This plan will undoubtedly be more convenient for the reader than the original one with a separate Atlas. The editor has also compiled an alphabetical index of more than a thousand entries, which he believes will be of great service in rendering the book more practical as a work of reference. A glossary of foreign words and phrases used in dancing and music has also been compiled for this edition.*

---

*The Editor desires to acknowledge his gratitude for the able and conscientious assistance of his translator, Mr. Benjamin P. Coates of Boston, to whose untiring exertion and enthusiastic coöperation the accuracy of this edition is largely due. The assistance of so capable a translator is seldom obtainable and is greatly appreciated.*

*At the Convention of the American National Association of Masters of Dancing held at Columbus, Ohio, June 12–17, 1905, the dedication of this edition of the Grammar was accepted and the work adopted as the standard of authority. The resolution also strongly recommends the book as a text-book for students and teachers.*

*The Appendix, which relates to deportment, has been purposely omitted for the reason that, while it is the duty of teachers of dancing to pay some attention to that subject in the course of their instruction, it does not in itself, technically, form a part of the art of dancing.*

*Again, rules of deportment are largely local in their application and of too transient a nature to be of authority after a lapse of twenty years. Social customs are, for the most part, creatures of fashion, and fashion is too fickle a goddess to submit to the tyranny of settled rules.*

*Herr Zorn himself expresses the belief that persons who contemplate teaching dancing will get more practical ideas regarding deportment from their experience as teachers than it would be possible to obtain from any book.*

*And now having set forth the principal points of this edition and the fact that it has been prepared to supply a great and increasing demand, the Editor wishes, in conclusion, to register the hope that the movement toward abandoning the use of French technical terms will be given up.*

*These terms now form the only common ground upon which the dancing profession of the world can meet, and to discontinue them would be to indefinitely postpone the date of a possible Universal Academy. Let us not only learn these terms which have acquired such important technical significance, but let us use them. Of course there is no call for a pedantic display of them in teaching social dances, and such a use of them would be in poor taste, but it would be a distorted allegiance to the mother tongue to so far over-look our manifest advantages as to insist upon the substitution of our own language for terms that have for centuries been accepted without cavil by other nations who do not speak French. In truth, what has the English speaking dancing world done for the art that entitles it to make so radical a change? Would it not be more logical to first determine the true meaning of the expressions which we seek to discontinue? The Editor, for one, thinks so, and that should his colleagues closely study the works of the foreign masters, they would agree with him.*

*Let us rather seek to increase the common bonds of the profession than endeavour to destroy them, for by that method, and by no other, can dancing attain that rank among the arts beautiful to which it is so certainly entitled.*

THE EDITOR

*Brookline Massachusetts*
*October 1905*

# Author's Preface

TO the average reader, the following pages will probably reveal a vast amount of research and labour, but the specialist in the subject should not, merely because the names, definitions and principles involved are treated in a different manner from what is usual, allow that fact to prejudice him or cause him to cast the work aside as of no value. Let him rather give it a fair and conscientious examination, and undoubtedly much that may at first glance appear to be fanciful will be satisfactorily demonstrated to be true.

In preparing this work, the author has carefully considered all probable objections, has scrupulously examined all obtainable authorities upon dancing, many of which were in foreign languages, and has made many journeys, regardless of expense, in order to consult with noted specialists.

In 1885 he held a personal conference with ballet-master P. Taglioni in Berlin, and he has for many years been in correspondence with that great teacher and ballet-master, Arthur de St. Léon; and now after fifty years of experience he has received the favourable judgment of Herr A. Freising, teacher of dancing at the Royal Academy in Berlin, upon the result of his studies as set forth in this book.

The Grammar is highly commended in the report of the members of the Royal Academy, May 24–25, 1885, and the author has been thereby induced to prepare a revised and enlarged edition of the work, in which he has received the valuable assistance of Herr A. Freising, president, and of Herr Otto Stoige, ballet-master and teacher of dancing at the University of Koenigsburg. He takes this opportunity to tender to those gentlemen his heartfelt gratitude. Also, to Herr Bernhard Klemm of Leipsic, the author offers his warmest thanks for valuable advice and the kind permission to quote from his "Catechism."

_____

The Author earnestly recommends this Preface to the attention of readers, for it contains a key to the Grammar, without which a proper understanding of the subject cannot be gained.

Notwithstanding the favourable criticism of specialists, the author is well aware that the work is still incomplete, and he will gratefully receive any reasonable suggestions and incorporate them in a future edition, should he be favoured by a demand for one. He believes, however, that the present work will be found quite satisfactory to those who study it carefully.

Those estimable choregraphs, Sultzer, Roller, Carlo Blasis, Arthur de St. Léon, and Bernhard Klemm express the hope that their system, the one most generally adopted by lovers of the art, might be improved and enlarged, thus elevating an art which is worthy, æsthetically, to stand in the first rank in matters of taste. To bring about such a result has ever been the ideal of the author.

Those great masters who have preceded us have accomplished much with the means at their disposal, and have left us far richer material than they found, but it devolves upon us who have had the good fortune to inherit the fruits of their labours to improve that inheritance, that our legacy to posterity may be greater still.

It would indeed be a false admiration that would deter us from advancing along the paths which have been left open to us, and the consideration that the publication of our experiences and discoveries might injure our personal advantages should be cast aside as unworthy of our attention. Let us rather emulate the example of our predecessors and direct our endeavours to the improvement of our art for the benefit of all who are interested.

Dancing is incontestably one of the fine arts, and not the least of them. It borrows from each of the others that which is most beautiful and blends all into a still more lovely unity. It presents, in vivid form, the highest ideals of the sculptor and the painter, by means of the most graceful attitudes and movements of the human body under the inspiring influence of music; and the ballet, which has been brought to so high a point of perfection, is an indisputable evidence of its artistic possibilities and value.

There is now lacking only a proper system of describing dances, by which they may be perpetuated and handed down to posterity — a script analogous to that by which the compositions of Mozart, Haydn, Beethoven, Meyerbeer, Wagner and Rubenstein have been preserved. Where, let us ask, would music stand .to-day without its script?

Perhaps that result which has always beckoned to the author like a good genius, lending him strength and courage when he has been cast down, may soon be accomplished, and he may yet live to see examples of his ideas upon the subject published in practical form.

The author considers his system of script appropriate for the representation of any dance or ballet, and that any such composition, so written, would at least be sufficiently intelligible to students of the "Grammar" for them to determine whether they had acquired sufficient skill to execute it. The author would feel amply compensated for his life's work, were his system to be accepted, and he is confident that the application of his ideas would be of signal benefit to the art.

In preparing this "Grammar" the author has been many times most forcibly reminded of the imperative need of an academy of the art of dancing to which questions of doubtful authority might be submitted and final decisions as to the best methods and solutions be made.

These findings might be promulgated through the agency of a journal or other medium, which should circulate among interested persons, and which would in a large measure overcome the influence and wanton speculations of those who masquerade as teachers, but who have no actual knowledge of the art of dancing.

If the unworthy designs and demoralizing influence of such persons could be counteracted, the dancing profession would have advanced a great step toward that position in the public esteem to which it is entitled.

In a copy of the German magazine "Über Land und Meer," which found its way to the author in Russia, he accidentally read of the formation of the German Academy of the Art of Teaching Dancing in Berlin, and, having investigated the matter, he had the great honour and pleasure of being elected a member.

He has much for which to thank that society, and association with its different members has been of immense practical benefit to him. Their kindly words and friendly interest have added greatly to his strength and confidence, and the members of the Academy have not only urged but aided him to complete this work at as early a date as possible.

At the annual meeting of the Academy, 29th and 30th May, 1887, it was resolved that each member of the association should procure a copy of the "Grammar" and after a careful and thorough examination submit a written report of his findings to the Academy, from which symposium such suggestions or additions as might be thought beneficial should be embodied in an Appendix, or if of sufficient importance to warrant it, in another edition of the "Grammar." The combined endeavours of so many competent masters could hardly fail to greatly enhance the technical value of the work.

The author has used the term *Choregraphy* and not *Choreography* for the reason that the former word is given in the Dictionary of Noël and Chapsal, published in 1857, which contains the most reliable information respecting dance terms. The same form of the word was used by two of the most distinguished of our recent choregraphs, Carlo Blasis and Arthur de St. Léon.

The term "grammar," which is ordinarily applied to a system of language, has been selected as a fit title for this work because of the analogy of the author's system with the system of teaching language.

The term "catechism" was originally applied to religious instruction in the form of questions and answers, but the recent application of the term to other than religious subjects has changed its significance and it is now applied to that form of instruction regardless of its subject.

This "Grammar" has been put forth with the object and hope of elevating and extending the scientific art of dancing, and to accomplish that purpose the author has exercised his utmost strength and all of his faculties.

He will consider himself not only fortunate but amply rewarded for the fifty years of labour which it has cost him, if this book meets with a favourable reception and recognition; for such will be an indication that the goal toward which he has striven so earnestly and so long has not only been discovered but in some small measure approached.

FRIEDRICH ALBERT ZORN.

ODESSA, 1887.

# Contents

Raising-Marching Steps (*Pas Marchés Elevés*) — The Steps upon the Points (*Pas sur les Pointes*) — Running Steps (*Pas de Course*) — Courante Step (*Temps de Courante*) — Changements of the Legs or Feet (*Changements de Jambes ou Pieds*) — Escaping Syllables (*Temps Echappés*) — Falling Syllables (*Temps Tombés*) — Spreading Syllables (*Temps Ecartés*) — Collecting Step or Syllable (*Pas ou Temps Assemblé*) — Throwing Steps (*Pas Jetés*) — Scissor Syllable and Scissor Step (*Temps et Pas de Sissonne ou Ciseaux*) — Double Scissor Step or Syllable (*Pas ou Temps de Sissonne Double*) — Hunting or Chasing Steps (*Pas Chassés*) — Gliding Steps (*Pas Glissés* — *Glissades*) — Gliding Half-Steps (*Demi-Glissés*) — Whip Syllables (*Temps Fouettés*) — Cutting Steps (*Pas Coupés*) — Cutting Half-Steps (*Demi-Coupés*) — Tossing Steps (*Pas Ballotés*) — Stuffing Steps (*Pas de Bourrée*) — Stretched or Zephyr Steps (*Pas Tendus ou Pas de Zéphire*) — Basque Steps (*Pas de Basque*) — Ball Steps (*Pas Ballonnés*) — Ball Syllables (*Temps Ballonnés*) — Twisting Steps (*Pas Tortillés*) — Body Turns (*Tours de Corps*) — Turn of the Trunk or Rump (*Tour de Torse*) — Choregraphy of Turning — Occupation of the Free Leg in Turning — Turns in the Air (*Tours en l'Air*) — The Pirouette (*La Pirouette*) — Thigh-Beating Syllables (*Temps de Cuisse*) — The Beating Steps (*Les Pas Battus*) — Changement of the Legs (*Changements de Jambes*) — Crossed Jump (*Capriole ou Entrechat*) — Half Counter-Beating (*Demi-Contretemps*) — Whole Counter-Beating (*Contretemps Entier*) — Broken Syllables and Steps (*Temps et Pas Brisés*) — Pigeon-Wing Steps (*Ailes de Pigeon* — *Pistolets*).

Theory of the Quadrille Positions — The First Person in a Quadrille — Figure and Strophe or Couplet — Division of Time — Measure — Signal (*Ritournelle*) — Prelude — Original Steps — The French Contra-Dance (*La Contredanse Française*) — Pantalon — L'Eté — La Poule — La Trénis — Les Trois Crochets ou La Coquille — La Pastourelle — Les Grâces — La Finale — La Rose — Pas de Galop — Moulinet des Dames — Grandes Rondes — Rondes Opposées — La Guirlande — The Polonaise (*La Polonaise*).

Minuet of the Queen (*Menuet de la Reine*) — Minuet of the Court (*Menuet de la Cour*) — Minuet Steps (*Pas de Menuet*) — Execution of the Minuet of the Court.

## CHAPTER XV

## CHAPTER XVI

## CHAPTER XVII

# Introduction

# Introduction

TO thoroughly understand an art, it is necessary to learn its source and to follow its development to the highest possible and attainable point of perfection; thereby reaching the capability of judging what is still to be accomplished and the best method of going about it.

The source of dancing lies in the nature of mankind. If in good humour, one moves quickly, and if the feeling is more pronounced the movements are correspondingly heightened and one jumps and raises himself involuntarily. This is natural dancing; it is to be found in all zones, at all times and among all nations.

To do away with dancing entirely, as is the wish of some persons, it would be necessary to change human nature.

It is quite comprehensible that these natural expressions of pleasure or spiritual excitement vary in accordance with the temperament of the individual, and that he who has the greatest nobility of mind will present the most noble expressions. Expressions of joy are truer mirrors of the mind than those of the more severe emotions.

As mankind began to form societies, to divide into nations, and to follow different courses of civilization, there grew up different dances, dependent upon and indicative of national characteristics; and when these nations changed place, occupation, political institutions, etc., their dances were correspondingly affected. This same process is operative to-day, and the statement which is made by many persons, that the character and civilization of a given man, or indeed of an entire nation, may be known by his or its dancing, is not all incorrect.

It is not the purpose of this work to record the history of the dance from ancient to modern times, for that has been most worthily accomplished by such writers as Albert Czerwinski, in his " History of the Art of Dancing," Rudolph Voss, in " The Dance and its History," and Franz M. Bahlme, in his "History of Dancing in Germany." There are many others who might be mentioned, but even these are seldom read.

3

Dancing, like every other art, has its childhood, its blossom time, its climax and its decay; but these periods are more uncertain than those of other arts, because of the lack of a generally accepted and efficient system of describing the accomplishments of the masters.

Without such a script even the works of our present generation cannot be preserved for posterity.

By means of the script of music we have retained the compositions of the early and middle ages and are enabled to reproduce, note by note, the masterpieces of the last three centuries; but what is left us of the works of the choregraphs of old — of the last century — even of the last few decades? Only a few programs and incomplete descriptions which serve rather to accentuate the extent of our loss than to aid us in reconstructing the works of which they treat.

If a ballet-master, even to-day, desires to produce the composition of another, there is only one way to do so. He must go where it is executed. And if he desires to reproduce one of his own that was presented five years before, he has nearly the same difficulty as at the original production, for the dancers are not the same. He must show them every step, because it is impossible to supply them with written parts with which they could practice alone.

In 1852, A. de St. Léon, first dancer and ballet-master at the Grand Opera in Paris, published the first numbers of his "Stenochoregraphy," employing with rare discrimination all the facilities and influence of his position, and thus opening the way to elevating the art in a most signal manner. His Majesty the Emperor Nicholas of Russia found opportunity, notwithstanding the serious duties of his kingly calling, to read the first part of the work, and by accepting its dedication proved conclusively that he appreciated the value of the invention.

It is greatly to be regretted that that gifted artist and author has been too soon taken from us, but he left us splendid material for perfecting the system set forth in his letters and published works.

An Academy of the Art of Dancing was founded in Paris by Louis XIV, in 1661, and was liberally endowed by that magnificent monarch. Little remains of the institution, however, save the names of its then thirteen members.

The German Academy of the Art of Teaching Dancing was founded in 1873 by several very thoroughly educated dancing masters, and if, as we most sincerely hope, that association succeeds in its objects, it will not be the first time that small enterprises with modest means have eventually accomplished great things.

There is a pressing need of firmly established rules, by means of which the art may be edified, and in formulating such precepts the members of the new Academy will, doubtless, strive to merit the approval and esteem of all who are interested in the dance.

It is certain that the purpose is commendable, and that the new Academy is composed of sincere and able teachers. The following names are a sure guarantee of the character of the Academy: A. Freising, Teacher of Dancing at the Royal University in Berlin, President; Otto Stoige, Ballet-Master in Koenigsburg in Prussia; Knoll, Senior, Ballet-Master in Hamburg; Bernardelli, Teacher of Dancing at the University of Leipsic, and many others of prominence.

Without governmental recognition and the establishment of the Academy as a board of examiners for those persons who desire to teach dancing, the association can never attain to sufficient authority to restrain unworthy persons from teaching.

Inasmuch as the Academy has submitted this work to a most rigid examination and has adopted it as the standard for teaching (May 25, 1885), it is unnecessary to state that examinations upon the theory of dancing will be based upon the principles laid down therein.

# *Dancing as a Branch of Education*

The importance of dancing as a factor in education is almost universally conceded, notwithstanding that many persons of unquestionable learning and good intention unhesitatingly condemn it and seek to substitute gymnastics in its place.

It is true that gymnastics develop the physical powers, increase courage and endurance, improve health and render one more robust, but they tend toward coarseness and impress one with a certain recklessness and lack of delicacy, unless taught by persons who are properly informed as to the true art of movement.

It would, however, be impossible to teach dancing by means of gymnastics, or gymnastics by means of dancing, although their combination is quite practicable and useful. Schiller says, "To couple the strong with the delicate makes an agreeable combination."

Still, those who are opposed to dancing are not wholly wrong, for if we contemplate the salon and the theatrical dances of to-day, we are compelled to admit that, with few exceptions, we find them objectionable to good taste. We have retained but little of that elegant deportment and that exquisite delicacy which marked the dances of the 18th century, and we frequently witness upon our stage indecencies of a most flagrant character, which are so earnestly applauded by the majority of the spectators that the "artists" are led to believe that they have done something highly commendable; while the less scrupulous managers and directors encourage such exhibitions on account of the returns which they guarantee.

The same state of affairs exists in the dance-halls, for custom has so shortened the vision of the majority that even the least criticism of this nature is astonishing to them, true though it is.

One has but to examine in an unbiased manner most of our round dances, noting the nonsensical running and racing therein, and the still more objectionable hugging which is not only possible but actually *à la mode* in certain places, to realize why it is that clergymen, physicians, parents, and conscientious educators and governesses disapprove of so degenerate a style.

The Lanciers Quadrille came into favor in 1856, and was generally hailed as a step toward better taste, but the supposition has not been confirmed by experience, for that beautiful dance has been long since banished from our orders and we dance worse, if possible, than before its introduction.

Dancing teachers there are and always have been who realize the dignity and responsibility of their profession, and who, in so far as possible, resolutely oppose objectionable taste; but the great majority practice for a livelihood and dare not struggle too persistently against common customs lest such resistance react upon their schools, and pupils who might otherwise be theirs bestow their patronage upon masters who are less severe. Unfortunately, there are teachers who lend themselves readily to every caprice of custom or fashion that they may line their pockets, regardless of its ethical or æsthetic value or result.

Proper dancing gives one that grace which should form a part of all our movements, and which, although advantageous to all, is absolutely essential to those who are obliged to go through the world unaided.

Upon meeting a person for the first time we are involuntarily impressed by his presence and manners, and as there is frequently neither opportunity nor time to become more intimately or fully acquainted, our treatment of him must necessarily be gauged by the impression thus obtained.

First impressions, therefore, are never of indifference, whether favourable or otherwise.

Carefully kept and tasteful clothing, cleanliness and good manners, and above all, lack of affectation or conceit, never fail to create good impressions, but an elegant carriage and a pleasing appearance should neither be regarded as the only valuable traits, nor should they be held to compensate for vice or ignorance; for indeed, unless they be in harmony with nobility of thought and action, they can but form a mask that will, sooner or later, be torn away and disclose the real person in his true ugliness.

Modern society demands of all who enter it, a certain attention to appearance and behaviour, which if neglected reacts in a most serious manner upon the delinquent, often destroying what might, with such slight concessions as it demands, be a most successful career, and dancing and deportment are as important accomplishments for girls as for boys.

That grace which comes from dancing, however, does not depend solely upon the good fortune of finding a competent and conscientious teacher, for unless one possesses a natural aptitude or talent he can never accomplish more than commonplace results.

There are in most places worthy dancing teachers, but it is often hard to distinguish them from those of lesser merit, as they usually refrain from thrusting themselves into prominence, and instead of glorifying their achievements by means of disparaging others, wait modestly until their services are demanded.

Still there are places where, although there are many persons to whom instruction would be welcome, there is no teacher of dancing, and for these persons there is nothing better than the books — many of which are of value — which have been carefully written upon the subject.

It is of course entirely impossible to write in such a manner as to equal the effects of proper vivid instruction, but where that is unobtainable, written instruction is better than none.

No system of written instruction is so effective or appropriate as choregraphy, and the time required to understand the script is far from wasted. It rests with that art alone to elevate dancing to a fitting place among the arts beautiful, for by that, and that alone, is it possible to so describe the dance as to withstand criticism.

If, therefore, we can promulgate a system containing proper rules for position and movement, and physical and æsthetic development, such as will receive the approval of the critics, it is certain that we shall be aided by the best masters, whose coöperation and backing will insure our ultimate success.

We already have the works of Blasis, St. Léon and Klemm, which contain the quintessence of previous authority, but it appears that these are not given that study which they deserve.

It should never suffice that a teacher of dancing earn a living, nor that a ballet-master please the public; each should strive to elevate his art and raise its morals.

Dancing is of no small importance viewed from a hygienic standpoint. Indeed, the exercise it provides is of peculiar physical benefit, particularly for the gentler sex.

This does not necessarily refer to the style of dancing now in vogue, but rather to the method known as "pedal calisthenics," which contains those strengthening and developing exercises that produce greater physical strength without destroying feminine grace.

Those physicians who forbid young persons to dance have usually a clearer understanding of the abuse than of the truly useful aspect of the exercise. It is only to be expected that if persons who are still growing and weakly avoid all exertion during the year and then dance immoderately a whole evening, and, becoming overheated, indulge freely in cold drinks and ices, they will become ill. If, however, they limit their dancing to a regular attendance at a reliable and worthy dancing-school, the exercise cannot fail to be beneficial.

# The Classification of Dances

Dancing is generally divided into two grand divisions, namely, social and theatrical, or salon and show dances. The social or salon dance, having been devised solely for social pleasure, is of such a nature that persons who do not make dancing a profession may acquire a knowledge of it.

Nearly every country possesses its peculiar dances, of which the French Minuet and Contra-dance may be considered the greatest, for they are replete with grace and modesty.

The "waltz position" in the so-called round dances should be conscientiously regarded.

It is to be regretted that the round dances, such as the Waltz, Galop, and Polka, are generally preferred to others, for they do not merit the distinction, from the standpoint either of art or of grace. This liking for that form of dancing is quite unaccountable, but as it would be futile for the dancing profession to attempt to stem the tide of public favour, it has been obliged to overcome its artistic scruples and teach what it must dislike.

Impartially considered, the so-called "waltz position" is wholly objectionable, as it places the lady absolutely within the power of her partner. Such an attitude would never be tolerated beyond the duration of the music of the dance.

After the Minuet, the Mazurka, which is the national dance of Poland, may be properly called the queen of social dances, for it affords every gentleman opportunity to display his peculiar talents and grace in such a manner as not to overexert himself; at the same time permitting the ladies to exhibit the most perfect grace. Again, the figure may be as widely varied as that of the Cotillion, thus offering never-ending charm and novelty.

Column and line dances are now out of style, although they afford much pleasure and make an agreeable change. In that class we have Ecossaise, Triolet, Tempête, Anglaise, and others. All of them belong to the class of "social choir dances," which is still further divisible into the figure and the round dances. Bernhard Klemm, in his "Catechism," gives the more minute division into dances of periodical and of full figure which is quite logical.

There are besides the "social choir dances," certain "social show dances" which may be danced by either one, two or four persons. It is true that these are usually representative of the manners and customs of certain peoples, but as they arise from and form a part of the national life which they typify, they are not technically "show" or "theatrical" dances.

This class contains such dances as the Gavotte, Cancan, Cachucha, Gitana, Fandango, Tyrolienne, Styrian, Hungarian, Cossack, Cracovienne, Russian, and others too numerous to mention. Any of these may, however, be raised to the class of "theatrical" dances if properly arranged to accord with stage requirements and executed with sufficient skill.

The second division comprises all those dances which are executed by professional dancers upon the stage, and which are, properly, Theatre dances. They are divided into five degrees.

Those of the lowest degree are styled "Grotesque." Their character is unsteady or, perhaps better, of an adventurous nature. Their movements are often imposing, but demand skill rather than gracefulness.

Those of the second degree are called "Comic," and are less unsteady than those of the first. They generally represent the customs, pastimes, or romances of the lower classes.

The third degree is known technically as "Demi-caractère." They exemplify affairs of ordinary life by representing upon the comic stage a love-story or a plot in which the characters are from the common people. This class is replete with grace and elegance.

The fourth degree contains what are known as the "Serious" dances. They represent such characters as are found upon the tragic stage. The highest possible degree of skill and elegance is displayed in these dances. They include solos, *pas de deux*, *pas de trois*, etc., and represent emotions or ideas. They demand the exercise of the entire art of position and movement.

The fifth degree is of a still higher order, representing entire tragedies. These dances are known as "Pantomimic," and are so divided into acts as to convey the entire idea without the agency of words. Such dances may be properly termed "Ballets," and our century has been especially rich in that class. The ladies have particularly excelled in this degree.

Most prominent among the artists of this class we may mention Carmargo, Marie Taglioni (mother and daughter), Fanny Ellsler, Fanny Cerito, Carlotta Grisi, Nadeschda Bogdanowa, and Messrs. Pecour, Beauchamp, Didelot, Noverre, Vestris (father and son), Blasis, Perrot, Bournonville, Philip and Paul Taglioni, A. de St. Léon, Petitpas, Lepitre, Laucherry, and Manzotti.

The amounts expended in producing a single ballet at this time are astounding, and in them so much elaboration and ingenuity is called into play that the spectator may easily imagine himself transported to fairyland, and he awakens to reality only at the conclusion, as from a beautiful dream.

It is much to be deplored that up to this time there has been no adequate or satisfactory script, by means of which these magnificent masterpieces might be preserved for future generations, and it is the object of this "Grammar" to supply that demand; the complete realization of which will yet necessarily require much time and labour.

The acquisition of such a script would enable ballet-masters to so describe the single parts — and indeed the entire compositions — that they could be read as easily as one reads a sheet of music. Thus it would be possible not only to communicate their achievements to persons at a distance, but also to transmit them in intelligible form to posterity.

# Grammar

# Chapter I

## METHOD

THE first condition of success or of accomplishment in science or in art is a method based upon the natural principles of the subject and so adjusted to the capabilities of the student as to lead from the base to the acme of perfection, without unnecessary waste of time.

Without such a method or system, and without the necessary specific names for even the most minute details and objects, progress in the Art of Dancing will be rendered well nigh impossible, on account of the numberless difficulties and apparent contradictions that must naturally arise.

Such a system should be devised as will lead the student easily and gradually from the simpler to the more complicated portions in such a manner as to enable him not only to comprehend but to demonstrate as he goes. A competent teacher is not often at a loss to thoroughly communicate his ideas.

The first necessity is, therefore, what we may term a Grammar of the Art of Dancing which shall contain a system analagous to those employed in teaching language or drawing, and which shall so clearly define the principles of the dance, that, while it does not exceed the comprehension of a child, it shall be none the less valuable and useful to teachers and to professional dancers.

A grammar of this sort will quickly be appreciated by educators and by dancers, and, indeed, by the general public, as a means of promoting correct principles, and at the same time of leading to an understanding of the true objects of conscientious dancing-masters and of overcoming the present degradation of dancing in society and upon the stage. May it not also, perhaps, induce careless and indifferent teachers to work more diligently for their own improvement, by raising the standard of professional requirement through the enlightenment of the public?

From the foregoing one may plainly discern the object of the author and his ideal of the nature of a Grammar of Dancing. Time and experience alone can determine the degree of success with which he has performed his task.

# GRAMMAR

1. Dancing is the expression of pleasure or of other sentiments by means of prescribed movements, which are regulated by music, either imagined or expressed.

2. Its factors are Position, Movement, Figure and Measure.

3. Before or after a movement, a Position may be either correct or incorrect.

4. Transition from one position to another is accomplished by means of Movements which are either simple or compound.

5. The lines described upon the floor by the dancers constitute the Figure.

6. The division of the movements into periods of equal duration to correspond with the music is called Measure.

7. To compare dancing to language, the positions correspond to vowels; simple movements to consonants; compound movements to syllables; steps to words; enchainments to phrases or sentences; and the combinations of enchainments to paragraphs.

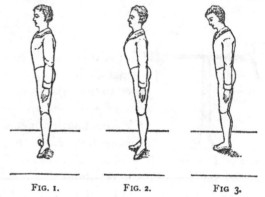

FIG. I.          FIG. 2.          FIG 3.

Simple figures correspond to verses, compound figures to stanzas, and the connection of compound figures or strophes, as in a Quadrille, to an entire poem.

# CARRIAGE

8. Before dealing with the various positions we must refer to the carriage of the body, for good carriage is the first essential to a dancer. The head must be held straight, and the eyes directed neither up or down, but to the face of the person opposite, the neck perpendicular, the chest expanded and thrust forward, the shoulders back and down, the abdomen drawn in, the legs turned outward from the toes, the knees stretched, and the arms hanging naturally at the sides [Fig. 1].

Hold the fingers as shown in Fig. 4 and touch the side line of the leg with the thumb and first and second fingers. It is

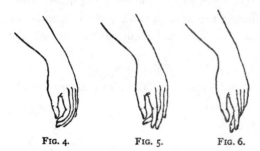

FIG. 4.          FIG. 5.          FIG. 6.

as incorrect to force the position, as in Fig. 2, as it is to neglect it, as in Fig. 3. The correctness of the position may be determined by the position of the arms: if proper, the arms hang naturally in such a way that the fingers touch the middle of the sides of the legs. If incorrect, the hands will hang either before or behind that point.

9. Three positions of the hand and fingers have been proposed [Figs. 4, 5 and 6]. All are good, according to the circle of the arms.

10. The curvature of the arm should correspond to an arc of a regular circle, from the shoulder to the tip of the little finger. The more fully the arm is stretched the more the fingers must be stretched. In Fig. 7 the little finger is bended properly; in Fig. 8 too much; and in Fig. 9 not enough.

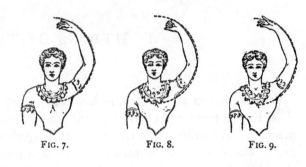

FIG. 7.          FIG. 8.          FIG. 9.

There is a mathematical correctness of beauty, and perception thereof is as keen a sense as musical perception. A circle not exactly round is as much an offence to the eye as a false chord or note is to the ear. Taste can be so far debased as to accustom itself to improper positions, but it is the object of art to enable one to perceive the difference and to distinguish the correct from the incorrect.

The positions and movements of the arms are given in §§ 268 and 320.

# Chapter II

## POSITIONS OF THE FEET

A S the modern art of dancing has been largely evolved and fostered in France, the French terms and expressions are more or less used in all countries where dancing is practiced; and while in this Grammar the English terms will be employed wherever practicable, the French equivalents are given where they differ from the English, and teachers should in all cases acquire a knowledge of them.

### Simple Positions

**11.** There are generally accepted five principal positions of the legs. These are subject to numberless variations, which are still further qualified, as in the sole, ball, point, heel and flowing positions which follow.

### Sole Positions

**12.** When the entire base of the foot touches the floor, it is in sole position.

**13.** First Position. In the 1st position the heels are brought firmly together, the points turned strongly outward and the knees held close together. This position is the one most commonly used [Fig. 10].

**14.** Second Position. In the 2d position the foot is extended directly to the side as far as possible without raising the sole from the floor or transferring the centre of gravity [Fig. 11]. If the foot corresponds to the ideal proportion, the width of the separation in this position — that is, the distance between the heels — will be about the length of the foot, which is said to be the norm of width in the open positions. It may be observed that as the supporting

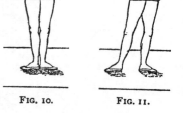

FIG. 10.          FIG. 11.

18

foot has not yet moved, it is still in 1st position. If both feet are carried to 2d position, the distance is doubled [Fig. 12]. In walking or dancing sidewise the 2d position comes into use, and the length of a common step to the side is, therefore, the length of one of the feet, in accordance with the rule above mentioned.

15. **Third Position.** There are two phases of the 3d position. If, for example, one places the right foot in 3d position forward (anterior) its heel touches the inner middle of the left [Fig. 13]; but if the same foot be placed in 3d position behind (posterior), its inner middle (instep) touches the heel of the left foot, as in Fig. 14. This position occurs in nearly all of the steps in social dancing, and, after the 1st position, is that most used.

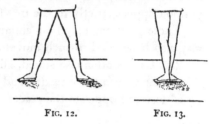

FIG. 12.          FIG. 13.

16. **Fourth Position.** The 4th position is attained by extending the foot in a straight line, either forward or backward, the length of one of the feet, as shown in Figs. 15 and 16. The ordinary walking step is an alternation of the 4th position. The figures are drawn from the side for the sake of clearness; if drawn from the front it would be difficult to distinguish them from the 1st position.

NOTE. — The statement made by some teachers that, as the 4th position is opposite to the 3d and 5th, the foot should be carried forward on a line with the supporting foot, is without logic, for the principal positions undoubtedly have their basis in *natural attitudes*. In natural walking the feet are carried forward upon parallel lines of the heels, and the legs are not crossed. The crossed 4th position, therefore, can hardly be considered as other than an intermediate position, and will be referred to later under that head.

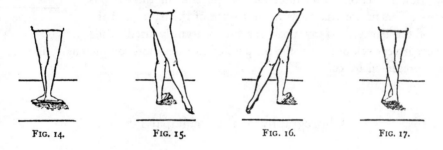

FIG. 14.          FIG. 15.          FIG. 16.          FIG. 17.

17. **Fifth Position.** In the 5th position the legs are so strongly crossed that the heel of each foot touches the point of the other [Fig. 17].

## Open and Closed Positions

18. All positions in which the feet touch one another are called closed positions. The open positions are those in which the feet are separated.

## Crossed Positions

**19.** The 3d and 5th positions and all their derivatives are called crossed positions.

**20.** In order to determine a position we may state as a basis that the supporting foot is always in 1st position, and that the term position as applied to all other than the 1st position applies strictly to the free foot.

These positions may be maintained with either the right or the left foot, and this rule may also be applied to such movements and positions as will be hereafter described.

**21.** Unless otherwise stated, all drawings of the positions and movements represent the dancer as facing the reader, and the terms right and left refer to the dancer, who is supposed to stand opposite the reader.

## Ball and Point Positions

**22.** When the foot is held in such a position that only the front portions rest upon the floor, it is said to be in "ball" or "half-point" position [Fig. 18].

**23.** When the sole is raised to such a degree that only the tips of the toes touch the floor, it is in "point" position [Fig. 19].

**24. Sole Direction.** The direction of the sole in the various positions differs in accordance with the nature of the dance and the ability of the dancer. Many positions are constantly used, while others occur very seldom. For the purpose of clearness and completeness, however, nearly all are represented by cuts.

FIGS. 18, 19.

## Choregraphy of the Principal Positions

**25. First Positions.** Below Fig. 20, which has been explained in § 13, we find two signs which represent the position. The upper one is the symbol employed in the script of Arthur de St. Léon, who called the invention by the name of "Stenochoregraphy." The lower sign is that designed by the author, who has amplified and perfected the system of St. Léon.

**26.** In the stenochoregraphic signs the lower limit of the body is shown by the horizontal line at the top of the figure. The legs are represented by the two perpendicular lines, and the lower horizontal line represents the floor.

The other symbol is self-explanatory, being merely a skeleton drawing of the legs and feet.

27. Fig. 21 represents the 1st sole position with the weight upon the right foot; and as such a position throws the right leg out of the perpendicular, the figure is slightly inclined to the right. In the stenochoregraphic signs the supporting foot is indicated by shading the right leg. Fig. 22 shows the same position, but with the weight upon the left foot.

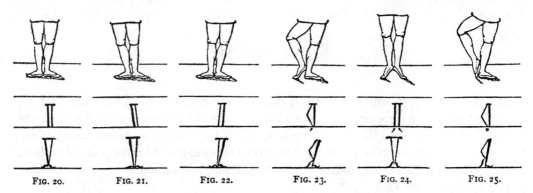

FIG. 20.        FIG. 21.        FIG. 22.        FIG. 23.        FIG. 24.        FIG. 25.

28. In Fig. 23 the right foot is held in 1st ball position, with the heel touching the supporting leg.

The ball position is indicated in the stenochoregraphic signs by a comma below the line of the floor. The skeleton sign explains itself.

29. Fig. 24 shows both feet in 1st ball position; and it must be noted that if in raising the heels they are separated, even in a very slight degree, the position changes from a 1st to an intermediate one.

30. Fig. 25 represents the 1st point position of the right foot, and in this the sole of the right foot touches the left leg.

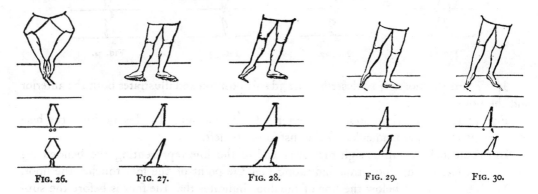

FIG. 26.        FIG. 27.        FIG. 28.        FIG. 29.        FIG. 30.

In the stenochoregraphic sign, the point position is indicated by a small circle beneath the line of the floor.

Fig. 26 shows both feet in 1st point position, and, although this position occurs very seldom, it is well to know it and, if necessary, to be able to describe it.

**31.**  Second Positions.  Fig. 27 shows the 2d sole position of the right foot.  This position has already been explained in § 14.  The symbols are too clear to need explanation.

Fig. 28 shows the right foot in 2d ball position.

Fig. 29 represents the right foot in 2d point position.

In Fig. 30 the right foot is in raising 2d point position.

## Raising Positions

**32.**  All positions in which the heel of the supporting foot is raised from the floor are said to be "raising" positions; and it is well to remember in this connection that the term "raising" always refers to the supporting foot, which may, according to the ability of the dancer and the requirements of the occasion, be carried either to the ball or the point of the foot.

**33.**  When the supporting foot is in raising position, it is indicated in the stenochoregraphic symbol by the sign ($_o$).

Fig. 31 shows both feet in 2d point position.

If the distance between the heels in the double 2d position is greater than the length of both feet, the position is called "amplified" [§ 109].

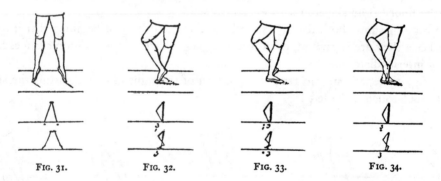

FIG. 31.          FIG. 32.          FIG. 33.          FIG. 34.

**34.**  Third Positions.  § 15 describes the 3d sole position and illustrates both the anterior and the posterior forms.

Fig. 32 shows the right foot in anterior 3d ball position.  In this position the heel of the right foot is perpendicular to the instep of the left.

In the stenochoregraphic sign the lower end of the line representing the bended leg touches the line of the floor, thus indicating that the point of the foot touches the floor.

**35.**  The number 3 below the line of the floor indicates that the foot is before the supporting one.  This numeral always signifies that the foot is in anterior position.

A point is placed below the line of the floor to indicate a posterior position.

**36.**  Fig. 33 represents the right foot in posterior 3d ball position.  In this position the heel is in a line above the inner middle of the supporting foot.

**37.** In the stenochoregraphic sign the comma indicating the ball is placed below the point which indicates the posterior position.

In the lower sign, the number and point are placed below the symbol to indicate that the foot is in posterior ball position, and to show that the line of the position leg is cut by that of the supporting one.

**38.** Fig. 34 represents the right foot in anterior 3d point position.

The point of the foot touches the inner middle of the supporting foot in this position, and the small circle is used to indicate the point position, as before mentioned.

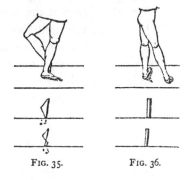

**39.** Fig. 35 shows the posterior 3d point position of the right.

**40. Fourth Positions.** Fig. 36 represents the right foot in anterior 4th sole position; the drawing being in profile to distinguish it from the 1st position.

FIG. 35.    FIG. 36.

**41.** In all illustrations of the 4th positions the position leg is shown turned toward the reader in order to avoid the interception of the supporting leg.

**42.** Fig. 36 shows only a partial view of the heel of the supporting foot, in order to obviate confusion; for if the foot were turned entirely out, it would be impossible to say whether the supporting foot were in 1st or 2d position. It is intended to show that foot in 1st position.

**43.** For similar reasons a portion of the body is added to the drawing, and, where distinctness calls for it, the entire figure is occasionally shown.

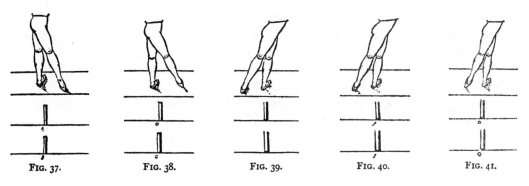

FIG. 37.    FIG. 38.    FIG. 39.    FIG. 40.    FIG. 41.

**44.** The front view, however, is the basis for the stenochoregraphic signs. But owing to the form of the symbol and the shading, the number and point are unnecessary in Fig. 36, the distinction of the advanced foot being apparent, because:

**45.** The shaded perpendicular line always shows the supporting, and the thin line the position leg. If the short connecting line is at the top, the position is anterior. If at the bottom, it is posterior. The ball and point symbols are the same as for the positions already described.

**46.** If, however, for the sake of clearness, the drawings are in profile, it is necessary to put the qualifying marks below the line of the floor.

Fig. 37 represents the right foot in 4th ball position.

Fig. 38 shows the right foot in 4th point position.

Fig. 39 displays the posterior 4th sole position of the right.

Fig. 40 represents the posterior 4th ball position of the right.

In Fig. 41 the right foot is in posterior 4th point position.

**47. Fifth Positions.** Fig. 42 represents the 5th sole position as described in § 17. The symbol is distinguishable by the number 5 which is placed below it.

Where the 5th position appears it should show the exact location of the feet, and particular care is necessary in indicating this.

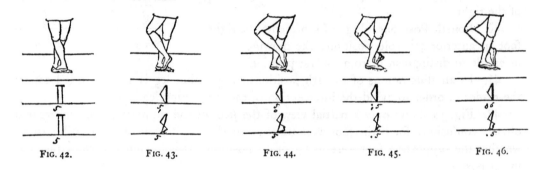

FIG. 42.        FIG. 43.        FIG. 44.        FIG. 45.        FIG. 46.

**48.** Fig. 43 represents the anterior 5th ball position of the right foot. In this the heel of the position foot is perpendicular to the point of the supporting one, while in the corresponding 3d position it stands perpendicular to the instep.

This difference is of great importance, especially in writing the stenochoregraphic script, and the drawings should therefore be carefully noted.

**49.** Fig. 44 shows the anterior 5th point position of the right foot. The point of the right foot stands directly above that of the left.

Fig. 45 shows the right foot in posterior 5th ball position, with its heel directly over the point of the supporting foot.

Fig. 46 represents the right in posterior 5th point position.

NOTE. — This last position is in reality physically impossible, and it is only given to complete the theory of the system.

The symbols have now been so fully described that further repetition of their significance will be avoided wherever possible.

**50.** It must be remembered that one foot may be in either ball or point position, while the other — that is, the supporting foot — is held in a "raising" position.

## Heel Positions

**51.** These positions are very clear and simple. The front portions of the foot are raised from the floor, and while this can be done in nearly all positions, the heel positions are usually open.

**52.** While the heel positions may seem at first thought to be superfluous, they are absolutely essential to many dances, and their omission would cause serious inconvenience in dances of the Hungarian, Russian and Spanish class, in which they occur very frequently.

Fig. 47 shows the right foot in 2d heel position. This is used in the third *pas* of the Spanish "Gitana," for the *tortillé*, etc.

**53.** The stenochoregraphic sign is similar to that for the ball, being an inverted comma ( *ı* ). The other symbol explains itself. Fig. 48 shows the right foot forward in 4th heel position. This position is frequently used in Russian dances.

**54.** Fig. 49 represents the 2d heel position of both

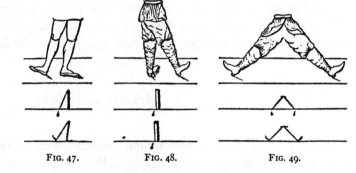

FIG. 47.    FIG. 48.    FIG. 49.

feet, which forms an important factor in Cossack dancing.

These few illustrations are sufficient to clearly define all of the heel positions.

## Flowing Positions

**55.** If one foot is lifted from the floor, and the entire weight supported upon the other, the free foot is said to be in a flowing position.

**56.** The French call such a position *une position en balance*, and the term *se balancer*, as applied to position, means to support the body upon one foot.

**57.** If both feet are lifted from the floor at the same time, as in the leaping and springing steps, the position is called "aerial" or "air position" (*position en l'air*), which will be fully explained later [§ 76].

**58.** As one foot is always in the air in the flowing positions, it may be very readily seen that their variety is manifold.

**59.** The direction of the sole may vary greatly in the flowing positions. If held as in the sole positions it is said to be "horizontal"; if as in the ball position, "diagonal" or "inclined"; if as in the point position, "vertical" or "perpendicular"; and if as in the heel position, "upward" or *rebroussale*.

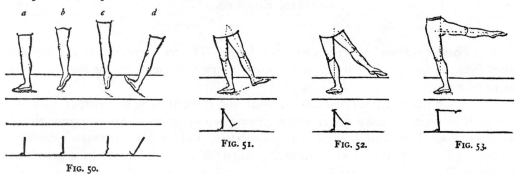

FIG. 50.          FIG. 51.          FIG. 52.          FIG. 53.

In Fig. 50, *a* shows the horizontal sole position; *b* the diagonal; *c* the vertical; *d* the *rebroussale*. In the open flowing positions, the direction of the sole usually follows the line of the leg, as in Figs. 51, 52 and 53. This will be further explained in § 72.

## Measure of Height

60. For the purpose of establishing a standard measure for the height in flowing positions, specific terms have been adopted. For instance, the closed flowing positions in which the foot can be only slightly lifted from the floor are called "low" flowing positions.

In Fig. 54 the right foot is shown in the horizontal low flowing 1st position.

61. In the stenochoregraphic script the flowing positions are indicated by auxiliary horizontal lines such as are used in music script, placed below the line of the floor. A single line shows the "low"; two, the "half-high"; three, the "high"; and four, the "super-high." And the sole direction is indicated as follows: ⌐ horizontal; ⌐ diagonal; ○ vertical; and ⌐ *rebroussale*.

62. In the above stenochoregraphic symbol, the line representing the position of the flowing

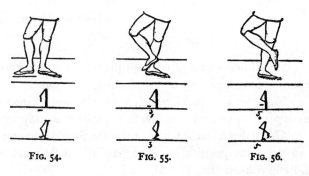

FIG. 54.          FIG. 55.          FIG. 56.

leg is shortened to indicate that the foot does not touch the floor, and the sign below the level of the floor shows that the sole is in a horizontal direction. The other symbol is self-explanatory.

Fig. 55 represents the low anterior flowing 3d position of the right foot, with diagonal sole.

Fig. 56 represents the right foot in anterior 5th flowing position, with perpendicular sole.

## Half-High Closed Flowing Positions

63. If the foot is lifted in the closed positions to the height of the calf, it is said to be in "half-high" position.

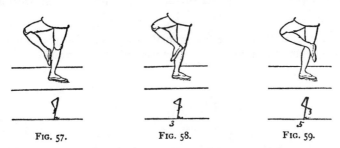

FIG. 57.          FIG. 58.          FIG. 59.

Fig. 57 represents the right foot in the half-high flowing 1st position, with perpendicular sole. In the symbol the bended line touches the supporting line at half-height, and the sign otherwise explains itself.

Fig. 58 shows the half-high anterior flowing 3d position of the right foot with sole inclined (diagonal).

Fig. 59 shows the half-high anterior flowing 5th position of the right, with perpendicular sole.

## High Closed Flowing Positions

64. The high closed flowing positions are those in which the point of the foot touches the supporting leg at the height of the knee.

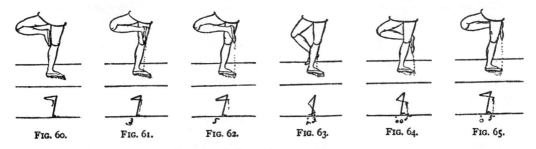

FIG. 60.      FIG. 61.      FIG. 62.      FIG. 63.      FIG. 64.      FIG. 65.

Figs. 60, 61 and 62 represent respectively the 1st, the anterior 3d, and the anterior 5th high flowing positions of the right foot, with perpendicular sole.

All of these positions may be assumed with the left foot.

Fig. 63 shows the posterior low 3d flowing position of the right foot, with diagonal sole.

Fig. 64 is the half-high posterior 5th position of the right, with perpendicular sole.

Fig. 65 shows the right in high posterior 5th flowing position, with perpendicular sole.

Thus we have shown all positions in which the foot is raised backward, and from this we can see that it is not difficult to write any position that can be imagined. Their execution is, however, a different matter; for some are quite impossible, save in the intermediate positions, which are fully explained further on [§§ 97–101], or with a bended supporting leg.

The use of the word " half " in connection with the height of raising is always imperative, but, except in extraordinary cases, it is unnecessary to say " entirely " high position or " whole " height.

## Open Flowing Positions

**65.** Any position in which the legs do not touch is called an open position, and the class therefore includes the 2d and 4th positions and all their derivatives [§18].

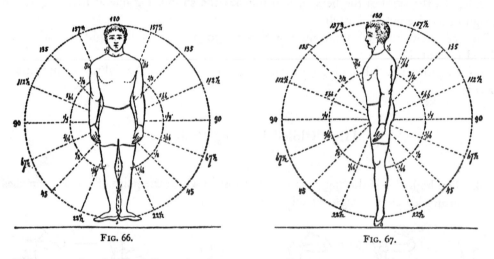

FIG. 66.                    FIG. 67.

When one foot is lifted from the floor and the weight of the body rests entirely upon the other foot, we have what is termed a "balancing" or flowing position [§55].

The rules of the degree of height to which the foot is carried in the open balancing positions are in accordance with Figs. 66 and 67.

When one foot is lifted slightly from an open sole position, it comes into low balancing position, as in Fig. 68.

**66.** But if the leg is raised to a horizontal position, as in Fig. 69, it is in high balancing position.

**67.** The half-high balancing position, shown in Fig. 70, is midway between the perpendicular and horizontal lines.

**68.** If the circle of height be divided into eight equal parts, as in Fig. 66 (front diagram), counting from the lower centre (between the heels and indicated by a zero), $\frac{1}{16}$ will represent the low; $\frac{1}{8}$ the half-high, and $\frac{1}{4}$ the high balancing positions.

**69.** If the leg passes the height of the horizontal position it reaches a super-high balancing position [Fig. 71].

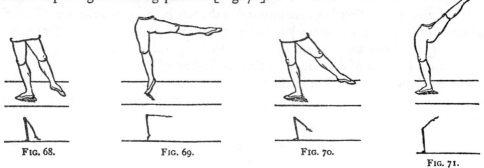

FIG. 68.  FIG. 69.  FIG. 70.

FIG. 71.

**70.** These positions occur only in the *grands battements*, and in grotesque and acrobatic dances.

**71.** The larger circle is also of use, as it gives the degree of height in mathematical form, but the fractional system above described is most readily understood by pupils.

**In** Fig. 66 (front diagram)

$\frac{1}{16} = 22\frac{1}{2}$ degrees, and represents the low,

$\frac{1}{8} = 45$    "    "    "    " half-high,

$\frac{3}{16} = 67\frac{1}{2}$    "    "    "    " three-quarters high,

$\frac{1}{4} = 90$    "    "    "    " high,

$\frac{3}{8} = 135$    "    "    "    " super-high,

open balancing positions. The front diagram applies to the 2d and the side diagram to the 4th positions.

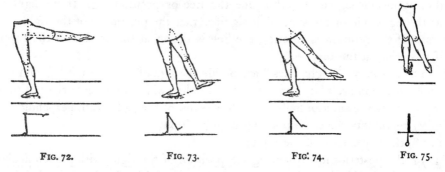

FIG. 72.  FIG. 73.  FIG. 74.  FIG. 75.

Fig. 68 represents the left foot in the low balancing 2d position, with diagonal sole.

Fig. 70 shows the half-high balancing 2d position of the left foot, with diagonal sole [§72].

Fig. 71 represents the 2d super-high balancing position, with perpendicular sole.

**72.** The direction of the sole in the open-balancing positions is called by the same name as the direction of the leg, regardless of the geometrical position.

Fig. 72, for instance, shows the left leg in the horizontal position, and notwithstanding the fact that the foot is also geometrically horizontal, the sole is said to be perpendicular in a technical sense, because the toe is pressed entirely down.

If the geometrical direction were to stand as the rule in this particular, the name of the sole direction would vary with every measure of height to which the foot might be carried.

**73.** Fig 73 shows the horizontal, Fig. 74 the diagonal or inclined, and Fig. 72 the perpendicular position of the sole, according to the line of the leg.

Fig. 75 shows the right foot in the anterior low balancing 4th position, with perpendicular sole. As before explained [§ 40], the cut is drawn in profile for the sake of clearness.

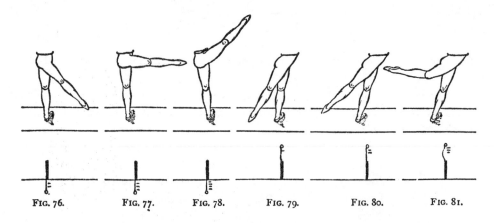

FIG. 76.          FIG. 77.          FIG. 78.          FIG. 79.          FIG. 80.          FIG. 81.

**74.** The stenochoregraphic symbol is drawn in front view, but is vastly different from the signs of the 4th positions in which both feet touch the floor. The thick line represents the supporting leg and the thin one the free or position leg. If the light line be made at the right side of the symbol, it signifies that the position is of the right foot, and vice versa. If the position is anterior, the line is drawn at the bottom of the supporting line; if posterior, at the top.

**75.** The auxiliary "height lines" are beside the sign of the position leg, and the signs for the sole direction are placed at the end of the line which represents the position leg.

Fig. 76 shows the anterior half-high 4th position of the right, with perpendicular sole;

Fig. 77 represents the corresponding high position;

Fig. 78, the super-high of the right;

Fig. 79, the posterior low balancing 4th position of the right, with perpendicular sole;

Fig. 80, the half-high position corresponding; and Fig. 81 the entire height of the posterior position.

### Air Positions (*Positions en l'air*)

**76.** When both feet are lifted from the floor at the same time, the dancer is in air position.

Fig. 82 shows both feet in 2d air position, with perpendicular soles.

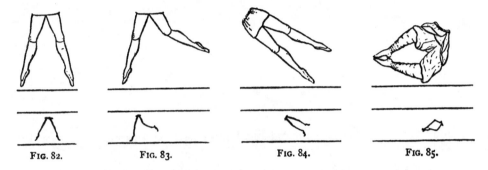

FIG. 82.　　　FIG. 83.　　　FIG. 84.　　　FIG. 85.

**77.** While in the air, the legs and feet may execute different movements, such as *pas brisés*, *ailes de pigeons*, *entrechats*, etc., and the direction of the upper body may also be changed, as shown in Figs. 83, 84 and 85.

### Inward-Turned Positions

**78.** There are, in many national dances, positions in which the feet are turned inward, and although no authority upon dancing has before written regarding them, they are of

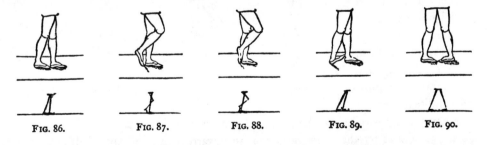

FIG. 86.　　　FIG. 87.　　　FIG. 88.　　　FIG. 89.　　　FIG. 90.

manifest importance in Hungarian and in Russian dances. They may be found in sole, ball, point, heel and flowing form.

**79.** Fig. 86 shows the right foot in inward turned 1st sole position.

The stenochoregraphic sign explains itself. It differs from that of the 1st principal position only in the sign of the inward turned foot of the position leg.

80. Fig. 87 represents the inward turned 1st ball position of the right foot.

In the script the inward turned positions are represented by the inward bended lines of the position leg, and the ball sign appears, as usual, below the line of the floor.

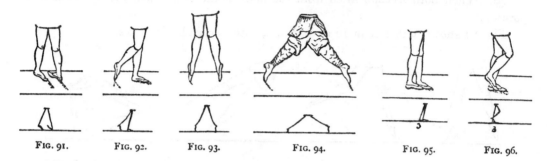

FIG. 91.          FIG. 92.          FIG. 93.          FIG. 94.          FIG. 95.          FIG. 96.

81. Fig. 88 represents the point and Fig. 89, the heel expression of the inward turned 1st position.

The author's script is well adapted to the writing of inward turned positions.

82. Since the balancing positions differ from the floor positions only in the fact that the free foot does not reach the floor, it is unnecessary to represent them by drawings and for this reason many of them will not be illustrated.

Fig. 90 shows both feet in inward turned 1st sole position.

Fig. 91 represents the right foot in inward turned 1st ball, and the left in inward turned 1st heel position.

These two positions occur frequently in the so-called *pas tortillés* of the Russian dances.

In Fig. 92 the right foot is shown in the inward turned 2d point position, which is often found in the Hungarian dances.

Figs. 93 and 94 show respectively the inward turned 2d point position of both feet, and the prolonged or amplified form of the same. All Cossack dances contain this position in amplified form.

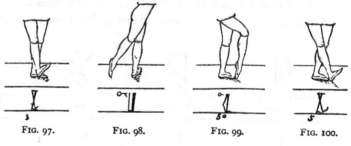

FIG. 97.          FIG. 98.          FIG. 99.          FIG. 100.

The amplified positions will be more fully dealt with in § 108.

Figs. 95, 96 and 97 show the right foot in inward turned 3d sole, ball and heel positions.

Fig. 98 shows the right foot in the posterior inward turned 4th point position, and Fig. 99 the anterior inward turned 5th point position.

In Fig. 100 the right foot is shown in the inward turned 5th heel position.

83. Wherever distinctness is wanting in the script it is well to add the number of the position, as in the above sign.

## Bended and Stretched Positions

84. Many — indeed most — of the sole and open positions may be assumed with either bended or stretched knees; while the closed ball and point positions necessitate bending; and the open heel positions cannot be executed save with stretched knees.

85. Specific names have been assigned to the various degrees of bending and may be illustrated by the following drawings which show the stretched, half-stretched, rounded, half-bended and entirely bended positions of the leg respectively [Figs. 101, 102, 103, 104 and 105].

86. In the entirely bended positions, the thigh and calf nearly touch one another. Fig. 106 shows the legs in the entirely bended 1st position.

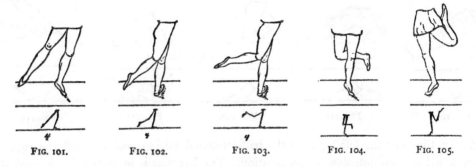

FIG. 101.  FIG. 102.  FIG. 103.  FIG. 104.  FIG. 105.

The drawing represents the heels as raised, because such a position is well nigh impossible in sole position.

87. In the half-bended positions the thigh and calf are at right angles.

88. The half-stretched positions contain an angle of 135 degrees, and may be called quarter-bended.

89. The rounded position is that in which the leg forms a portion of a circle.

90. Figs. 107 and 108 show respectively the half and quarter bended 1st positions of both legs upon the soles.

Fig. 109 is the amplified 2d heel position of the left, with the supporting leg three-quarters bended (Cossack step).

Fig. 110 shows the left in the amplified inward turned 2d point position with the supporting leg three-quarters bended, while Fig. 111 shows the more exaggerated form of the same position, which may be found in a very effective Hungarian dance, and in which the top of the left foot nearly touches the floor.

Fig. 112 illustrates a position in which the weight rests upon the left knee and the right leg is in the half-bended 4th position upon the sole.

The position shown in Fig. 113 occurs frequently in a popular Cossack dance and shows the prolonged anterior 4th heel position of the right leg, with the supporting leg in a bended raising position.

Fig. 114 shows both legs in a half-bended air-position.

The last mentioned positions are much more clearly shown by drawings than by any choregraphic signs.

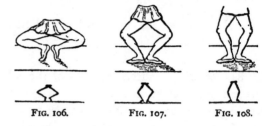

FIG. 106.   FIG. 107.   FIG. 108.

**91.** In Fig. 115 the left leg is in an entirely stretched supporting position, while the right is held in the low balancing 2d, and Fig. 116 represents the left leg in bended raising position on the ball and the right in the high balancing 2d position.

All minor or auxiliary symbols should be placed as near as possible to the leg whose position they qualify.

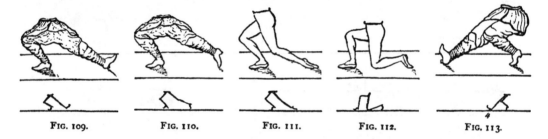

FIG. 109.   FIG. 110.   FIG. 111.   FIG. 112.   FIG. 113.

**92.** In Fig. 117 the left leg is in the half-stretched raising position, and the right is half-stretched in half-high flowing 2d position. The left foot is in diagonal sole position.

Fig. 118 shows the fully stretched half-high 4th balancing position with perpendicular sole and supported by the half-stretched left leg in raising position.

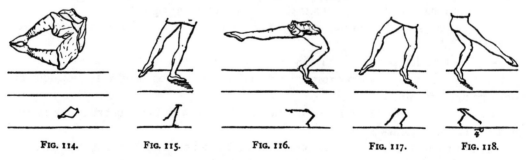

FIG. 114.   FIG. 115.   FIG. 116.   FIG. 117.   FIG. 118.

In Fig. 119 the right leg is in a half-stretched raising position supporting the left, which is held in the entirely stretched posterior low 4th balancing position.

In Fig. 120 the left leg supports the weight in a fully stretched sole position, while the right is held in the anterior high half-bended 4th position, with the sole nearly horizontal.

93. In all open balancing positions the height is determined by the direction of the thigh when the knee is bended, as explained in §65 and §71; the degrees of bending are described in §§85 to 89.

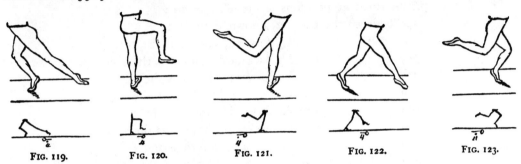

| FIG. 119. | FIG. 120. | FIG. 121. | FIG. 122. | FIG. 123. |

Fig. 121 represents the left leg stretched and supporting, and the right half-bended in the posterior half-high 4th balancing position.

Figs. 122 and 123 represent the ordinary running steps. In Fig. 122 the step is commenced by the extension of the right leg into the amplified anterior low 4th balancing position, with diagonal sole, while the left is half-stretched and supporting.

Fig. 123 shows the completion of the running step in which the right leg is carried back to the posterior high 4th balancing position.

## Intermediate Positions

94. The foot is sometimes carried into a position between the 2d and 4th positions, thus standing in a diagonal relation to the line of position. Such a position as lies thus — between two principal positions — is called an intermediate position.

95. Intermediate positions may be classified as simple, double, whole or half-intermediate.

96. Simple or whole intermediate positions which lie between two principal positions are shown in Figs. 124 and 125, in which the left foot is to be regarded as free, and is, therefore, omitted and indicated by the position numbers, which are placed at various points upon which the heel rests in the positions given.

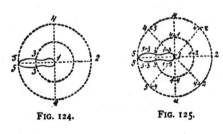

| FIG. 124. | FIG. 125. |

St. Léon used musical signs to indicate the open intermediate positions, the "sharp" ($\sharp$) representing the amplified, and the "flat" ($\flat$) representing the narrowed positions, and these symbols were placed upon that side of the leg to which the changement would carry the foot. The exact positions can be best represented by numbers.

97. To avoid confusion, the intermediate positions are more properly represented by writing the numbers, as 2-4, 3-5, etc., rather than in the form of common fractions, as $\frac{1}{2}$, $\frac{1}{4}$, $\frac{1}{8}$, etc.

98. The simple intermediate positions of the left foot are:

      1st, between the 1 and 2, known as the 1-2.

      2d,    "    "  1 and 3 forward, known as the 1-3.

      3d,    "    "  1 and 3 backward, known as the 1-3.

      4th,   "    "  1 and 4 forward, known as the 1-4.

      5th,   "    "  1 and 4 backward, known as the 1-4.

      6th,   "    "  2 and 4 forward, known as the 2-4.

      7th,   "    "  2 and 4 backward, known as the 2-4.

      8th,   "    "  3 and 4 forward, known as the 3-4.

      9th,   "    "  3 and 4 backward, known as the 3-4.

      10th,  "    "  3 and 5 forward, known as the 3-5.

      11th,  "    "  3 and 5 backward, known as the 3-5.

      12th,  "    "  4 and 5 forward, known as the 4-5.

      13th,  "    "  4 and 5 backward, known as the 4-5.

These positions may also be assumed with the right foot.

## Half Intermediate Positions

99. The half intermediate positions are those in which the foot does not stand midway between two principal positions, but is half-way between such a point and a principal position. These positions are represented in Fig. 126.

100. The ruling position is designated by doubling the number of the principal position to which the foot stands in closest proximity.

NOTE.—These half-intermediate positions occur but seldom; however, they are represented here for the purpose of completing the script, so as to enable one to write all possible positions.

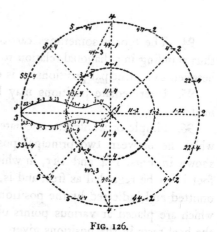

FIG. 126.

## Double Intermediate Positions

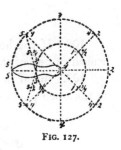

FIG. 127.

**101.** The double intermediate positions lie at points which are in direct relation to three principal positions. They are shown in Fig. 127.

## Crossed Positions

**102.** The 3d and 5th positions and all their derivatives are called simple crossed positions.

**103.** If the foot be carried around the supporting leg it comes into double-crossed position.

Fig. 128 represents the right foot forward in 3d point position.

Fig. 129 shows the right leg in the anterior double-crossed 3d point position.

In Fig. 130 the left foot is in anterior 5th point position.

In Fig. 131 the left leg stands in anterior double-crossed 5th point position.

**104.** Double-crossings must always be designated; although such a course is unnecessary in the case of the single-crossed positions, which are self-evident.

**105.** In the choregraphic signs the double-crossed positions are indicated by a cross (×) placed over the line of the supporting leg.

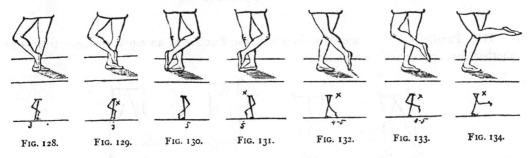

FIG. 128.    FIG. 129.    FIG. 130.    FIG. 131.    FIG. 132.    FIG. 133.    FIG. 134.

Special attention should be paid to drawing the feet in the symbols, as absolute distinctness is imperative.

**106.** Fig. 132 represents the right foot in the amplified double-crossed anterior 4-5 point position.

**107.** Figs. 133 and 134 represent the same position in half-high and high attitudes respectively.

These positions can be most easily represented by the skeleton symbols.

The three last shown positions come into use in the *pas de basques*.

## Prolonged Positions

**108.** If the heel of the free foot be placed within a circle of which the radius is the length of one of the feet, it is in an intermediate position.

**109.** But if the heel of the free foot passes beyond such a limit, which is only possible in the open positions, it comes into a prolonged or amplified position.

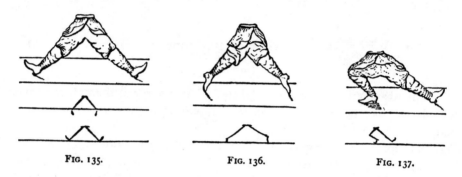

FIG. 135.                FIG. 136.                FIG. 137.

Figs. 135 and 136 show the prolonged 2d heel and point positions of both feet.

Fig. 137 shows the left foot in the prolonged 2d heel position and supported upon the wholly bended right leg.

## Parallel Positions

**110.** Parallel positions are those in which the feet are at an equal distance from one another throughout their whole length.

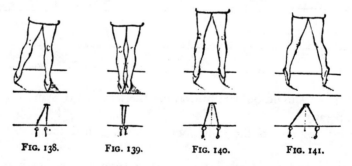

FIG. 138.        FIG. 139.        FIG. 140.        FIG. 141.

**111.** Parallel positions may be either sole, ball, point or flowing; indeed, one foot may be sole and the other balancing, and still be in parallel position.

NOTE. — These positions are frequent in Russian, Polish and other national dances.

Fig. 138 shows the right leg stretched and held in low balancing 2d position, and the left in a stretched raising position, while the feet are parallel and the points directly forward.

In the sign, the parallel position is indicated by small symbols to represent the soles, which are placed below the line of the floor.

112. Fig. 139 shows both feet in parallel 1st position.

In Fig. 140 the feet are in the parallel 1-2 position. The dotted line is drawn to indicate the intermediate position, and shows the width to be less than that of a principal position.

In Fig. 141 the feet are both in parallel 2d position on the points.

From the foregoing it can be seen how manifold the positions are — there are thousands of them — and although it is hardly possible to illustrate them all, the dancer or choregraph should, if he has attentively studied such examples as have been given, be able to classify any that may occur.

The proper name and sign for each, however, demand thoughtful consideration, and in order to clearly express every quality in such a manner that the dancer may understand and interpret them, special attention must be given to their form.

# Chapter III

## MOVEMENTS

TRANSITION from one position into another is accomplished by means of one or more movements. These may be either simple or compound. If compound, it is necessary to analyze the movements and reduce them to the simple movements of which they consist. The ability to write the compound movements is therefore dependent upon the ability to write the simple; and he who has learned to do that can surely handle any combination.

114. If we study the anatomy of the leg, we find the following capabilities of movement:

(a) The toes may be either spread or contracted.

(b) The ankles may be either drawn up or stretched down; thus raising or lowering the instep.

(c) The knees may be either bended or stretched.

(d) The thighs may be either raised or lowered; and a turning movement, in which the other portions of the leg participate, may be accomplished at the joint of the hip.

(e) Both legs may, by coöperating, effect a transfer of the weight from one foot to the other.

115. By means of these possibilities of movement human beings are able to execute the following simple movements, all of which are exercised in dancing: bending, stretching, raising, lowering, lifting, putting down, turning and transferring.

116. The clutching or contraction of the toes which occurs in the point positions, and their spreading, as in most heel positions, are so natural that it is unnecessary to deal with them as independent movements; and there are therefore no special choregraphic symbols to represent them.

117. The following French terms will be explained, as they are inseparably connected with the art of dancing. There may perhaps be a time when such words as are now employed in the language of art will be eliminated and our tongue be entirely free from foreign words and expressions; but at present any attempt to obviate their use in a technical manner would only serve to confuse the student, and we can be of far greater service to our language by explaining these technical terms and by using them properly, than by seeking to avoid them.

40

# The Simple Movements

**118. Bending (*Plier*).** This movement may be made with either or with both legs, and is absolutely essential to elasticity of motion. The various degrees of bending have been exemplified under the heading " Bended and Stretched Positions" [§§ 84 to 104]; and while it is true that bending is for the most part so natural as to render its description unnecessary, there are cases in which the intention of the composer may be somewhat indefinite. The system has therefore been extended to the bending signs for the sake of absolute distinctness.

**119. Stretching (*Redresser — Allonger — Tendre*).** Stretching is that movement which is opposite to bending, and without it no new bending is possible. The term *redresser* means to straighten a bended member. *Allonger* means to stretch it to the limit. These terms are used to designate the different forms of stretching which the term *tendre* (to stretch) is sometimes insufficient to clearly express.

**120. Narrow and Distant Legs (*Jarreté et Arqué*).** Very few persons possess entirely straight legs, and few therefore find it easy to hold them straight.

Those whose knee-joints nearly or quite touch, and whose calves stand close together, while the heels are separated, are said to have narrow legs. In such cases the knees are large and thick, and it is usually impossible or at least difficult to stand with the heels together.

Those persons whose heels touch, but who have a space between the knees, are said to have distant legs. Such persons are usually of a lively temperament, and are especially fitted for the execution of *entrechats* and steps of a similar nature in which the knees are often a hindrance to properly formed persons. Such persons as have distant legs should exercise particular care to bring the legs as near parallel as possible.

**121. Raising (*Élever*).** Raising is that movement which results from pressing down the front portion of the foot, by which the body is slightly raised from the floor. The movement may be made with either or with both feet, and the raising may be extended until one stands upon the extreme point of the foot, as in the case of many female ballet dancers. To do this, however, the toes must be very strongly contracted. No light and easy dancing can be imagined without raising.

To raise the body from a sole position carries the foot into ball or point position; and to apply the same movement to a flowing foot, creates a diagonal or perpendicular position of the sole.

**122.** By raising upon both feet from sole position, the heels are separated and the position is either amplified or changed.

**123. Lowering (*Abaisser*).** Lowering is merely the resumption of sole position which results from raising. In this movement, the heel merely sinks to its normal position. As applied to a flowing foot, the movement creates a *rebroussale* sole direction.

**124. Lifting (*Lever*).** Lifting is a movement which starts at the hip, by means of which the entire leg is carried from a position upon the floor. The movement may be executed in either bended or stretched position. §§ 60 to 64 show the various degrees of lifting in the closed, and §§ 66 to 71 those of the open positions. They are clearly set forth in the diagrams accompanying these sections.

**125. Putting Down** (*Baisser*). To put down signifies the replacing of a foot which has been lifted. Do not confound this movement with lowering (*abaisser*).

**126. Turning** (*Tourner*). Turning is that movement by means of which the leg is turned either inward or outward. This movement cannot be made unless the entire leg participates in the motion.

This differs from the movement by which the single members are turned, and from that by which the whole body is carried around upon one foot or in the air.

If the leg is carried from an outward position, without turning the body, it is a simple foot-turning. Such movements are common in the Russian and many other national dances.

Turning may be executed in sole, ball, point, heel or flowing position.

**127.** The French term *se tourner* is understood to mean changing the direction of the body. Such a movement may be made without really turning the leg.

Most of the rapid Pirouettes are executed by swinging the arms and body and one of the legs, whereby the supporting leg, which is really not turned, is carried around upon the ball. In the slow Pirouettes turning is the principal factor.

**128. Transferring** (*Dégager*). The term *dégager* is applied to that movement by which the weight is transferred from one foot to the other. Such a movement may be made in all positions, but is more frequently found in the open ones. Its importance as a movement is demonstrated by the fact that no step can be made without a transfer. Movements which do not contain this transfer are merely parts of steps, and are called *temps*.

In § 27 the position of the weight is clearly illustrated by drawings.

**129.** By transferring the weight, a new position is always taken; as the free foot, which denominates the position, is made to support the weight, while the supporting foot has been relieved of its burden and becomes free. This is true even though the feet are not moved.

*Dégager* will be more fully dealt with in § 253 and §§ 289 to 291, in which the transferring exercises will be found.

## Choregraphic Signs for Movements

130. The choregraphic symbols for the movements which have just been described are as follows:

| MOVEMENT. | RIGHT. | LEFT. | BOTH. |
|---|---|---|---|
| Bending.—*Plier.* | | | |
| Stretching.—*Tendre.* | | | |
| Raising.—*Élever.* | | | |
| Lowering.—*Abaisser.* | | | |
| Lifting.—*Lever.* | | | |
| Putting down.—*Baisser.* | | | |
| Turning.—*Tourner.* | | | |
| Transferring.—*Dégager.* | | | |

All symbols of the movements represent the dancer as facing the reader.

131. The movement signs differ from the position signs in the fact that the body is not represented above them, and in that they are usually made in smaller proportion than the position signs. The symbols of the sole directions may be placed either below or at the side of the movement signs. The application of the signs for movements is demonstrated in the following preparatory exercises.

# Chapter IV

## PREPARATORY EXERCISES

A GREAT variety of preparatory exercises may be composed of the simple movements. It is important to adapt these exercises to the ability of the pupil. If for young grown persons, who desire only social dancing, they must be limited to those which are necessary, as more than these would render the instruction tiresome.

In teaching children, or at private houses, more attention may be devoted to the work and more difficult exercises are both possible and desirable.

133. In the case of courses which extend over a longer period, still others may be used with good results, for here the training is rather for æsthetic development than for education in the various dances. Even here, however, care should be taken to introduce only such exercises as may be given without lessening the interest of the pupil, or dulling the pleasure of learning, for without these factors it is impossible for the most conscientious and competent teacher to achieve worthy results.

134. In ballet schools, and in courses for persons who desire to make dancing a profession, the system of preparatory exercises should be applied in its entirety.

Of these exercises the most necessary are: *pliés, élévations, battements, changements de jambes* and *dégagements* (bending, raising, beating, alternating, and transferring).

### Bending Exercises (*Plier*)

135. These exercises, which are composed solely of the two movements, bending and stretching, are first in importance; for without them it would be impossible to acquire any degree of flexibility or ease of movement, and without these qualities dancing is ridiculous. These bendings must be made in all positions, and as low as possible; and the exercise is as necessary to the most proficient dancer as to the novice.

136. The trunk must be held perpendicular, the knees turned outward and the heels remain upon the floor, thus supporting the weight upon the whole sole. The arms should hang naturally at the sides with the forefingers touching the side lines of the legs. The ladies may raise their skirts, if desired; in which case the arms should be rounded.

If the knees are bent forward, the body is not only ungraceful, but also unsafe; if the

44

heels are raised, the ankles receive no training; and if the body is allowed to bend forward, the entire attitude is absurd.

**137.** In order to render the exercises agreeable to pupils, only the first eight measures should be counted. The remainder should be accompanied by suitable, simple music. Pupils will practice more zealously and more willingly if the aim of the movements is explained in every case where it is possible.

The measures of the metronome show the various degrees of speed, from the simplest slow movements to the most rapid and the most difficult. Teachers should commence with that degree most in accordance with the temperament of the pupil, and work upward to the more difficult by easy degrees.

Variety is of great assistance to a teacher.

In the Music Book the measure of the metronome is given, so that the teacher may indicate the exact tempo to his musician; and the pieces have been arranged for the piano with simple accompaniment. The melody is written upon a separate line for the violin, and can be used without accompaniment.

**138.** Exercise 1. Staccato Bendings (*Pliés staccato*) [Fig. 142].

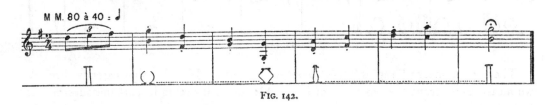

FIG. 142.

(Beginning with 80 beats a minute and changing to 40, in accordance with Maeltzel's metronome.)

NOTE.—As a musical example appears here, it seems necessary to refer to music, measure, accent, metronome and kindred subjects; but such information on these subjects as is required will be found in Chapter V.

The dotted lines between the choregraphical signs indicate the continuation of the movement. For this the French term is *continuer*.

After this exercise has been taken in all simple sole positions, it should be made gliding, with music.

**139.** Exercise 2. Legato Bendings (*Pliés legato*) [Fig. 143].

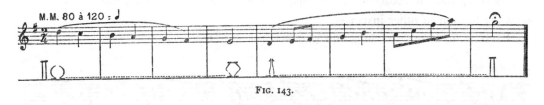

FIG. 143.

For the sake of variety in these exercises, which might otherwise become tiresome to the pupil, vary the speed from M.M. 69 to 144, and change the rhythm by either bending slowly and stretching quickly or vice versa, pausing a longer or a shorter period between the positions, as shown in the following examples.

140. Exercise 3. Quick Bendings [Fig. 144].

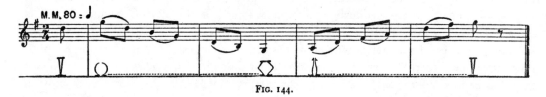

FIG. 144.

It is readily seen that the "slurs" belonging to the notes have a gliding influence upon the exercise.

141. Exercise 4. Slow Bendings and Quick Stretchings [Fig. 145].

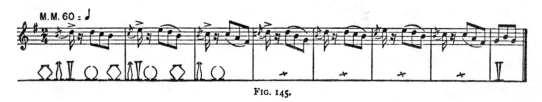

FIG. 145.

The sign ✕ means "repeat" (*répétition*), as in music. If such a sign extends through two measures it means the repetition of both (✕); and if it occurs in part measure, repeat the preceding part measure.

142. Exercise 5. Slow Bendings and Quick Stretchings [Fig. 146].

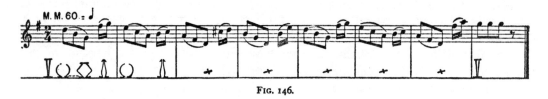

FIG. 146.

In this example the position signs are omitted after the first measure because they are understood; and the reader must not imagine that the author has forgotten them if such signs are left out in other instances.

Exercise 6. Slow Stretching and Quick Bending [Fig. 147].

FIG. 147.

Exercise 7. Quick Bending and Slow Stretching [Fig. 148].

FIG. 148.

Exercise 8. Slow Bending and Quick Stretching of One Leg, with Balancing Position of the other [Fig. 149].

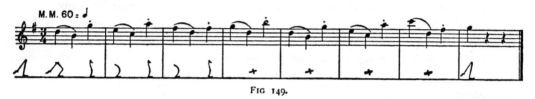

FIG 149.

Exercise 9. Quick Bending and Slow Stretching of the Supporting Leg [Fig. 150].

FIG. 150.

Exercise 10. Bending and Stretching of the Supporting Leg in Equal Duration [Fig. 151].

FIG. 151.

Repeat music, transfer weight and execute with other leg.

By varying the position of the free leg, this exercise may be changed in many ways.

143. After the above exercises have been practiced in all simple sole positions, they should be executed in the various ball, point, heel and flowing positions.

144. After these, the bending and stretching exercises may be applied to the free leg; but as they are quite difficult, it is better to defer them until after the pupils have learned the small and large *battements*, when they will be referred to as *battements sur le cou-de-pied* [§ 164].

145. Inasmuch as dancing is rather an art than a science, all of these exercises must

be repeated often and with precision. Knowledge is the first requirement, but the ability to execute what is learned demands a great deal of careful practice.

146. But as these strictly necessary repetitions are tiresome, especially to children, the great desideratum of teaching is to render the instruction agreeable.

147. It is a well known principle of teaching that if one would not tire his pupils, he must retain their good-will. Experience has demonstrated that grace, ease and freedom of movement can only be acquired by constant practice of elementary work; it is therefore necessary from time to time to introduce changes which will not interfere with the course of the instruction.

148. Teachers must always adapt the work to the ability, knowledge and requirements of the pupil; as it is impossible to set up a standard of accomplishment for a given time, on account of the difference in pupils. Any teacher whose method is practical can, however, always conform to circumstances.

149. Intelligible explanations are of the first importance to pupils, and any teacher whose knowledge is well founded will be enabled to impart his instruction in a satisfactory manner.

Teachers should give the reason for each exercise, and be able to correctly answer all questions regarding the work. Answers which may be given upon the instant and are not accurate or well grounded, are soon discovered, and react in no favourable manner upon the instructor.

150. No one thing is so sure to secure a teacher the esteem of his pupils as a demonstration of his ability and of his knowledge; for although many succeed for a short time, and with certain persons, by means of boasting, the only real success comes from wide and appropriate knowledge and a constant endeavour to succeed. Besides all this, the teacher's conduct must be dignified and refined; his speech free from levity or immoral suggestion, and his dress tasteful and neat.

151. By friendly ways, a teacher may, if he possesses great patience, effectually gain the confidence and esteem of his pupils, thereby overcoming their lazy, careless and even vicious instincts, if such exist. Private reproof, administered in a kindly manner, can only result pleasantly, but unkind or ungentlemanly manners usually destroy that confidence which, once disturbed, is lost forever.

## Raisings (*Elévations*)

**152.** These exercises are composed of only two movements — raising and lowering. They strengthen and train the muscles of the lower leg and foot, thus increasing endurance; without this factor, the dancer would tire very soon, and become slow and unsteady and finally lose the measure.

The exercises should be practiced in all positions, increasing in height from the sole to the extreme point positions. Slow movements are more beneficial and likewise more difficult than rapid movements. They should be done by counting at first, and then by music; and particular care should be paid to the carriage of the trunk. Pupils should never be allowed to make ridiculous grimaces, or to move the shoulders, or to stretch the fingers in an awkward manner, as all of these things tend to ruin the work.

**153.** It is more difficult to lower one's body slowly than to raise it slowly, but the heels must be allowed to sink noiselessly at all times.

Exercise 11. Pushed Raisings [Fig. 152].

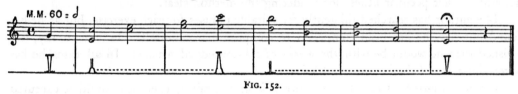

FIG. 152.

Exercise 12. Bound Raisings [Fig. 153].

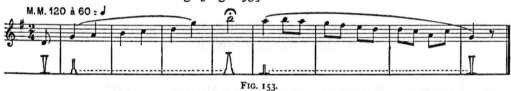

FIG. 153.

Exercise 13. Quick Lowering and Slow Raising [Fig. 154].

FIG. 154.

Exercise 14. Slow Raising and Quick Lowering in ⁴⁄₄ time [Fig. 155].

FIG. 155.

Exercise 15. Intermittent Raising and Lowering [Fig. 156].

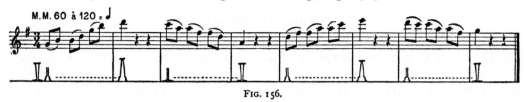

FIG. 156.

Exercise 16. Slow Raising and Quick Lowering, in ¾ time [Fig. 157].

FIG. 157.

154. For the sake of variety, innumerable passages may be chosen from existing musical compositions which will fit these exercises; those given having been selected on account of their peculiar fitness for rendering the method clear.

The author has searched diligently for suitable phrases for each exercise, but as he has found but few, he has been compelled to compose many himself. He is, naturally, less satisfied than he would be with the works of acknowledged masters. In all cases he has given the name of the composer, if known.

When it is possible to apply the entire system, the raising exercises should be executed upon one foot only in all stretched, bended and intermediate positions.

## Combined Bendings and Raisings

155. Exercise 17. Bending and Raising in one Measure [Fig. 158].

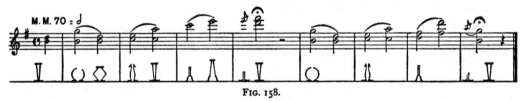

FIG. 158.

Exercise 18. Bending and Raising in ¾ Time [Fig. 159].

FIG. 159.

Exercise 19. Quick Bending and Raising [Fig. 160].

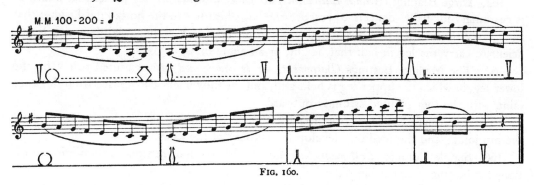

FIG. 160.

All exercises should be executed in all possible positions.

**156.** If in the raising exercises in 3d or 5th position, we so vary the movement that, in lowering, one heel and then the other falls in front, we have what are termed the alternate crossed raising exercises — *des élévations croisées alternatives.*

**157.** These exercises have been called *changements de jambes*, or rubbing of the heels. However, as a *changement de jambes* is literally a changement of the legs, such as occurs in every step, and it is unnecessary in so doing to rub the heels, it is perhaps better to refer to these exercises in such a manner as to signify their peculiar quality by sticking to the term "alternate crossed raisings."

**158.** Inasmuch as the front direction of the trunk is not changed in these exercises, they can only be executed in ball and point position, in which it is possible to turn the feet. They will therefore be found in the department relating to the turning of the feet [§ 246].

## Remarks Upon the Raising and Lowering Exercises

**159.** When the foot is carried from a closed to an open position the leg is raised, and when carried from an open to a closed one the leg is lowered.

## Beating Exercises (*Battements*)

**160.** If one foot is pushed strongly against the other, the movement is called a beating (*un battement*) from the French word *battre*, to beat.

**161.** These beatings are either small, medium, large, simple, crossed, changed or alternate.

**162.** Small Beatings (*Petits Battements*) are those in which the feet are not separated beyond the point at which the tip touches the floor when the leg is fully stretched. Their width, therefore, can never exceed the length of the foot.

**163.** Large Beatings (*Grands Battements*) are those in which the leg passes that limit. It is customary for ballet-dancers to practice the large beatings to the horizontal height; that is, to carry the free leg to a horizontal position in the air. For the social dances, it is sufficient to carry the leg to half that height, or an angle of 45 degrees.

**164.** The Medium Beatings (*Battements sur le cou-de-pied*) are executed solely by the lower leg, in which the upper leg is held still, and the movement takes place from the knee joint, with the foot pointed strongly outward.

**165.** The Small Beatings are especially adapted to training the ankle; the large affect the hip joint; and the medium develop the activity of the knee.

**166.** Simple Beatings (*Battements Simples*). If the free foot returns to its original position, the beating is called Simple.

**167.** Crossed Beatings (*Battements Croisés*). If it is carried to the crossed (3d or 5th) position, it is a Crossed Beating (*croisé*).

**168.** Changed Beatings (*Battements Changés*). If the beating be with the same foot forward and backward, it is called changed (*changé*).

**169.** Alternate Beatings (*Battements Alternatifs*). And if it is made first by one foot and then the other it is termed alternate (*alternatif*).

**170.** Beatings may be executed in all directions, from an open to a closed position, but are usually commenced from a preparatory closed one.

**171.** They may be either glided or carried, and therefore may be either audible or inaudible.

## Gliding  (*Glisser*)

**172.** The word *glisser*, which is the French term for gliding, also expresses in that language those other forms of movement which, in English, are known by the more specific names of sliding, slipping and tracing.

In our language, the difference is as follows:

**Gliding** is a simple leg movement by means of which the foot is moved from one position to another lightly touching the floor in transit.

**Sliding** is a voluntary movement in which the body is propelled along a surface by means of its own weight, or the momentum derived from a previous movement.

**Slipping** is an involuntary or unintentional movement by means of which either one or both feet move upon a surface.

**Tracing** (French, *tracer*) is the indication of movement, or the lines of movement, upon the floor without transfer of weight.

**173.** *Glisser* should not be confounded with the terms *glissez*, *un glissé*, and *un glissement*.

*Glisser*, being the infinitive, means to glide.

*Glissé* is the technical term which signifies a gliding step or *battement*; *un glissé* designates a glided step (*un pas glissé*), and *glissement* is the term by which a gliding movement is known.    More particulars may be found in § 480.

**174.** Gliding may be executed upon either the sole, ball, point or heel, and is written as follows: sole ⌢, ball ⌢, point ⌢, and heel ⌢.

## Carrying  (*Porter*)

**175.** All beatings that are not glided are said to be Carried, and this includes that class in which the free foot does not touch the floor in transit.

**Carrying** (*Porter*) is of so self-evident a nature that it is seldom necessary to express it in dance-writing.  There are cases, however, in which clearness is gained by employing a symbol, and the following signs may be used: upward ╱, horizontal ──, and downward ╲.

## Crossing Before and Behind (*Dessus et Dessous*)

**176.** If in a crossed beating the foot passes before the supporting leg, it is called *dessus* (over), and if it passes behind the support, it is called *dessous* (under).  Strictly speaking, these movements should be referred to as crossing before or behind, but it is preferable in the technical sense to omit the word and to adhere to the French usage; thus obviating the confusion that arises from the employment of similar terms to express different attributes.

## Direction of Movements

**177.** Movements may be either forward, backward or to the side, in either straight or curved lines.

**178.** **Straight movements** may be either directly forward, backward, to either side, over or under crossed; and oblique movements, to either side forward or backward, over or under crossed.

**179.** **Curved movements** may describe either whole or part circles, or elliptical, waving or spiral lines.

It is plain, therefore, that the beatings may be combined in almost endless variety, and the more deeply the student studies the art, the more arduously must he practice, in order to properly execute the steps and movements.  For the choregraph, or dance-writer, the *battements* are doubly important.

## Beatings for Social Dancing

**180.** Only the following *battements* are imperatively necessary for social dancing:

1. The small crossed beatings from the 3d into the 2d position (*les petits battements croisés de la 3ième à la 2ième position*).

2. The same forward or backward from 3d into 4th position.

3. The same forward and then backward, alternately.

4–6. The corresponding large *battements* in all above directions, to the half height.

7. The medium changed *battements* in different degrees of speed (varying tempo).

# Chapter V

## THE APPORTIONMENT OF TIME

SOME remarks relating to the coincidence of music and dancing may have appeared necessary in connection with the bending exercises, but they have been deferred until now in order to more clearly demonstrate their importance to the student by creating an imperative demand for them in his mind.

It will be unanimously conceded that without this coincidence, dancing becomes disagreeable both to the dancer and to the observer; and although this fact is based upon a sense of measure which is instinct to most persons, there are comparatively few who clearly understand the reason of it.

Now, while an imperfect sense of time may be sufficient to satisfy most social dancers, the professional dancer, the dancing teacher, and the choregraph, must be so completely informed on the subject that he is conscious of what he is doing at all times. We are hardly surprised, however, at the present time, to find not only social dancers, but professionals who demonstrate by every step and movement their imperfect conception of time, rhythm and accent.

182. Exercises and steps for dancing are usually practiced by counting, before they are combined with music, and in so doing, the measures of music are not expressed, the count relating merely to the beats, or part measures, which constitute the step-syllables; for there are in dancing steps of more than one beat, which may be compared to words of more than one syllable; and the dancer counts the number of time or step-syllables in the same manner as the poet does the sound-syllables in completing his scansion. These dance-syllables are called *tempi.*

### Measure of Speed (*Tempo*)

183. Every movement consumes a certain period of duration which varies in accordance with its length and form. This applies most conspicuously to the jumped steps. A long jump consumes more time than a short one, as the falling back takes longer, in accordance with the natural law of falling bodies. Glide dances may be executed in quicker tempo

than those in which the feet are lifted from the floor, and it is, for that reason, nonsensical to urge musicians to play in more rapid tempo than the quality of the step requires.

The proper tempo may be decided by the metronome.


## Metronome


**184.** In the days before the invention of the metronome by Maeltzel, certain Italian words, such as Adagio, Allegro, Presto, etc., were used throughout the world for the expression of the various degrees of speed in rendering musical compositions, but since that time this ingenious little pyramidal machine, which divides the duration of a minute into equal parts, has been universally adopted. The pendulum, which marks these divisions by audible strokes, is so arranged that a scale shows the various divisions from 40 to 208; or, in other words, it is arranged so that it may swing at a rate varying from 40 to 208 strokes to a minute.

One of these machines should be in the possession of every teacher of dancing, for by it alone may the exact tempo be determined. It is not necessary that the dancing teacher should be a performer upon any instrument, but some knowledge of music is absolutely imperative; without it he can never hope to succeed, either as a teacher or as an artist.

For the information of the student who is perhaps only slightly acquainted with the subject of music, the following explanations have been inserted, and careful consideration thereof is earnestly recommended, not only to dancers but also to dance musicians and to composers.


## Explanation of Musical Terms*


**185. Measure.** 1. In music the term measure is applied to the division of sounds into periods of equal duration, and these are indicated upon the "staff" by means of perpendicular lines, which express the form or rhythm of the composition.

2. The term is also applied, in a qualifying sense, to the regular succession of such periods of duration.

Of the various kinds of music measures, the most common in dancing are what are known as 2-4, 3-4, 4-4, 3-8 and 6-8.

The term measure, as applied to dancing, signifies the division of the dancing steps and movements into periods of duration to correspond with the music and to the maintenance of such periods throughout the dance composition.

---

*The writer has drawn largely upon the "Catechism of the Art of Dancing," by Bernhard Klemm, for these explanations. That excellent work contains a masterly exposition of the terms used in music.

**186.** To dance without measure is therefore to move out of harmony with the music, in either more or less rapid tempo, or to vary the speed regardless of the rhythm of the sound. Such lack of measure in dancing is due either to ignorance as to measure, or to inattention or carelessness.

**187. Accent** is that quality of speech by which the sense of words is conveyed or affected by means of a stronger or a lighter pronunciation of certain syllables. In music it is the demonstration of the theme by means of strengthening the tone which forms a certain portion of the measure, and without which the melody would not be properly expressed. In dancing, the term is applied to that part of the descending step which coincides with the heavy part measure in music, and if the dancer accents the wrong portion of the measure he is said to dance in false measure (*en fausse mesure*), even though he maintain the proper tempo. Accent usually applies to the first part of the measure, but there are certain exceptions to this rule.

**188. Down-Stroke and Up-Stroke** (*Thesis et Arsis*). If, in beating the measure, a musician lowers his baton on the first part-measure, it is called "beating down" (*Thesis, frappé*, ∧); and if he raises his baton upon the last part-measure, it is called "beating up" (*Arsis, levé*, ∨).

**189.** Preparation for a step is made by raising the leg during the beating up.

**190. Syncope** in music is the continuance of an unaccented into an accented note, and in dancing it is the execution of an unaccented step closely joined to an accented one.

**191. Rhythm** is the symmetrical regulation of time and the periodical repetition of the same arrangement. In poetry, rhythm is applied to the arrangement of syllables; in music to the division of tones; and in dancing the term refers to the coincidence of movement and music.

**192. Cadence,** which is derived from the Latin word *cadere*, to fall, is the term applied to the final down-beat in a passage of music. Cadence is the quality which expresses the intent of the dancer by means of rests and pauses, in the same manner as cadences of speech and song aid the expression of the speaker and the singer by means of raising or lowering the voice, or of lengthening or shortening the enunciation of a syllable, or the emission of a tone. If, therefore, a dancer finishes a certain chain of steps either before or after the corresponding musical cadence, he is said to be in false cadence.

## Sentences and Phrases (*Enchaînements*)

**193.** If two dance movements are connected, the combination is called *une phrase* (a phrase), and the combination of several such phrases constitutes what is known technically as an *enchaînement*, or a step-sentence.

**194.** If the step-sentence or *enchaînement* is repeated in each measure, the accent falls upon the first syllable, thereby clearly demonstrating the measure; but in cases in which the enchainment extends through two measures, as in the Waltz, the Galop, the Polka, etc., the dancers often begin upon the accented first part of the second measure, thereby dancing in false measure, although in accordance with the time. This is best explained by the term "dancing across the music." Special attention to measure must be paid in those dances whose enchainment requires four music measures for their execution, such as the Mazurka, the Polka, the Schottische, etc., and in those in which the combination of steps extends through eight measures; as, for instance, the Cracovienne, the Hongroise and the Varsouvienne, where it is easier still to fall into incorrect measure.

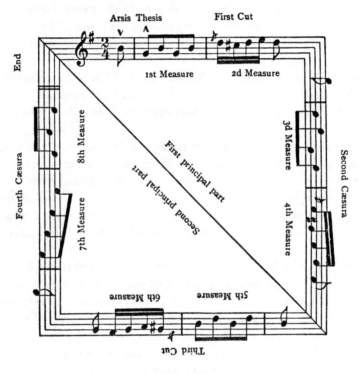

FIG. 161.

195. In the Varsouvienne the tempo remains the same, although the rhythm is changed, and one is therefore doubly liable to miss the measure.

196. **Faulty Composition of Dance Music.** Dancers frequently step into false measure because of faulty composition or poor rendering of the music.

197. Each strain of a piece of dance music contains, ordinarily, eight measures, which may be compared to a square [Fig. 161]. This square, which contains the melody (*Clausula*) may be divided into its eight measures, each two of which constitute a "cut" or "*Cæsura*," and two such "cuts" form a principal part; two principal parts making up the entire melody. By thus analyzing a composition, it will be seen that the first and third "*Cæsuras*" are of like rhythm. They are therefore said to be "parallel"; but while the

second and fourth are also similar, there is the distinction that, while the second indicates a continuance of the melody, the fourth contains its conclusion.

**198.** Fig. 161 demonstrates the necessity for composing dance music in strains of eight measures; but if such a number is insufficient for the composer he may sometimes use ten measures, without seriously disturbing the dance, but melodies of twelve measures should be avoided in such figure-dances as the Mazurka and the Quadrilles. It is to be regretted that this fault is very common in Mazurka music, for such compositions can only be used in the execution of "free" figures, such as the "Serpent," the "Pyramid," etc.

**199.** Ballet music is either written originally for the dance or else the ballet-master composes the dance to correspond with a certain composition to which it is always executed. In such cases the number of measures is immaterial; it is left to the judgment or taste of the composer or choregraph.

**200.** In Social Figure Dances, however, the number of measures is unchangeable, and as the dances may be executed to different musical compositions, such music must be so arranged as to coincide with the enchainment.

**201.** An introduction of several measures often precedes the melody of a dance composition, and although it is left entirely to the judgment of the composer to prefix such an introduction as may be necessary, it should be as short as possible and should end with a decided cadence, in order that the dancers may recognize the commencement of the dance melody. The prelude should never be repeated during the execution of a dance, and even the "to place" which occurs in Quadrille music as an introduction to each strophe or couplet is, in reality, entirely superfluous.

**202.** No prelude whatever should precede the "*trio*" or any other part of a dance composition, for a prelude would render the execution of the regular figure impossible; as indicated in Fig. 162.

FIG. 162.

**203.** Many of the most celebrated composers make this mistake, and in the "Wine, Woman and Song" Waltz, No. 2, this error is especially annoying, for the prelude contains only three measures [Fig. 163]:

FIG. 163.

These three measures invariably throw the dancers into false cadence, as a waltz rotation requires two measures of music.

The same annoyance, with similar results, arises from the addition of a few measures at the end of a strain, as in Fig. 164, which has been taken from a popular polka:

FIG. 164.

If, therefore, a composer finds it necessary to insert certain chords in order to change to another key, such chords should extend through at least four measures; although they would be more acceptable to the dancers if embodied in a melody of eight or sixteen.

204. In the matter of part measures, special care should be taken; for if they are improperly constructed, they mislead the dancers, who mistake them for the commencement of the melody. In 2-4 time, for instance, only an eighth note should be used; and not more than two eighth notes in 6-8.

FIG. 165.

FIG. 166.

In Fig. 165 we find this mistake, while Fig. 166 is correct.

A similar example in 2-4 time may be found in a popular Quadrille from *La Fille de Madame Angot* [Fig. 167].

FIG. 167.

This error could have been obviated if it had been written as shown in Fig. 168.

FIG. 168.

Thousands of such instances might be cited, but these will suffice to cover the point.

205. A dance musician who has a correct understanding of cadence and accent will clearly interpret the music by placing a strong accent upon the first syllable of the measure, but composers should write their music so that misinterpretation will be impossible, instead of leaving it to the player to properly express their meaning.

206. All dancers can hardly be expected to possess a knowledge of music, but dance

music must, nevertheless, be written for all, and should therefore be composed so that it may be readily understood. Unless a composer understands enchainments, movements and figures, and their rhythm, he should consult a scientifically educated master of dancing before publishing dance music; for even the most perfect musical masterpiece is unfit for dancing if it does not assist the dancer; and the number of incorrectly composed dance compositions is surprising.

**207.** Another, and still more annoying evil must be mentioned, and this is the tendency upon the part of certain musicians to vary the tempo in order to render the music "soulful." In the programs of garden and house concerts, there are usually some numbers of dance music, and of these the musicians frequently render certain measures more slowly and others more rapidly than is proper for dancing. To render music in this manner is destructive of the sense of measure, for if a composition be played several times with a certain variation of tempo, the hearer becomes so accustomed to the variation that it becomes fixed in the mind as the correct form of the piece, and this ruins the conception of the dance rhythm.

**208.** No one is better qualified to make observations regarding the sense of measure than the dancing master, for the contemplation of properly measured dancing develops and refines this sense.

There are, at this time, many more persons who lack a conception of measure than in the days when it was fashionable to dance correctly. Indeed, while there was scarcely one in a hundred dancers who lacked that sense fifty years ago, there are more than ten to-day.

# Chapter VI

## THE BEATINGS

### Raising and Lowering Exercises

IN the raising and lowering exercises which follow the holding of the body must be correct; the knees stretched, and the entire sole should remain upon the floor as long as possible, thus exercising the ankles. Special attention should also be paid to the positions.

It is especially necessary to execute all exercises with such precision as to ennoble the work and to give the dancer that elegance of carriage and manner which tends toward beautiful dancing.

**210. Bad Habits.** It is better to make ten proper movements than a hundred careless ones, as the muscles so quickly become accustomed to either good or bad habits. If the first exercises are carefully executed, a person will dance easily and well, but if they have been neglected with the intention of making corrections later, it will be found that it is much more difficult to make these corrections than it would have been to learn properly from the beginning, because the muscles will have become accustomed to careless movements.

As it is self-evident that one can glide from one sole position to another, no particular instructions in relation thereto will be given.

**211.** Most of the musical examples for the following exercises are extremely simple and old, and may be replaced by any others, so long as the rhythm is correct. Of course, all musical compositions grow old, but although the various compositions may be succeeded by later ones, the necessity for the coincidence of the music and the dance remains the same.

**212. Exercise 20.** Small Simple Beatings (*Petits battements simples*). [Fig. 169].

The signs above the notes upon the rhythm line indicate the manner in which the exercise should be counted before executing it with music.

The sign ( ‿ ) shows the unaccented, and the sign ( — ) shows the accented counts. Counting is of special importance to those pupils who do not understand music, or whose sense of measure is imperfect.

**213. Exercise 20** *a* [Fig. 169] is called Small Simple Beatings of the Right Foot from the 1st into the 2d Position (*Petits battements simples du pied droit de la première position à la seconde*).

**214. Correct Order of Words.** The expressions are given both in the English and the

62

French languages for the benefit of teachers and pupils, and for the purpose of demonstrating the advantage of the correct order of the words, which, if properly systematized, forms a great help to the memory.

These *battements* are called small because they do not pass the limit of the length of one of the feet; and simple, because the foot returns to its original position.

Repeat the music and go through the exercise with the left foot before proceeding to Exercise 20 *b,* and apply the same method to each of the succeeding exercises.

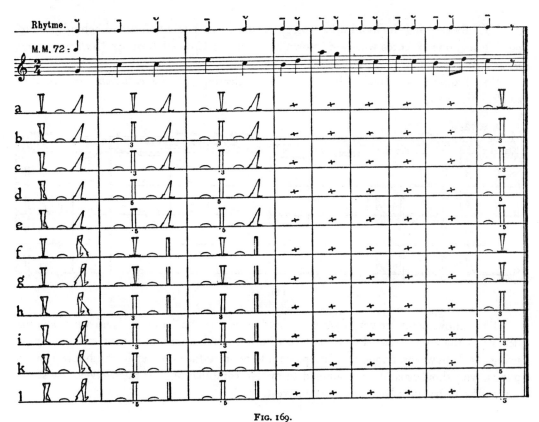

FIG. 169.

**215.** Exercise 20 *b* [Fig. 169] is known as Small Simple Beatings of the Right Foot from the Anterior 3d into the 2d Position (*Petits battements simples du pied droit de la troisième position dessus, à la seconde*).

**216.** Although the 3d is a crossed position (*une position croisée*) the exercise is not called a crossed beating, for the purpose of avoiding confusion, and the word "simple" is sufficient to show that the foot returns to 3d position.

The names for Exercises 20 *b* to 20 *l* [Fig. 169] are easily determined by comparing them with those already described.

It might now appear to be the natural course to extend the execution of these exercises to the intermediate positions, but as the intermediate positions seldom permit a movement of the length of a foot, no complete movement of the ankle could be contained in them and they are therefore not only unnecessary but useless.

## Small Changed Crossed Beatings (*Petits battements croisés changés*)

217. By carrying the foot into a crossed position alternately before and behind the supporting leg, one executes what are known as Alternate Crossed Beatings (*Battements croisés changés*).

218. Exercise 21. Small Alternate Crossed Beatings (*Petits battements croisés alternatifs*) [Fig. 170].

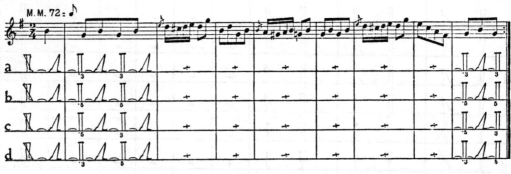

FIG. 170.

These movements are very frequently used, especially "a" and "b" and are of so great benefit to the ankles that they cannot receive too much attention and practice. In practicing them, however, enough variations should be introduced to retain the interest of the pupils, who should also be encouraged to evolve combinations for themselves. By such a course the instruction becomes more interesting.

## Small Alternate Beatings (*Petits battements alternatifs*)

219. If the changes are so executed that one beats first with one foot and then the other, these movements are called Alternate Beatings (*des battements alternatifs*), and if they return to the original position they are called "simple." If they are in the crossed positions they are called "crossed."

220. If the position be first before and then behind, or vice versa, the movement is called Alternate Changed Crossed Beatings (*Battements alternatifs croisés changés*).

If they begin with the foot which is in the rear, they constitute a movement forward; and if they begin with the advanced foot the movement is reversed.

Exercise 22. Small Alternate Simple Beatings (*Petits battements simples alternatifs*) [Fig. 171].

FIG. 171.

**221.** Exercise 23. Small Alternate Crossed Beatings (*Petits battements alternatifs croisés*) [Fig. 172].

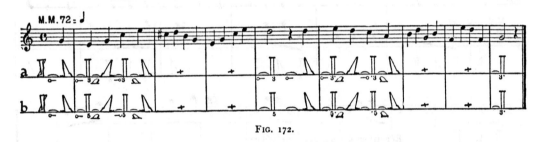

FIG. 172.

These exercises differ from Exercise 22 both in position and in rhythm. The rhythm in Exercise 22 shows the movement continued to the end of the *clausula*; while in Exercise 23 there is a pause (rest) in the fourth measure, for the purpose of changing the direction of the movement. In repeating, begin the movement with the other foot.

**222.** The transfer sign (*dégager*, $\Omega$ or $\Omega$ ), which is to be found below the line of the floor, indicates the proper time for transferring from one foot to the other.

The sole symbol shows which foot should execute the movement.

The terms *clausula*, *cæsura*, and "principal part" were explained in § 197.

The following variations of the foregoing exercises will render still other changes easy.

Exercise 24. Three alternate beatings, rest, and repetition with other foot; four measures walking forward, and four measures walking backward. (*Trois petits battements alternatifs dessus, intervalle et répétition commencée de l'autre pied: 4 mesures. Répétition de ces battements mais dessous: 4 mesures*) [Fig. 173].

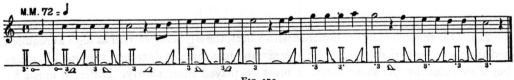

FIG. 173.

Exercise 25. Three Alternate Beatings in a Cut (*cæsura*). First phrase forward, second backward. The second principal part (*clausula*) is executed in the same way as the first [Fig. 174].

FIG. 174.

Exercise 26. Enchainment of Eight Measures (*Variation avec des Intervalles*). Two alternate beatings forward, rest, and repeat. Four measures. Same backward 4 measures. Repeat entire eight measures [Fig. 175].

FIG. 175.

Exercise 27. Two Beatings in Complete and three in Broken Measure; first *clausula* forward, second backward [Fig. 176].

FIG. 176.

## Large Beatings (*Grands battements*)

**223.** These movements commence with a beat, the leg being carried as high as required, and they may be varied in the same manner and to as great a degree as the small beatings; but if executed by the same music it must be played more slowly. Different music has the advantage of being an agreeable change for the student, and its use is therefore recommended.

224. The weight of the entire body, resting as it does, balanced over one foot, renders the outward turned position of the feet more difficult to maintain than if the point of the free foot reached the floor. The *grands battements* are therefore more difficult in execution than the *petits*, and their difficulty increases with the decrease in the tempo. They are usually commenced at M. M. 72, that tempo being gradually diminished to 40.

NOTE. — Although it is customary to practice the large beatings with the aid of a bar or support, they should also be executed in free manner, as greater benefit is to be derived from that form of exercise, after the bar work has been accomplished.

225. Exercise 28. Large Simple Beatings (*Grands battements simples*) [Fig. 177].

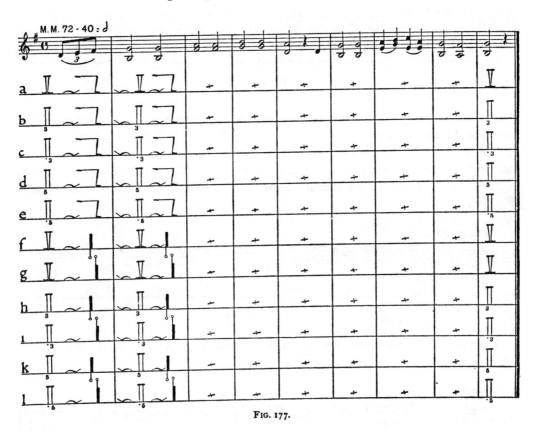

FIG. 177.

Exercise 28 *a* is called large, simple beatings of the right foot, from the 1st sole into high 2d position, with perpendicular sole-direction. This verbal description clearly shows the advantage of the signs over the words, as it takes many words to explain what may be conveyed by the use of very few signs.

226. The sign ⌒ represents the beating of the point of the foot upon the floor

which precedes the movement of the leg into a horizontal or "high" position; and the opposite sign, ‿⌒ signifies that the leg is lowered and the foot beats back again to its original position.

227. Exercise 28 *b* is known as large simple beatings of the right foot from the anterior 3d into the high 2d position. The word "simple" signifies that the beating returns to the original position.

In Exercise 28 *c* the right foot stands in posterior 3d position.

These exercises should also be executed with the other foot.

Exercise 29. Large Beatings to Half Height (*Grands battements à demi-hauteur*) [Fig. 178].

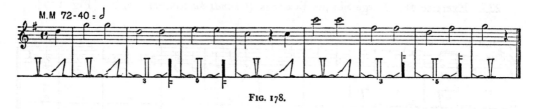

FIG. 178.

This Exercise is composed of those movements contained in Exercise 28 which are carried to the half height.

The choregraphic symbols of the degrees of height were explained in §§ 61 and 75 and illustrated therein by cuts and diagrams. Some of these signs are used in this Exercise.

Exercise 30. Large Simple Beatings upon the Ball (*Grands battements à demi-hauteur*) [Fig. 179].

FIG. 179.

Exercise 31. Large Simple Beatings upon the Point (*Grands battements simples sur le pointe*) [Fig. 180].

FIG. 180.

Exercise 32. Alternate Large Crossed Beatings (*Grands battements croisés changés*) [Fig. 181].

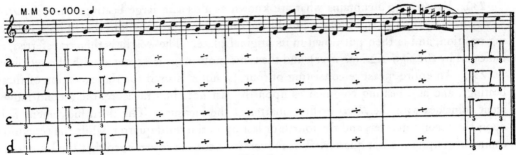

FIG. 181.

228. The signs of movement have been purposely omitted, as they have been rendered unnecessary by the full descriptive titles of the exercises.

229. Exercise 33. Alternate Large Beatings (*Grands battements alternatifs*) [Fig. 182].

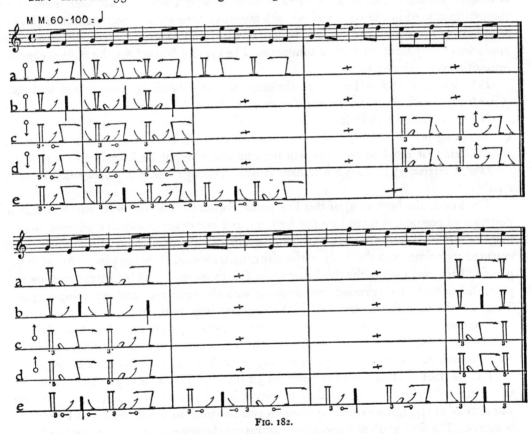

FIG. 182.

At the commencement and in the middle of this Exercise appears a sign that has not been used before. It is called the "key" and it indicates the movement of the free foot in the air. This sign will be fully explained in § 353.

**230.** Exercise 33 *a* contains what are known as alternate large beatings (*Grands batte-ments alternatifs*). The right foot is lifted from the 1st sole position into the 2d high balanc-ing position, and is then put down in its original place. The weight is then transferred, as indicated by the sign ⏜ (*dégager*), and the same movement is executed with the left foot.

**231.** An entire measure consisting of four ¼ notes is used for the execution of these beatings, and as a beating commences upon the last note in a measure, the second move-ment coincides with the *thesis* or first quarter of the measure. The third movement falls upon the second quarter, and the fourth or last upon the third quarter, while the repetition commences upon the last quarter. The movement has been so arranged that the last move-ment coincides with the third part measure, for the purpose of distinctly expressing the cadence.

**232.** It will be noted that in the second measure the transfer sign, and in the third and fourth measures the lifting and putting down signs have been omitted, and that they have been again written in the fifth measure. This is because a new line has been used. The abbreviations used in the sixth and seventh measures have already been explained [§ 141] as indicating a repetition of the preceding measure; and as they are regular signs from music-script they need no further comment. The symbol is used for the mutual conven-ience of reader and writer.

**233.** Exercise 33 *b* is known as the alternate large beatings forward and backward (*Grands battements alternatifs en avant et en arrière*).

In this exercise the right foot is lifted from the 1st sole position into the high anterior 4th balancing position, and put down in its original place; when the weight is transferred, and the left foot lifted to posterior 4th position and brought back again to 1st position.

**234.** Exercise 33 *c*. Large alternate crossed beatings (*Grands battements alternatifs croisés*).

The key at the beginning of this line points forward. The left foot, which stands in posterior 3d position, is lifted into the high 2d, and put down in anterior 3d position; the weight transferred, and the same movement made with the other foot. This movement is executed four times and the body is thereby carried forward from the place. Another key pointing backward follows the third part of the fourth measure, and indicates that from that point the movement is reversed, commencing with the right foot and returning to place. These are the most frequently used of the alternate large beatings.

Exercise 33*d* differs from 33 *c* merely in position, starting from the 5th instead of the 3d.

**235.** Exercise 33 *e* contains the alternate large beatings with direction sidewise and for-ward (*Grands battements alternatifs avec changement de direction de côté et en avant*).

The left foot is lifted from the posterior 3d into the high 2d and put down in anterior 3d position, then again lifted to high anterior 4th and put down in anterior 3d position. The symbol of repetition extending through two measures means to repeat both preceding measures. The fifth, sixth and seventh measures are the same as the first, second and third, but the eighth ends upon the third quarter.

All of these exercises should be practiced in different directions and various heights, according to different rhythmic arrangement.

**236.** It requires much more space to explain the various choregraphic signs and abbreviations than to express their meaning by applying them to the musical score, but it is no more difficult to acquire skill in reading them than in learning to read the script of language or of music.

**237.** The exercises which now follow, although belonging, on account of their construction, to the bending and stretching exercises, have been deferred until this time, because their difficulty has rendered them impracticable up to this point [§ 144].

**238.** The Intermediate Beatings (*Les battements moyens, ou les battements sur le cou-de-pied*).

In lifting the right foot into the low 3d balancing position, as in Fig. 183, it will be noticed that the right leg is bended, thereby throwing the knee strongly outward. The uninterrupted extension of the right leg, through this position into the 2d low balancing position, followed by so bending the knee as to carry the foot again into the 3d low balancing position, is technically known as the *battements sur le cou-de-pied*. These beatings tend to train and develop the knee-joint.

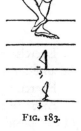

FIG. 183.

**239.** This exercise is styled Intermediate Beatings (*battements moyens*), because, while the free foot may beat upon the supporting leg, and the movement of the leg may be greater than the length of a foot, which is the limit of the small beatings, it is impossible to so execute the movements as to fill the specifications of the large beatings.

**240.** The French term, *Le cou-de-pied*, which finds its equivalent in the Italian as *Il collo del piede*, may be literally translated into English as *the neck of the foot*, or ankle. While this term may be appropriately applied to that portion of a horse's leg known as the fetlock, there is really no part of the human leg which resembles a neck.

**241.** For the purpose of obtaining a complete bending of the forefoot, the pupil should be made to execute each beating with an audible tap upon the floor; and to perfect his sense of measure, the first part of each measure should be accented by a stronger and more audible beating. This audible beating is known technically by the term *terre-à-terre*. This practice, while it renders the exercises more difficult to learn, will give greater ease and pleasure in execution as the pupil progresses.

Exercise 34. Intermediate Simple Beatings (*Battements moyens simples*). To the greatest possible degree of speed [Fig. 184].

**242.** Exercise 34 *a*. Intermediate simple beatings of the right foot from 1st ball to half-high 2d flowing position, with inclined sole, in which the foot is put down in its original position, palpably touching the supporting leg.

These movements would be simply bending and stretching exercises if the free foot did not touch the supporting leg; that attribute alone constitutes them *battements*.

The choregraphic signs for these movements are the usual bending and stretching signs. If the movement is executed in a flowing position, the fact is made evident by the appropriate sign under the floor line.

Exercise 34 *b* differs from the preceding only in the perpendicular sole direction.

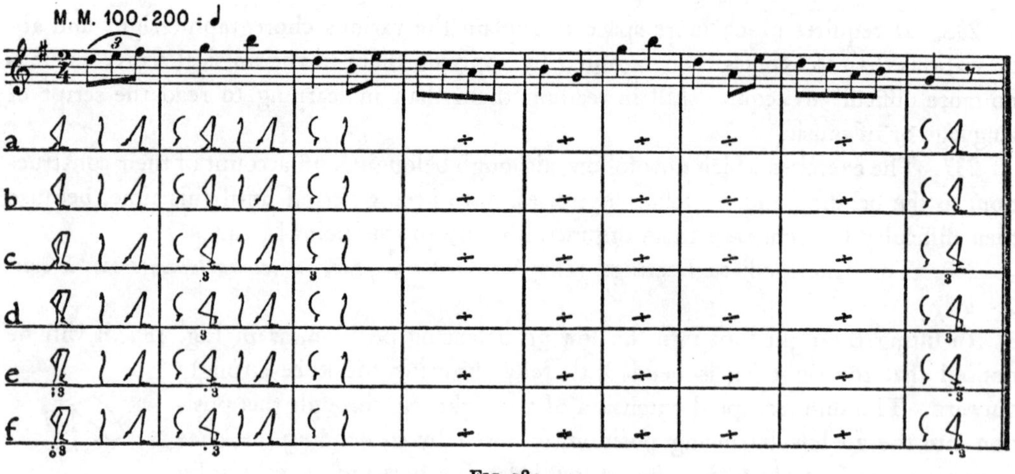

FIG. 184.

Exercise 34 c is composed of the intermediate simple beatings of the right foot, from the anterior 3d ball position into the half-high 2d.

Exercise 34 d differs from 34 c in sole direction.

Exercise 34 e contains intermediate simple beatings of the right foot, from the posterior 3d ball position into the half-high 2d, and back to its original position.

Exercise 34 f is the same as 34 e, but with perpendicular sole.

These exercises may be executed in 5th position by extremely skilful pupils who are able to hold the legs turned completely outward.

243. Exercise 35. Alternate Intermediate Beatings (*Battements moyens changés*). To the greatest degree of speed [Fig. 185].

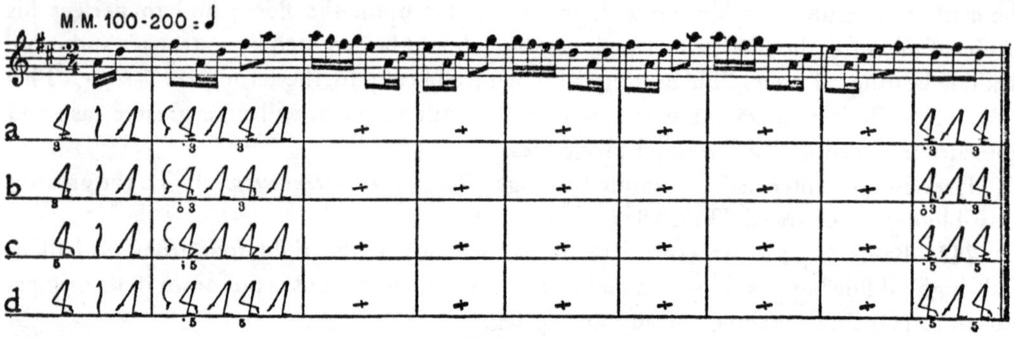

FIG. 185.

Exercise 35 a. The right foot is extended from the anterior 3d ball position (*dessus*) into the half-high 2d, and then put down in the posterior 3d ball position, palpably touching the supporting leg. Repeat in opposite direction.

244. The changement from the anterior to the posterior 3d position renders this move-

ment different from the simple beatings. These positions are illustrated by Figs. 186 and 187. This is the most important of the exercises known as *battements sur le cou-de-pied*.

Explanations of Exercises 35 *b*, 35 *c*, 35 *d*, are not necessary.

245. Exercise 36. Alternate Intermediate Beatings in Varied Rhythm (*Battements moyens changés avec changement de rhythme*). To the most rapid tempo [Fig. 188].

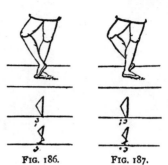

FIG. 186.          FIG. 187.

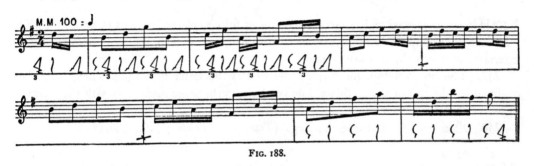

FIG. 188.

This exercise may be practiced in different rhythms. Such practice aids in the appreciation of rhythmic arrangement and educates the musical sense.

# Chapter VII

## TURNING EXERCISES

THE terms *tourner* and *se tourner* have been fully explained in §§ 126 and 127, while the choregraphic symbols are given in § 130, and §§ 156 and 158 contain Raising Exercises in which the feet are turned.

**247.** The simplest sign for turning the foot is the letter *v* [§ 130], which is further qualified by the use of the auxiliary sole symbols, in the same manner as with the position signs.

**248.** Exercise 37. Turning the Legs (*Tourner les jambes*) [Fig. 189].

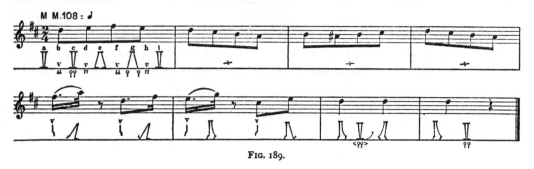

FIG. 189.

In this exercise (*a*) shows the first sole position; (*b*) means to turn both feet upon the heels; (*c*) the feet in parallel first position; (*d*) turning both feet upon the balls; (*e*) inward turned 1-2 intermediate position of both feet; (*f*) the same as *b*; (*g*) parallel 1-2 position; (*h*) the same as *d*, and (*i*) the first position. The first and last mentioned (*a*) and (*i*), are without auxiliary symbols, as it is understood that the feet are turned outward in the 1st position unless otherwise noted; indeed the symbols themselves show the feet in that position. If the turn be executed in a balancing position, the sign (v) is placed above the line of the floor. If the accent sign (∧) be placed horizontally, near the sole sign, as in the seventh measure of this exercise, it indicates that the movement is to be executed sidewise.

**250.** Whether the leg is turned inward or outward is always indicated by the succeeding position sign.

**251.** Twisting (*Tortiller*). The term *Tortiller* signifies twisting, or the simultaneous turning of one foot upon the toe and the other on the ball. This is not a simple move-

74

ment, as it consists of two turning movements, and it will therefore be explained more fully under the head of compound movements and steps in § 532. The choregraphic sign for *Tortiller*, is a double *v* or *w*.

**252. Transferring (*Dégager*.)** This has been explained in § 128 and its symbol is explained and illustrated in § 130.

The transfer of weight in the open positions may be combined with elevations upon the balls or points. Such exercises are usually practiced in 2d position, but the movement should be more thoroughly practiced in the intermediate 2-4 position, as more benefit is to be derived therefrom than is afforded by the 2d.

**253.** These exercises affect the spine, as well as the legs, as no transfer can be made without a certain degree of movement thereof. One may avoid losing the balance by moving the upper body.

Certain movements of the head and arms, combined with the transferring exercises, contribute much to the acquirement of grace [§ 289].

The choregraphic sign of transfer, which is found in Exercise 38, which follows, is in most cases omitted, as the transfer is usually so evident that it is superfluous to indicate it. In such cases, however, as there may be more or less ambiguity as to the exact moment of transfer, the symbol should always be used.

Exercise 38. Raising and Transferring (*Élever et Dégager*) [Fig. 190].

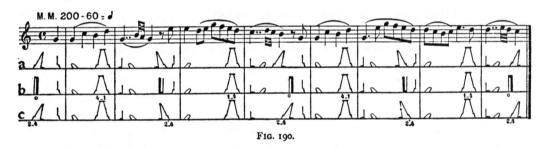

FIG. 190.

Exercise 38 *a*. Stretch right leg to second point position, raise left foot as high as possible, thus throwing both feet into intermediate 1-2 point position [Fig. 191] then lower the right foot to sole position, by which movement the left comes into 2d position. The transfer in raising and lowering is so natural that it needs no comment.

Exercise 38 *b*. Standing in anterior 4th point position of the right, raise the left foot and transfer weight to right, thereby leaving the left in posterior 4th position. At the instant when both feet are entirely raised, they are in intermediate 4-1 point position, and therefore separated by the length of a half step.

Exercise 38 *c* consists in raising and transferring the weight from the anterior 2-4 position of the right to the posterior 2-4 position of the left.

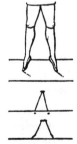

FIG. 191.

## Foot-Circles (*Ronds de jambe*)

The-foot circles differ from the small beatings only in the fact that their transition is curved, while that of the *petits battements* is in straight lines. They are therefore very closely related.

254. A foot-circle is, as its name indicates, a circle described by the foot. In the French language the term *rond de jambe*, which means, literally, circle of the leg, is applied; but as the circle is actually described by the point of the foot with the assistance of the leg, the term "foot-circles" is considered proper.

255. The various foot-circles (*ronds de jambe*) may be classified as follows:

(*a*) Into whole, double and triple or more, and half, quarter and eighth circles.

(*b*) Into large and small circles.

(*c*) Into circles forward, backward, or to the side.

(*d*) Into inward or outward circles.

(*e*) Into bended or stretched circles.

(*f*) Into beaten or carried circles.

256. (*a*) Whole, half and double circles are known by their geometrical form.

(*b*) Small circles are those whose diameter does not exceed the length of the foot; all others are called large circles.

257. A circle forward does not pass farther back than the line of the 2d position, nor does a circle backward reach in front of that line. Circles to the side are exactly bisected by the same line [Fig. 192].

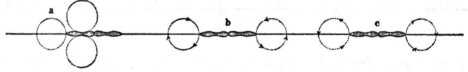

FIG. 192.

258. The circles to the side usually start from 2d position, and if the foot is carried backward, the circle is called "outward," if carried forward, the circle is called "inward" [*b* and *c*]. If a circle to the side starts from 1st position, an "outward" circle is described by carrying the foot forward, and an "inward" by the opposite movement. Any circle which starts forward from an anterior closed position is "outward," and all those which begin with a movement to the side are "inward."

Circles starting backward from a posterior closed position are "inward," while those which start sidewise are "outward."

A circle which starts from the anterior 4th and passes through the 1st and 2d positions is "inward," but if it passes the 2d and then the 1st position, it is an "outward" circle.

Circles beginning from the posterior 4th position and passing through the 2d and 1st are "inward," and those in countermotion are "outward."

Circles starting backward from open intermediate positions are "outward," and those starting forward are "inward." All circles which go in the direction indicated in the preceding figure [*b*] are "inward," and those in [*c*] are always "outward."

**259.** Circles are either "bended" or "stretched," in accordance with the state of the leg.

**260.** Circles which are described upon the floor by the point of the foot are called "glided" circles. If the foot does not touch the floor they are called "carried" or "balanced." These latter may be executed at any height.

**261.** The signs for the various foot circles are as follows:

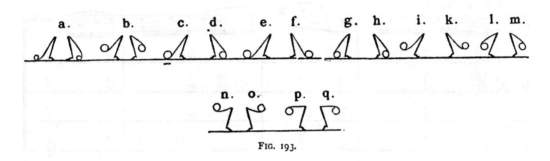

FIG. 193.

(*a*) "Small," of the right and left.
(*b*) "Medium," of the right and left.
(*c*) "Forward" (*dessus*), indicated by auxiliary line under free foot.
(*d*) "Backward" (*dessous*), shown by point over supporting leg.
(*e*) "Outward glided," of the right.
(*f*) "Outward glided," of the left.
(*g*) "Inward glided," of the right.
(*h*) "Inward glided," of the left.
(*i*) "Half-high outward," of the right.
(*k*) "Half-high outward," of the left.
(*l*) "Half-high inward," of the right.
(*m*) "Half-high inward," of the left.
(*n*) "High outward," of the right.
(*o*) "High outward," of the left.
(*p*) "High inward," of the right.
(*q*) "High inward," of the left.

The position from which the circle starts is indicated by the form of the sign.

**262.** Double or repeated circles are designated by the letter "t" (meaning *tours*) which is placed below the line of the floor, accompanied by the number of times the circle is executed, and half and quarter circles are shown by the form of the circle in the drawing or the fraction which is placed below the line of the floor [Fig. 194].

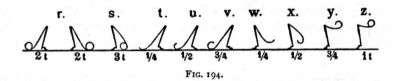

FIG. 194.

Exercise 39. Stretched Glided Foot-Circles to the Side (*Ronds de jambe glissés latéralement*) [Fig. 195].

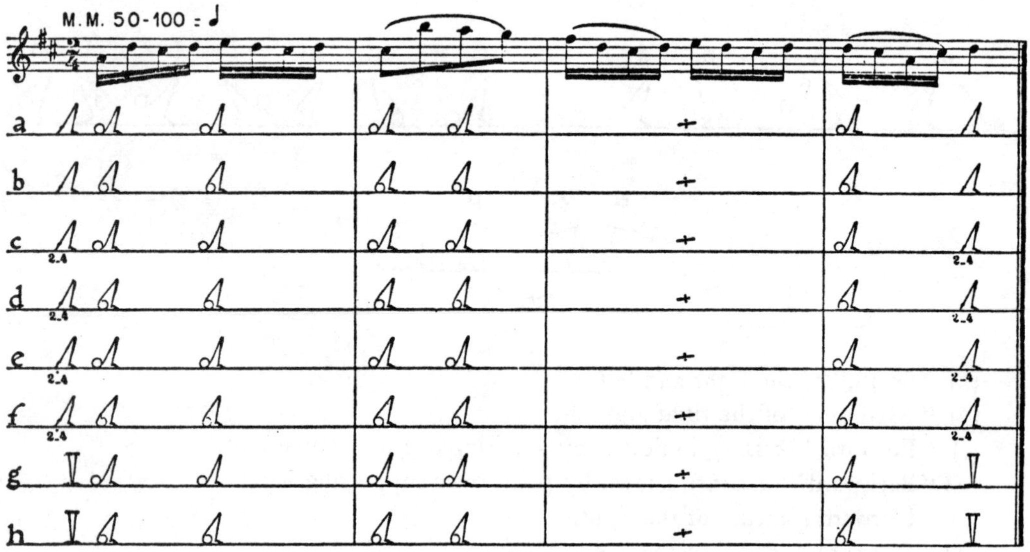

FIG. 195.

Repeat the music and execute the movements with the left foot.

Exercise 40. Stretched Carried Foot-Circles to the Side (*Ronds de jambe portés latéralement*) [Fig. 196].

FIG. 196.

This exercise differs from Exercise 39 only in the fact that the foot does not touch the floor.

Exercise 41. Stretched Glided Foot-Circles Forward (*Ronds de jambe glissés dessus, en dedans et en dehors*) [Fig. 197].

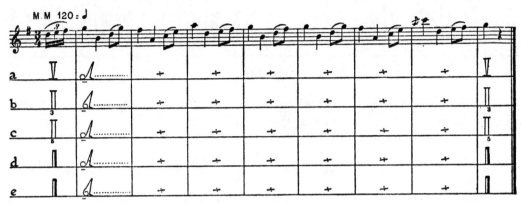

FIG. 197.

Different music for Exercise 41 *b*, without choregraphic symbols, may be found in the Musical Score, arranged for piano accompaniment. The exercises above given should be practiced with that music, as well as with the melody provided above [Fig. 197].

Exercise 42. Small Stretched Glided Foot-Circles Backward (*Petits ronds de jambe glissés dessous, en dehors et en dedans*) [Fig. 198].

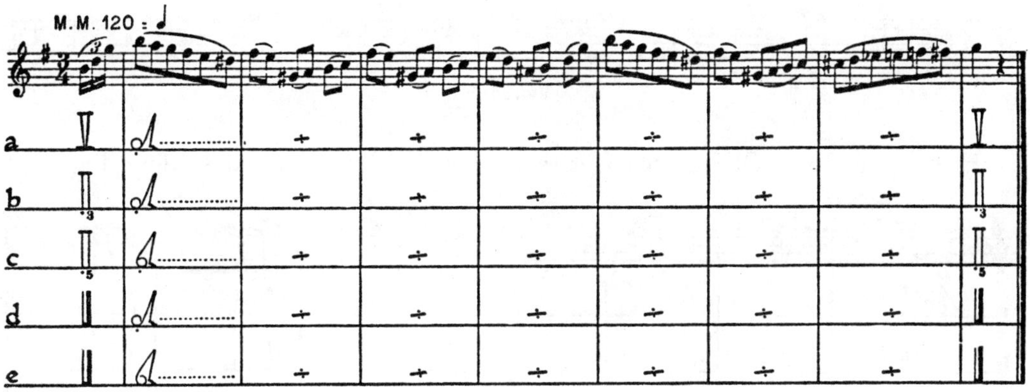

FIG. 198.

The corresponding carried circles may be executed with the same music.

Exercise 43. Three Carried Foot-Circles to the Side and a Transfer (*Trois ronds de jambe portés et un dégagement*) [Fig. 199].

While every movement is written by signs upon line *a* of this exercise, only the most necessary symbols have been expressed upon line *b*.

263. In such cases, as the movement is clearly understood, only the most necessary signs should be used.

FIG. 199.

Exercise 44. Foot-Circle Forward, to the Side, and Backward, and a Transfer (*Ronds de jambe dessus, de côté, dessous et un dégagement*) [Fig. 200].

FIG. 200.

Exercise 45. The same as Exercise 44, but commencing with circle backward and ending with circle forward [Fig. 201].

FIG. 201.

Exercise 46. Large Glided Foot-Circles, combined with Raising and Bending [Fig. 202].

FIG. 202.

Exercise 46 *a*. Raise upon supporting left leg, and bend and stretch same during the lowering. At the same time describe a large outward circle with the right foot, forward.

Exercise 46 *b*. Execute a large inward circle backward with the right foot, during the combined lowering, bending and stretching of the raised and supporting left leg.

Exercise 46 *c*. Execute movements similar to Exercises 46 *a* and 46 *b*, with large circles to the side.

## Accessory Qualities of Movement

**264.** The movements heretofore described may be expressed in other forms which have not yet been mentioned, such as stamping or pounding, rubbing, striking, etc.

**265. Stamping** (*Taper*). To "stamp" one puts his foot down forcibly; this is known in the French language as *taper*.

**Pounding** (*Frapper*). To "pound" with one's foot is to wilfully and forcibly put down the foot in such a manner as to produce sound.

"Stamping" is done with the leg stretched, while the knee must be bended in order to procure the force necessary to "pounding."

Either movement may be executed upon the sole, ball, point or heel, which may be indicated by the regular symbols of sole direction below the line of the floor.

These more than ordinarily strong accents are noted in the choregraphic symbolism by the same sign as is used in the script of music (∧). The difference between the two movements, stamping,—*taper* (∧), and pounding,—*frapper* (∧), is indicated by representing the former by thin and the latter by thick lines. The application of these symbols is fully explained by Fig. 203.

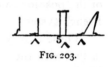

FIG. 203.

**266. Rubbing** (*Frotter*). By this term, as applied to the art of dancing, we designate the movement of the feet one against the other, and the choregraphic sign therefor is ═◖╼ or ─◗╼ . The proper sign is usually placed below the line of the floor, to designate what portion of the rubbing foot comes into actual contact with the other.

**267. Striking** (*Battre*), taken in its technical sense, means to touch the supporting leg sharply with the free foot, which is in transit from an open position. One may "strike" either with the entire leg, the calf, the sole, the edge of the sole, the heel, etc. If, in striking, the free leg touches the support only once, it is called a simple striking; two strokes constitute a double, and three a triple striking, etc.

The signs of these various strikings are as follows [Fig. 204]:

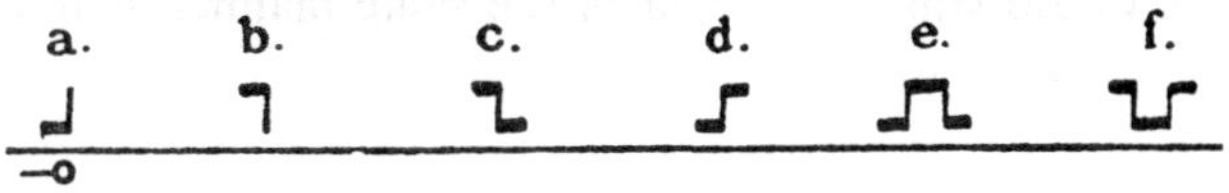

(*a*) Simple forward striking (*Battu simple dessus*).

(*b*) Simple backward striking (*Battu simple dessous*).

a.        b.        c.        d.        e.        f.

FIG. 204.

(*c*) Double striking, backward and forward (*Battu double dessous-dessus*).

(*d*) Double striking, forward and backward (*Battu double dessus-dessous*).

(*e*) Triple striking, forward, backward and forward (*Battu triple dessus-dessous-dessus*).

(*f*) Triple striking, backward, forward and backward (*Battu triple dessous-dessus-dessous*).

If the signs do not of themselves indicate the striking foot, the corresponding sole position should be written.

# Chapter VIII

## CARRIAGE AND MOVEMENT OF THE UPPER BODY AND ARMS

OF the many different systems which have been applied to this department of dancing, that of the so-called French school has become most widely known and adopted, and the exercises practiced according to this system are extremely beautiful and graceful. Still, the representation by the dance script, which describes the order and manner of succession of the positions and movements, makes necessary certain alterations and additions to the French system.

These changes are rather complemental than corrective to that system, and are quite in line with the published wishes of such distinguished writers upon dancing, as Sulzer, Blasis, St. Léon, and B. Klemm, as expressed by themselves. The latter distinctly states that "their systems might be employed, corrected and amplified by artistic masters, to assist in the advancement and development of an art which is able to fight for first place with all works of good taste in regard to æsthetic power" (Klemm's "Catechism of the Art of Dancing," p. 28).

The many fine exercises introduced by the French system may be very distinctly classified by means of a mathematically divided circle of positions.

Our predecessors have accomplished great results, and it is our duty to advance along the road which leads to the perfection of our art by means of the assistance they have left us; but it is only a false admiration for that which has gone before which would prevent corrections or improvements; indeed, had all former writers clung to that line of action, we would still be dancing in the same manner as did Adam and Eve.

### French System of Arm Positions

According to the French system, the horizontal position of the arms at the sides is called the 2d position. Now, if one arm is raised to the horizontal position at the side, and one to the horizontal position in front of the body (the 3d arm position), which arm is actually in proper 3d position? Both. But how is that possible with the arms so differ-

82

ently disposed? Has not one remained in the horizontal side position, while the other has passed into another? The same is true of the French 4th position. One arm is in horizontal side and one in horizontal front position. Which is in 4th position? The 5th position, according to that system, is with the arms raised and forming an oval above the head.

## Zorn's System of Arm Positions

If we hold to the principle that the perpendicular hanging position of the arms is the 1st position, and the perpendicular raised position is the 5th, there exists, theoretically, a circle, the centre of which is just below the gorge, which is described by raising the arms sidewise, and which is shown in Fig. 205.

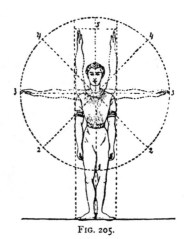

FIG. 205.

In the middle of the circumference, or, as we may say, half-way between the 1st and the 5th positions, we find what we may term the 3d position, and these points are horizontal to the shoulder line. The 4th position falls, consequently, midway between the 5th and 3d, and the 2d at a point equidistant from the 3d and 1st. The position of the arms, therefore, is known by the height to which they are raised.

For the purpose of representing whether the position be sidewise, forward, or backward let us suppose the dancer to be surrounded by a horizontal circle [Fig. 206], and we shall then be able to indicate, with mathematical precision, the exact position to which the arm is carried.

The system embodied in this Grammar is based upon this mathematical foundation, and the difference between our system and that of the French school is that we consider the horizontal position of the arms the 3d instead of the 2d position, and that the heights midway between the 1st and 3d, and 3d and 5th positions are taken as the respective 2d and 4th positions.

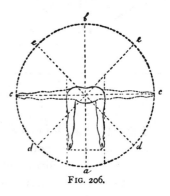

FIG. 206.

In the French system the harmonious coincidence of the arm and foot positions is maintained, the 3d arm position corresponding to the 3d foot position, etc.; while in our system it is necessary to name the position of each. By our method we are enabled to describe all positions exactly. The art of dancing is universal and its script must be capable of expressing all national dances.

## The Carriage of the Arms (*Port de bras*)

**268.** Let us then suppose five positions of the arms, corresponding to the five foot-positions, and from them we may derive all the variations and all the intermediate positions.

## The Principal Arm Positions

**269.** The pendant position of the arms is their natural attitude and is universally understood to be the 1st arm position.

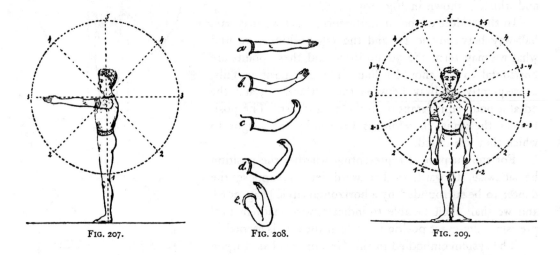

FIG. 207.                    FIG. 208.                    FIG. 209.

**270.** The line from the points of the middle fingers, when both arms are extended to their full length horizontally at the sides, is exactly equal to the distance from the crown of the head, perpendicularly, to the sole of the foot.

These two lines cross one another a little below the gorge, and taking this point as the centre of a circle, we may easily find the various arm positions by dividing the circle into eighths; for the arm positions are based upon this division in our system.

The lowest point in this circle is the location of the 1st position; the points at the ends of the horizontal diameter, that of the 3d; and the highest point, that of the 5th; while the lower intermediate points show the 2d; and the upper intermediate points the 4th position.

It will be noticed that the ends of the fingers touch the circumference of the circle in the 3d position only. This is because of the width of the chest, which affects and increases the distance in that position alone.

Fig. 209 shows all positions as viewed from the front, and stretched sidewise; and Fig. 207 represents them as viewed from the side, and extended either forward or backward.

271. The wholly stretched arm positions occur only in comic dances, for the representation of stiffness, but they are mentioned here for the purpose of more clearly demonstrating the system.

272. Five degrees of bending the arm are recognized. They are known technically as follows: (*a*) wholly stretched, *tendu;* (*b*) half-stretched, *demi-tendu;* (*c*) rounded, *arrondi;* (*d*) half-bended, *demi-courbé;* and (*e*) wholly bended, *courbé-entièrement* [Fig. 208].

FIG. 210.        FIG. 211.

The half stretched positions are most appropriate in serious dances and for tall persons.

The rounded carriage harmonizes with all positions and is most suitable for persons of medium height and full figure. This is the most usual position, and unless qualification is used, the term "arm position" is always understood to mean the rounded form. The half-bended positions occur in the small armcircles (*petits ronds de bras*) in the supporting positions, and in various national dances. Wholly bended positions are seldom used.

## The Intermediate Arm Positions

273. The intermediate arm positions, which lie between the five principal positions, may be found in Fig. 209, which shows not only the principal positions, but also the simple, double and half-intermediate positions.

## Crossed Arm Positions

274. If the arm passes beyond the perpendicular line of position which divides the circle into equal parts, it is said to be in "crossed position" [Figs. 210 and 211].

## Supported Arm Positions

Besides these, there are also what may be termed the interlaced, supported and mimic or imitative arm positions, which will be treated in the following sections.

**275. First Arm Position.** Assume the 1st position, as described in § 8, and allow the arms to hang naturally at the sides, with fingers rounded and the palms turned toward the legs [Fig. 212]. Gentlemen hold their arms in 1st position in Quadrilles and various other dances, and although it was formerly the custom for ladies to hold their arms in 2d position, and carry the dress, the fashion has been so far abandoned that that position now appears affected, and ladies as well as gentlemen usually adopt the 1st position.

FIG. 212.        FIG. 213.

**276. Second Arm Position.** The arms, though hanging, are so rounded as to form an oval, with the elbows turned outward, and the wrist neither noticeably bended nor stretched [Fig. 213]; but so rounded as to harmonize with the curvature of the arm, which, as previously stated, should form a portion of a regular circle. In this position, the little finger may be more fully stretched than the others, so long as it does not pass the arc of the circle of the arms. In theatrical dancing, the first finger is sometimes more fully stretched than the middle one.

**277. Third Arm Position.** The arms are raised (rounded) to the height of the shoulders, and form an open circle; and the forearms are held at an angle of 45 degrees from the straight line of the upper arms [Fig. 214].

FIG. 214.       FIG. 215.       FIG. 216.       FIG. 217.

**278.** This position of the arm occurs frequently in ordinary life as well as dancing. Even the common greeting of " shaking hands " is most gracefully done in this position.

**279.** To present the hand in a straight line, with fully stretched arm, appears stiff and ridiculous, and if the hand be carried higher than the horizontal position of the forearm, it must be lowered again to reach that of the other person. This also looks crude and affected. In the figures of the Quadrille, the Mazurka and the Cotillion, such a position occurs very frequently with either or both arms, and the theory of the " position " for the social round dances is based upon it.

**280.** The left arm of the lady is half-stretched and rests upon the half-stretched right arm of the gentleman. The proper height of raising the arms in this position depends upon the height of the dancers [Figs. 215, 216].

**281. Fourth Arm Position.** The arms are rounded and carried so far toward the perpendicular as to form a circle above the head, in which the breach, or distance between the hands, is equal to the width of the shoulders [Fig. 217]. This position is seldom used in social dancing, but it occurs often in theatrical dances.

NOTE.—The circle is taken as the model for the rounding of the arms, for well proportioned persons, but for persons who are more than ordinarily slender and who have long arms, the oval is more suitable.

**282. Fifth Arm Position.** The arms are raised, rounded, into a perpendicular attitude, and the middle fingers nearly touch. Although this position is never used in social dancing, it occurs frequently in theatrical and national dances, particulary in Spanish dances [Fig. 218].

FIG. 218.    FIG. 219.

## Closed Arm Positions

**283.** All positions of the arms in which the hands touch are called "closed" positions. They occur at all heights; the degree of height determining the number of the position.

## Open Arm Positions

**284.** All arm positions in which the hands do not touch are called open positions. The normal width (distance between the hands) in such positions is the width of the shoulders.

## Narrowed and Amplified Arm Positions

**285.** If the distance between the hands in the open arm positions is less than the width of the shoulders, they are said to be "narrowed"; and if the distance be greater, they are in "amplified" position.

Fig. 219 represents an amplified arm position which is very commonly used.

**286.** To determine the degree to which a position is narrowed or amplified, let us surround the body by a horizontal circle at the height of the shoulders, which will represent the various positions as seen from above.

Fig. 220 shows such a plan. A dotted line passes from the point *a* through the centre of the breast and spine to the point *b*, and marks the point from which the width of the position is determined. The horizontal line *c–c* shows the line of complete amplification; the points *d–d* represent the anterior half-amplified positions, and the points *e–e* show the posterior half-amplified positions.

The choregraphic signs representing these various positions will be found in § 336.

## Opposition

**287.** Opposition is the term which, in the art of dancing, is used to signify an exactly contrasted or opposed position or movement. If, for instance, one arm be in 2d and the other in 4th position, they are in opposition.

**288.** Opposed positions may be either coincident or harmonious, as shown in Fig. 221, which is agreeable to

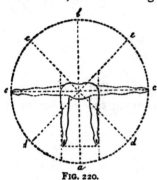

FIG. 220.

FIG. 221.

FIG. 222.          FIG. 223.

the eye; or they may be inharmonious, as shown in Fig. 222, which is not. The inharmony of the position shown in Fig. 222 lies in the fact that one arm is stretched and the other is rounded.

**289.** In walking, the right arm and the left leg are carried forward simultaneously, and vice versa. This may be said to be opposition of movement, and such opposition assists the movement by maintaining the proper balance of the body. The rules for the movements of the arms are all based upon this natural law.

**290.** To insure to the pupil a proper comprehension and appreciation of this law of opposition, the transfer exercises combining the corresponding arm and head movements should be practiced as soon as the simple arm positions have been learned [§ 253].

In practicing this exercise one should start from a position like that in Fig. 223, which shows the right foot in 2d point position, the left arm in 4th, and the right arm in 2d position, with the head turned ⅛ to the right. From this attitude the various members are gradually and simultaneously carried into the opposite

FIG. 224.

positions, while the left heel is raised and the weight is transferred to the right foot. This movement carries the body into the attitude shown in Fig. 224, which represents the left foot in 2d point position, the right arm in the 4th and the left arm in the 2d position, while the head is turned ⅛ to the left. This exercise may also be practiced from the anterior to the posterior 4th position.

**291.** These exercises, if practiced diligently and accurately under the direction of a competent teacher, are of great value (especially for girls). They should be practiced away from the dancing school before a mirror, or if no large mirror is accessible, a lamp may be placed upon the floor of a dark room and the movements followed in the shadow upon the wall.

Exercise 47. Transfer with Arm Movements (*Dégagements et mouvements des bras*) [Fig. 225].

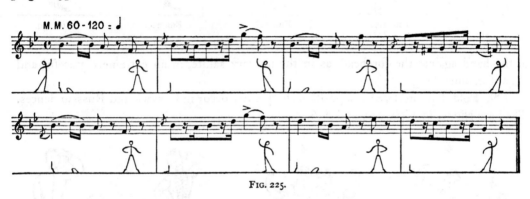

FIG. 225.

## Supported Arm Positions (*Demi-bras*)

**292.** In many dances, particularly those of the Slavic nations, positions may be found in which the arm is bended and the hand rests upon the hip. This is called a supporting position. The technical French term for this position is *demi-bras.*

**293.** The position shown in Fig. 226, in which the palm rests upon the hip, with the thumb backward and fingers forward, is usually reserved for gymnastic exercises.

**294.** The positions in which the closed hand is supported upon the hip are generally used by male dancers and occur most frequently in peasant dances.

**295.** Those in which the joints of the fingers rest upon the hip are usually adopted by female dancers, as they are more graceful than those in which the hand is closed [Figs. 227 and 228].

**296.** Positions in which the head or the elbow are supported upon the back of the hand occur only in mimic dances. They are used frequently in character dances [Figs. 229 and 230].

297. The resting of the hand upon the arm or shoulder of another person, as in Figs. 231 and 232, is very effective, and these attitudes are found in all round dances.

298. The palm of the hand is sometimes placed upon the back of the head in certain Hungarian dances [Fig. 233], and some persons execute the movement of placing the back

FIG. 226.          FIG. 227.          FIG. 228.          FIG. 229.          FIG. 230.

of the hand against the forehead, as in the military salute, in an extremely graceful and elegant manner [Fig. 234].

299. Folded or interlaced arm positions frequently occur in Cossack and Russian dances. They are shown in Figs. 235 and 236.

FIG. 231.          FIG. 232.          FIG. 233.          FIG. 234.

Interlaced fingers, with either inward or outward turned arms, are frequent in character dancing and are very graceful if well executed [Fig. 237].

Interlaced groups, such as are represented by Figs. 238 and 239, are found in unlimited number and variety.

## Mimic or Character Arm Positions

300. No dances are so rich in mimic positions as those of the Russians, unless, perhaps, we might descend to the indecent dances of the Moors and the Spaniards. The very title

of this class of positions so well demonstrates their nature that further explanation would be superfluous.

301. The Polish and the Hungarian dances and those of the Gypsies, the Tartars and the Bayaderes are replete with mimic arm positions; and while the native dancers in this class do not execute their steps with artistic finish and elegance, they certainly do instil into them sufficient of the national characteristics to make them typical of their race, and a thoroughly educated teacher of dancing can so arrange them that they will become presentable as artistic dances.

FIG. 235.          FIG. 236.          FIG 237.          FIG. 238.

## Arm Movements

302. The arm movements have been so beautifully and so clearly described in the "Catechism of the Art of Dancing" by Bernhard Klemm, that the author has, with the kind permission of Herr Klemm, transcribed many of them here.

303. The movements of the arms are entirely independent of, and often opposite to, those of the legs; although the object of each is to harmonize with the other, so as to present a beautiful whole. This independence may be best explained by stating that the arms represent the plastic, and the legs the rhythmic elements of the dance.

FIG. 239.

## Carriage of the Arms (*Port de bras*)

304. The expression *Port de bras* means the ability to carry or hold the arms gracefully, either in curved or in parallel positions, and to change easily and gracefully from

one position to another, by means of either straight or curved movements; consequently it also means the development of formal beauty in the lines described.

The *port de bras* are divided into two classes, the high and the low.

**305.  The Low Port de Bras** include all movements of the arms horizontal to or below the shoulders; and the high, all movements above the shoulders.  The low *port de bras* are used only in social dancing, and the high only appear in the art and national dances.

**306.**  The entire arm contains but five movable parts: the upper arm, the elbow, the lower arm, the wrist and the hand; and the fundamental movements of the arm are raising and lowering.  Each of these movements is executed in accordance with the same rule. In *raising* the movement starts with the upper arm and extends in easy transition to the elbow, forearm, and wrist, ending with the hand.  In *lowering*, the sequence is inverted.

**307.**  In the low *Port de bras* the movements are executed as follows: First, assume a closed position of the feet, observing the rules which apply to the correct holding of the body, and raise both upper arms, turning the elbows and forearms slightly to the front, and curving the wrists to correspond, while the forefingers nearly touch.  The arms are now raised to the height of the breast, where the hands, which are so held that the palms are visible, are separated and carried in their respective directions until an oval is formed before the body.  From this the hands, wrists, forearms, elbows and upper arms respectively are allowed to sink to the original position.  The low *port de bras* should be executed with the feet in 5th position and accompanied by bending and stretching.

**308.  The High Port de Bras** are commenced in the same manner as the low, but the raising continues beyond the shoulder height until the head, which should be thrown back, is framed in the circle of the arms, while the points of the forefingers nearly touch.  The arms should be swayed to right and left and in a circular manner, before they sink gradually to the original position.


## The Simple Arm Movements

**309.**  The simple arm movements are: bending, stretching, raising, lowering, carrying and turning.  The ability to bend and stretch lies in the elbow, the wrist and the fingers, and it may be exercised either in one or more of these joints simultaneously.  The script should clearly show this.

**310.**  The ability to raise or lower the arm, or to carry it horizontally from one position to another, resides in the shoulder-joint.


## Hand-Circles (*Ronds de bras*)

**311.**  In the execution of a regular movement, the hand describes a portion of a circle. If the elbow forms the centre, and the lower arm the radius of such a figure, it is called a small circle; but if the shoulder is the centre, and the entire arm the radius, it is a large circle. In the same manner that a circle described by the foot is called a *rond de jambe*, one drawn by the hand is termed a *rond de bras*.

312. While it is the rule in the *ronds de bras* to draw the circles as large as the radius will permit, in the small arm-circles (*petits ronds de bras*), the first quarter starts from the height of the breast and passes from the perpendicular or 1st arm position into the narrowed 2-3 position; the second quarter from that point to the height of the shoulder; the third quarter to the amplified 2-3 position; and the fourth quarter to the place from which the movement began.

313. The easy bending of the wrist in raising and the corresponding stretching in lowering the arms add much to the grace of the arm movements. Even the fingers must participate in all the movements, being bended to correspond with the degree of bending the arm, and stretched to correspond with the stretching.

## Presenting and Giving the Hand

314. In presenting the hand as in the ordinary salutation, the execution of a quarter circle enhances the grace of the movement; but to raise the arm beyond the 2-3 position, or to too strongly bend the wrist, renders it affected and absurd.

315. In dancing the gentleman always " presents " his hand palm upward ( ), and the lady " gives " hers palm downward ( ), thus signifying that the gentleman must guide, while the lady follows.

316. If a circle is composed entirely either of ladies or of gentlemen, the right hand is presented (palm upward) and the left is given (palm downward). If the circle is mixed (that is, if it contains both ladies and gentlemen), the gentlemen present both hands (palm upward) and the ladies give theirs. The thumb of the presented hand rests lightly over the fingers of the given one.

317. In the large arm-circles (*grands ronds de bras*) the arm is carried, in the first quarter, from the perpendicular into the narrowed 3d position; in the second quarter to the 5th, in the third quarter to the amplified 3d position, and again into the original (1st) position in the fourth quarter.

318. The sixth simple arm movement is known as " turning " or " rolling," but the former term appears to be the more appropriate for the language of dancing.

## Positions of the Hands

Positions in which the palm of the hand is held toward the body are called *inward turned* [Fig. 240], and those in which the palm is turned from the body are called *outward turned* hand-positions [Fig. 241]. The hands may also be held in forward or backward, upward or downward turned positions.

Figs. 242, 243, 244 and 245 show the hands in various positions which are sufficiently described by their names.

Fig. 246 shows the right elbow (*a*) turned outward and the right palm turned inward; while the left elbow (*b*) is turned backward and the left hand turned palm forward.

FIG. 240.                FIG. 241.

Fig. 247 represents the right elbow (*a*) and palm turned outward, and the left elbow (*b*) and palm turned inward.

319. In giving the hand, one should look at the person to whom it is given, thus causing the head to participate in the general movement of the body. This concerted movement is called *tournure*.

FIG. 242.                FIG. 243.                FIG. 244.                FIG. 245.

Forward turned palms.    Backward turned palms.    Forward turned fists.    Backward turned fists.

### Shrugging the Shoulders

320. The shoulders may be raised and lowered entirely independent of all other movements. This frequently occurs in Slavic and Russian dances.

### Carriage and Movement of the Head (*Tenue et Mouvements de la Tête*)

321. The head may be turned to the right or to the left, and inclined forward, backward or sidewise; and it may be moved in a circular manner in the inclined positions.

In turning, the head cannot be moved further than the limit of a quarter circle, as shown in Fig. 248. So complete a turning, however, appears forced, and the ⅛ turn, as shown in Fig. 249, is much more agreeable to the beholder. A slight inclination of the head to one side makes a very pleasing effect.

Many persons who do not possess exceptional beauty, carry the head in so beautiful a manner as to render themselves extremely attractive or " bewitching." Grace is often even more fascinating than cold beauty.

## Movements of the Trunk and Shoulders (*Mouvements de torse et épaulements*)

**322.** The trunk may be turned either to the right or to the left, or bended forward, backward or to the side; and it may be moved in a circular direction in the bended positions.

The limit of twisting in the turning of the trunk (*tour de torse*) is a quarter turn, but so complete a movement always appears forced and the most graceful attitudes are those in which only a one-eighth turn appears.

The movements of the trunk are most clearly noticeable in the shoulders, and are for that reason termed *épaulements*.

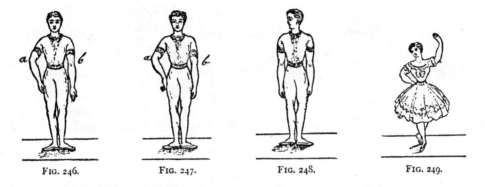

FIG. 246.　　　FIG. 247.　　　FIG. 248.　　　FIG. 249.

**323.** The art of turning is the most graceful and beautiful accomplishment connected with the dance, and is called *avoir une jolie tournure*. This phrase, however, cannot be properly translated to express beauty of carriage, nor regularity of outline, as the word *tournure* implies a movement (turning), and it cannot therefore be expressed by mere attitude or exterior form. The turnings of the body (*tours de corps*) are fully described in §§ 540 to 548.

**324.** In addition to the above movements, the weight of the body may be transferred from one foot to the other by means of turning or bending; but in this movement the muscles of the legs participate so naturally and unavoidably that the sign of transfer is seldom necessary in order to show the movement of the body.

**325.** The bending of the body forward, backward and to the side is particularly common in the Spanish dances and in the ballet.

## Harmony (Coincidence)

**326.** In the language of music, the coincidence of certain tones is called a chord. A combination of harmonious tones creates a pleasing impression upon even those persons who understand little or nothing regarding music, while inharmonious or discordant tones are unpleasant to every one; for the hearing organs of man are so delicately constructed that even the slightest discord is disagreeable to them.

The same is true of the sense and the organs of sight; and a house, a window or a human being whose outline is not symmetrical creates an impression upon the beholder quite as disagreeable to the sense of sight as is an inharmonious sound to the sense of hearing. A swollen cheek or a cross-eye will ruin the most beautiful face, and a lack of symmetry or harmony is equally destructive to beauty of movement.

FIG. 250.

The artist or connoisseur is always able to see such defects, and even those who have little or no technical understanding of the artistic are guided (by intuition?) to a proper sense of what is graceful and what is not. The harmonious disposition of the entire body may be said to constitute a " chord " for the eye.

## Attitude*

327. " Any significant position of the body, either in action or at rest, and upon either or both feet, which gracefully displays the lines of the figure by means of a harmonious holding of the arms and hands, is called an *Attitude*; and such a position expresses the liveliness of artistic repose, which precedes the development of graceful movement."

---

* The following definitions have been taken from " The Catechism of the Art of Dancing " by Bernhard Klemm, as the descriptions he gives cannot be more beautifully or more comprehensively expressed.

## Group

328. " The artistic assemblage of several persons, arranged according to their size, attitude and direction so as to form a harmonious and properly connected whole, is called a *Group*."

## Tableau

329. " The combination of several artistically arranged groups, for the representation of a larger unit, is called a *Tableau* — which is an animate picture instinct with vital energy." [Fig. 250.]

## Choregraphic Signs

for the Positions and Movements of the Head, the Arms, the Shoulders and the Trunk.
(*Signes chorégraphiques des positions et mouvements de la tête, des bras, des épaules et du tronc.*)

330. The head is represented by an oval ring, whose form and shading indicate the direction of the face, as in Fig. 251:

331. The long perpendicular line in this sign represents the body; the horizontal line the shoulders; and the short oblique lines at the sides, the arms.

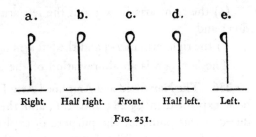

| a. | b. | c. | d. | e. |
|----|----|----|----|----|
| Right. | Half right. | Front. | Half left. | Left. |

FIG. 251.

332. The degree of bending in the arms is indicated by the shape of the sign:

— Stretched (*tendu*).
⌒ Half-stretched (*demi-tendu*).
⌣ Rounded (*arrondi*).
∨ Half-bended (*demi-courbé*).
V Entirely bended (*courbé entièrement*).

333. Unless specifically mentioned, the arm positions are always understood to be in rounded form.

**334.** The signs of the five principal arm-positions are as follows: —

These symbols show the choreography of Figs. 212, 213, 214, 217, and 218.

## Intermediate Arm Positions

**335.** Fig. 252, as has been already stated [§ 273], shows the height of the various intermediate positions which are denominated by the double numbers.

Therefore, if an arm appears in an intermediate position, it may be clearly indicated, either by the position of the arm-line or by the numbers themselves, or both, as shown in Fig. 253, which represents:

(*g*) the right arm in the 2-1 and the left arm in the 4-5 position;

(*h*) the right arm in 2-3 and the left arm in 3-4 position; and

(*i*) the right arm in 2-3 and the left arm in 3-4 position. The last sign is an abbreviation of the regular script.

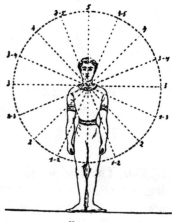

FIG. 252.

**336.** The Narrowed and Amplified Arm Positions have been explained in §§ 285 and 286, and the drawing referred to in § 286 is again introduced at this point for the purpose of explaining the manner of designating their various degrees [Fig. 254]. The letter *a* shows the point at which the hands touch before the body; *b* indicates the corresponding point behind the body; *c* the points of the greatest possible amplification; *d* the half-amplification forward; and *e* the corresponding points backward. These letters are written above the position signs [Fig. 255], which show respectively the 1st anterior closed; the 2d half-amplified; and the 3d wholly amplified positions.

The second example is an abbreviated sign.

**337.** The expressions "wholly narrowed" and "closed," while synonymous in meaning, contain a distinction and a difference, notwithstanding the fact that the fingers of both hands, or indeed both arms, may touch; as the term closed position can only be applied when both hands are brought together; while a wholly narrowed position may be assumed, with only one arm, the other remaining in an open position.

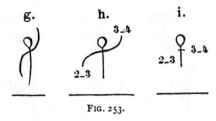

FIG. 253.

**338.** If an arm passes from the half-circle of its side, as in Figs. 210, 235 and 238, it enters what is called a crossed position, which position has already been explained in § 274. These positions may be indicated in the script either by the form of the sign or by a cross (×) placed above the arm-line [Fig. 256].

*n* shows the right arm crossed in front. (Observe the small a and the ×.) In cases which demand greater clearness, the side-lines of the body which complete the drawing may be added.

In *o* the left arm is represented as in posterior crossed position.

*p* indicates that both arms are in anterior 3d crossed position.

## Opposed Arm Positions

**339.** In Fig. 257, *q* the right arm is in 2d and the left in 4th position.

In *r* the right arm is half-backward in the 4th, and the left half-forward in the 2d position.

*s* represents the right arm in half-forward 2-3 position, and the left in half-backward 3-4.

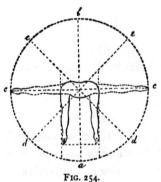

FIG. 254.

## Supporting Arm Positions (*Demi-bras*)

**340.** The sign of the supported hand ends with a fork, but in the usual drawing only the forepart appears. This fork touches the figure at the point of support (*t*).

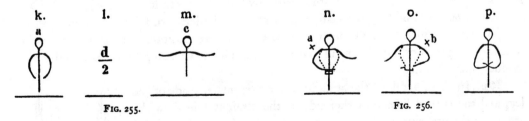

FIG. 255.                FIG. 256.

The sign of the supported knuckles is round and with palm turned outward (*v*), and that of the supported fist is a ring (*u*) [Fig. 258].

In Fig. 249 the right arm is supported upon the knuckles, and the left is in 4th position.

**341.** In cases where the choregraphic symbols are insufficient for showing the lay-

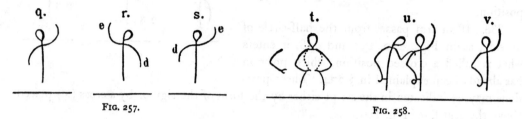

FIG. 257.                    FIG. 258.

ing on of the hand, or the crossed or the mimic hand positions, the figure must be more fully represented by means of a drawing.

## Arm Movements

**342.** The right arm (*bras droit*) is represented by this sign ⎯, and the left (*bras gauche*) by this one : ⎯.

A dotted horizontal line indicates the continuance of a movement, and the position sign which succeeds it shows the result of the movement by representing the position in which it ends.

**343.** If the movement is otherwise than in a horizontal line, the line of continuance is drawn so as to show the exact figure of movement, and an arrow point is placed at the end to show its direction. If the movement is curved, it is represented by a curved line ; and if it is undulating, a wavy line will show the course of the movement [Fig. 259].

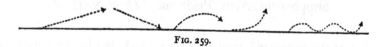

FIG. 259.

**344.** The signs for "raising" and "lowering" are similar to those for moving the arms, but may be distinguished by their unbroken lines :

**345.** *Tourner* (Turning) is usually represented by the letter *v*, followed by the sign of the position in which the movement terminates. As the position signs may at times be indefinite, signs showing the hand positions are added wherever they may render the symbol more distinct.

**346.** In these symbols the straight line represents the side of the leg, and the curved lines on either side of the straight line show the arms. In the first sign the hands are represented with the palms turned toward the body ; and in the second, which represents the hand in a convex position, the palms are turned outward.

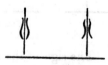

## Carriage of the Head

**347.** The degree of turning the head is indicated in the sign by the shape of the line, and by the shading which represents the hair; and the inclination of the head is shown by the line which represents the neck.

**348.** To indicate the turning of the shoulders, the musical sign # is placed on that side of the symbol toward which the movement is made [Fig. 260].

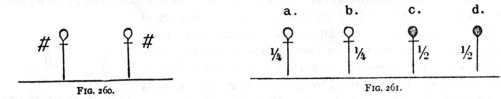

FIG. 260.          FIG. 261.

**349.** If the dancer does not stand fully facing the observer, the fractions showing the degree of turning are used instead of the double cross, as in Fig. 261, which shows:

    *a.* Quarter-turn to the right.
    *b.* Quarter-turn to the left.
    *c.* Half-turn to the left.
    *d.* Half-turn to the right.

**350.** If the body be inclined, the fact is shown by a corresponding inclination of the body-line in the sign, in the proper direction, as in Fig. 262, which shows:

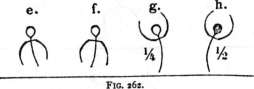

FIG. 262.

    *e.* Inclination of the body to the right with pendant arms.
    *f.* Same to left.
    *g.* Quarter-turn and inclination to right, arms raised.
    *h.* Half turn and inclination to right. This sign shows the dancer with his back toward the spectator, as a half turn would place the dancer in that relative position. In such drawings the right of the dancer is at the right of the figure, etc., and the entire symbol is opposite to that used for the representation of the front view. The darkening of sign of the head, to indicate the hair, is the best way to show this position by chorographic sign.

## Shrugging (Raising) the Shoulders

**351.** The shrugging or raising of the shoulders has been referred to in § 320. This movement is indicated in the script by means of the regular lifting sign, which is placed above the shoulder to which it applies. The lowering is shown by placing above the proper shoulder the regular sign of putting down. Each is shown in this drawing.

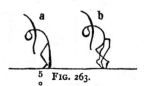

**351 a.** *Ramasser-Movements.* Strong bending movements, accompanied by deep lowering of the arms (as in picking up objects from the floor), are of frequent occurrence in Spanish dances, and are known as *ramasser-movements.* These movements may be represented by choregraphic signs, but in very complicated signs the script will be more intelligible if accompanied by drawings of certain positions of the figure [Fig. 263 *a* and *b*].

FIG. 263.

## Arm-Circles

**352.** In order to properly designate or describe an arm-circle, one must ascertain from which position, and in what direction, it is executed. In the script the starting point is

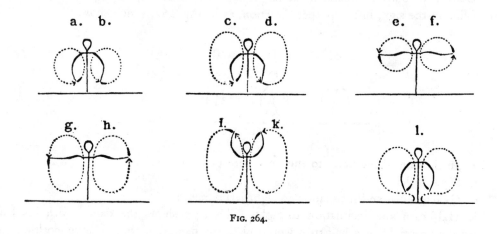

FIG. 264.

shown by a comma; the continuation by a dotted line; and the direction and finishing point by an arrow head [Fig. 264].

This sign shows (*a*) small inward circle of the right, and (*b*) small outward circle of the left, from the 1st position.

*c.* represents a large inward circle of the right, and *d.* a large outward circle of the left, from the 1st position.

*e.* shows a small downward circle of the right; and *f.* a small upward circle of the left, from the 3d position. A large downward circle of the right is shown by *g.*; and a large upward circle of the left from the 3d position by *h.*

*i.* represents a large outward circle of the right; and *k.* a large outward circle of the left from the 4th position.

*l.* shows large inward circles of both arms, from the 2d position, ending in the hip support.

## The Choregraphic Key (*La Clef*)

**353.** In the script of music a clef is a symbol which is placed upon a given line of the staff, to indicate the pitch of the note which is placed thereon. In the script of dancing a similar symbol is used to indicate the line of direction to be followed by the dancer. The effect of the key continues until it is superseded by another.

The form of such keys may be either straight, diagonal, circular, spiral, wavy or zig-zag, and indicates the figure which is to be described upon the floor. The first step always follows the direction of the key.

The twenty-five keys which are shown in Figs. 265*a* and 265*b* are used according to their various descriptions:

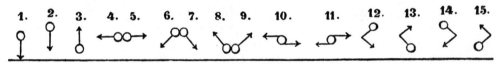

FIG. 265*a*.

1. Movement to be executed upon the place.
2. " " " " forward.
3. " " " " backward.
4 and 5. Movement to right and to left, respectively.
6 and 7. " diagonally forward to right and to left, respectively.
8 and 9. " diagonally backward to right and to left, respectively.
10. Movement alternating from right to left.
11. " " " left to right.
12. Zig-zag forward to right and left.
13. " backward to " "
14. " forward to left and right.
15. " . backward to " "

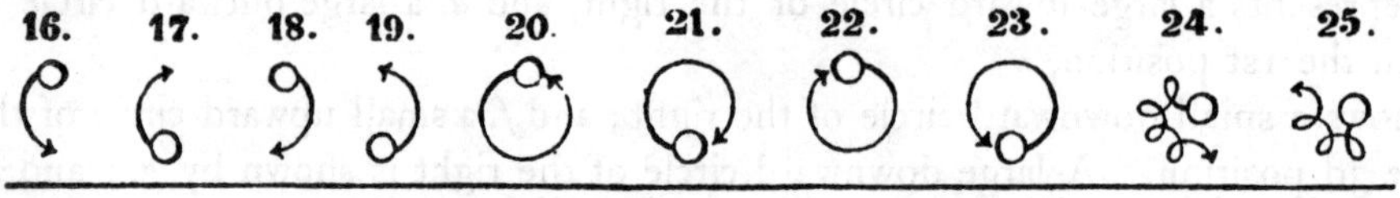

FIG. 265 b.

16.  Movement curved to the right, forward.
17.  Movement curved to the right, backward.
18.  Movement curved to the left, forward.
19.  Movement curved to the left, backward.
20.  Circular movement to the right, forward.
21.  Circular movement to the right, backward.
22.  Circular movement to the left, forward.
23.  Circular movement to the left, backward.
24.  Waltz turns to the right, with direction line running to the right.
25.  Waltz turns to the left, with direction line running to the left.

It must be remembered that the key refers to the direction of the entire movement in the room in which the person is dancing, and that it represents the figure described by the dancer upon the floor; and also that the dancer is supposed to be facing the reader.

# Chapter IX

## COMPOUND MOVEMENTS

THE combination of two or more simple movements produces a compound movement, which may or may not possess secondary attributes. The analysis of compound movements is, particularly to the inexperienced, very difficult. This is perhaps one of the principal reasons why written descriptions of dances are so imperfect.

It is often quite necessary to exactly describe the movement of the supporting leg as well as that of the free leg, in connection with compound movements, and wherever distinctness will be aided thereby, it is well to represent the figure or a certain part thereof in the script.

### Classification

355. Compound movements may be classified according to form, direction, and division of time (phrasing). For the purpose of instruction, it is well to explain the most commonly used compound movements before the classification is made.

356. A step differs from a compound movement in that it must contain a transfer of weight (*dégager*), while this is not always true of the compound movements.

### Music Syllable, Dance Syllable, Step (*Temps, Pas*)

357. The same difference that exists between a syllable and a word, exists between *temps* and *pas*. A step is a combination of movements which contains a transfer of the weight, and this last is an indispensable attribute of a step. A *temps* is a step-syllable; therefore, it is only a portion of a step.

358. A word is an entity, existing by itself, and having its own meaning; a step is also an independent entity. Steps may be made alternately.

359. A syllable must be pronounced with a single tone; a *temps* must be executed upon a single beat of music.

A syllable may contain many letters, but only one vowel sound; a *temps* may, in like manner, contain many movements without a transfer of weight, but must not exceed one beat of music.

As there are words of more than one syllable, so also are there steps of more than one *temps*.

## Definitions of Various Dance Terms (*Termes de Danse*)

**360.** Each of the sciences and arts and crafts has its own technical expressions, and these are often unfamiliar to those outside the profession or trade; indeed, they are sometimes not understood at all by the outsider. Many such expressions occur in the arts of dancing and choregraphy, and while they appear unreasonable or unnecessary to the inexperienced, they are not only reasonable and appropriate, but they are indispensable to the initiated.

The best definitions of the *termes de danse* may be found in the dictionary of Noël and Chapsal. They were probably furnished by A. de St. Léon, or others deeply learned and experienced in the art. These definitions follow and have been inserted because they are imperatively necessary to the proper understanding not only of the subjects which already have been treated, but also of those that are to follow in this work.

**361.** *Temps.* The literal translation of the word *temps* is "time," and many writers upon dancing and gymnastics use that word in preference to the French *temps*, or the Italian *tempo.*

**362.** The Italian word *tempo*, which has been adopted into the English language, is generally understood to refer to the degree of speed in the execution of a musical composition [§ 184].

**363.** The word "dance-syllable," which is often used in this work, is not current in the language and has been adopted by the author to fit the requirements of his system. Similar terms have recently been invented for use in teaching gymnastics; if the innovation is justifiable in gymnastics, why not in dancing?

**364.** *Un Temps Levé* (A Lifting Syllable) is a compound movement of one side, which consists of lifting one leg while the other leg is differently occupied. It usually occurs in the part measure, as preparation for the succeeding step. It may be represented in the script by an ascending sign, crossed by a raising one (*a*).

**365.** *Un Temps Baissé* (A Putting-Down Syllable) is the putting down of the lifted foot to coincide with the music-syllable. It is shown by (*b*).

**366.** *Levé et Élevé* (Lifting and Raising). There is a distinct difference in the meaning of these two words. *Levé*, which means to lift, applies only to the free leg; while *élevé*, which means to raise, refers always to the supporting leg.

## *Sauter*—Jumping

367. *Un Temps Sauté*, a jump, is the result of a quick pressure of the front portion of the supporting foot, by means of which the body is lifted from the floor. If the weight falls upon one foot only, while the other leg is lifted, it is called *un temps levé-sauté*, — a jumped lifted syllable, or a lifting syllable.

This is one of the most important of all the compound movements. A hop on the right is shown in *a*, and one on the left in *b*. The lifting sign does not touch the floor. This clearly shows that a jump has been made.

368. *Sautiller.* Although the word "hop" is seldom used, it is quite as correct as the words "spring" or "throw." Indeed, many of the new books upon gymnastics use the word frequently. The hop may be distinguished from the spring or leap, not only by the indispensable bending of the knee, but also by the fact that the weight is not transferred from one foot to the other. A high jump cannot be executed without bending the knees, and may be written as shown in the drawing. It must never show the sign of transfer.

369. *Pas Sauté.* If, as soon as the body is lifted from the floor, the weight is transferred to the other foot, it is a jumping step and is represented as follows :

370. *Bondir.* Although it has been stated that hopping and springing (*bondir*) have the same meaning, there is a technical difference. A child may be said to jump for joy, upon either foot or upon both feet, but in so doing he remains on or near the place ; while a man does not jump, but springs across a ditch ; for instance : A sparrow jumps over a straw, and a lion springs at his prey.

Inasmuch as a spring contains a transfer of weight, it is not a step-syllable or *temps*, but a step of one *temps, un pas.*

371. *Jeter.* The word *sauter* in the French language means "to jump," and the word *bondir* means "to spring." This latter word has been used by Delille and Blasis, but the word *jeter*, to throw, is more commonly used in the *termes de danse*, because in springing the weight is thrown from one foot to the other.

372. *Bond* (Spring). *Jet* (Throw). The term "spring" relates to the foot from which the force is derived, and the term "throw" refers to the one which receives the weight. If one springs from the right foot and lights upon the left, the left foot has been thrown, and the right, which is now free, may either during or after the movement be carried into any position.

373. In springing it is necessary to press the front portion of the foot strongly down, and to forcibly bend and stretch the knee.

These signs show the spring from the right and from the left foot, respectively. The sign of transfer is placed near the lifting sign to show that the movements follow in natural succession.

**374.** *Tomber* (Falling). Every jumping, springing or throwing movement is accompanied, inevitably, by a falling back, which may be executed either upon the sole, ball, point, or heel. If this movement is so strongly accented as to become audible it is called a fall, *une chute*; and if a step is executed, it is called a falling step, *un pas tombé*.

The choregraphic sign depends upon and corresponds to the movement which precedes it.

*c.* Jump (Hop) and fall on right foot.
*d.* Jump (Hop) and fall on left foot.
*e.* Jump and fall on both feet.
*f.* Spring from right and fall on left foot.
*g.* Spring from left and fall on right foot.

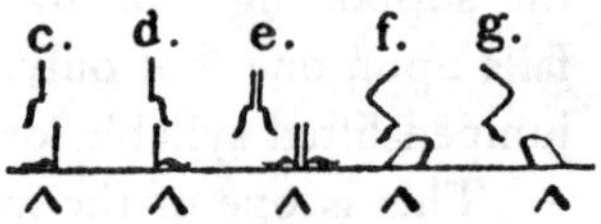

FIG. 266.

**375.** *Pliéments* (Bendings) are simple movements.

*Un temps plié* (a bending syllable) is the bending of one leg, while the other is differently occupied, upon one music syllable, in which no transfer of weight is made.

During the bending of the right leg, the left foot glides backward upon the ball into the 4th position. It will be noted by the sign that the supporting foot rests upon the line of the floor, and that the other is above it.

*Tensions* (Stretchings) are also simple movements. They have already been explained in §119.

**376.** *Élévations* (Raisings) are simple movements and are described in § 121. *Un temps élevé*, a raising syllable, is a raising of the supporting foot while the free foot is differently occupied. While the body is being raised upon the right foot, the left is carried to the half-high balancing 4th position.

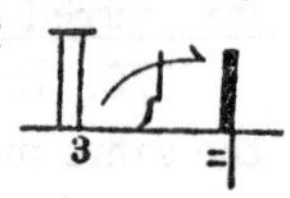

**377.** *Abaissements* (Lowerings) are simple movements and are described in § 123.

**378.** *Un Temps Abaissé* (A Lowering Syllable) is a compound movement, in which the body is lowered from a raised supporting foot while the free foot is otherwise occupied, and in which there is no transfer of weight.

**379.** *Une Levée* (a Lifting) is a simple movement [§ 124].

**380.** *Un Temps Levé* (A Lifting Syllable) is a compound movement which is executed upon one music-syllable [§ 364].

**381.** *Une Baissé* (A Putting Down) is a simple movement and is explained in § 125.

**382.** *Un Temps Baissé* (A Putting-Down Syllable) is the putting down of a lifted leg while the supporting leg is otherwise occupied, and without transfer of weight.

**383.** 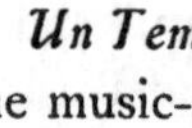 ⌐∘＼ *Temps Baissé.* ⌐∘＿ *Temps Abaissé.*

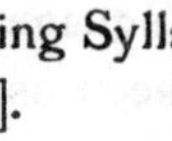

To avoid ambiguity regarding similar signs, the movement sign should be clearly executed, with lines showing the floor. The sole direction symbol may be omitted, if desired, in the above signs.

**384.** *Ruer* (To Kick) is to project the leg forcibly into an open position; and kicking movements should, therefore, be termed *ruements*. This term has been seldom used, except in referring to horses.

*Un Ruement* (A Kick) differs from a beating, *un battement*, because the accent in a *rue-*

*ment* applies to the movement of lifting the foot to an open position; while a *battement* is the opposite movement, that of knocking the free foot against the supporting leg.

**385.** The term *Marquer les Pas ou Temps* (Marking) is applied to the practice of describing the dance-steps and measures upon the floor without raising from it, maintaining precision of accent and time and correct lines of movement, but omitting all embellishments (especially the *battements*) or at least only faintly indicating them. (*Klemm.*) This is generally practiced for the purpose of memorizing the figure, and it is in reality the partial execution of steps, or dances, of which the dancer feels certain.

**386.** *Terre à terre.* This expression is used to designate the gliding style of dancing. It usually consists of small connected movements, in which the feet lightly touch the floor (Music: *legato*). (*Klemm.*)

**387.** *Équilibre* (Equilibrium) is the quality of balancing the entire body, which is effected by a proper and graceful attitude of the upper body, and maintained by it independently of the legs, although coöperating with them to present a harmonious appearance. (*Klemm.*)

**388.** *Aplomb* is the absolute safety in rising and falling back which results from the perpendicular attitude of the upper body and the artistic placing of the feet. By means of *aplomb* the dancer acquires a precision and an elegance which insure the successful execution of every foot-movement, however artistic and difficult, and thereby creates a pleasing and a satisfactory impression upon the observer. *Aplomb* may be compared with the sureness of touch of the pianist. (*Klemm*).


## Grace


**389.** Grace is the ideal of purity and beauty of movement and that ease and elegance in holding and moving the body which attracts and charms all beholders. "Grace is a beauty not given by nature, but produced by the subject itself; and as the beauty of the human form does honor to the Creator, so do cheerfulness and grace do honor to their possessor. One is a natural, the other a personal gift." (*Schiller.*) (*Klemm.*)

Gentle and natural, unconscious of its charm, and free from the effort to please, natural grace is most effective. Overstepping this tends to affectation, distasteful elaboration and grimace. Schiller says, "Grace must be always natural and involuntary (or at least must appear so), and a person must never display a consciousness of it." (*Klemm.*)

There are persons who possess so great a degree of natural grace, that a teacher may learn more from them than he can impart to them, but such cases are very rare. A competent teacher is generally able to assist his pupils by overcoming the impediments which naturally arise from weight and form.

The development of grace should be the principal aim of instruction in dancing.

# Chapter X

## TECHNICAL STEPS AND MOVEMENTS

### Steps — *Pas*

THE term "stepping" is generally understood to mean the movement of ordinary walking, and a common step forward extends from the posterior to the anterior 4th position. A step has, therefore, a beginning and an ending position, and a movement by which transition is made from one position to the other. The transfer of weight is so closely allied to the movement of the legs with which it coincides that it is impossible to separate the two; for that reason, wherever two or more steps are taken, it is unnecessary to consider the transfer.

391. As every step contains a change of position and a transfer (*dégagement*), both legs are more or less active therein. The legs may be engaged in either simple or compound movements. These are often so natural that they do not require description. At other times, however, not only the simple movements and the moment of their execution, but even the various positions through which the dancer passes in making the step, must be indicated so precisely as to enable the distinction from other and different steps to be easily seen.

392. Every step contains at least three necessary attributes, viz.: size, direction and duration. Frequently other qualities of a secondary nature may be found.

**Size.** As to size, a step may be either whole, half, or quarter, etc.; small, medium, or large; natural, diminished or prolonged.

393. **Direction.** As to direction, a step may be either on the place; forward or backward; in straight or diagonal lines; sidewise or crossed. Side-steps may be made either to the right or to the left, and either over or under crossed. The diagonal steps may be made either to the right or to the left, forward or backward, and either over or under crossed.

394. **Duration.** Steps are of one or more *temps*, and may be executed according to either slow, protracted, temperate, rapid or very rapid tempo.

#### REMARKS AS TO THE NECESSARY ATTRIBUTES

395. The regular marching step is a *whole* step, as it is made from the posterior to the anterior 4th position; but the first movement, which is *from* repose in a closed position, and the last, which is *to* repose in another closed position, are *half-steps*.

110

## Military March (*Marche Militaire*)

### (EXPLANATION OF THE CHOREGRAPHIC SIGNS)

**396.** The key indicates the movement forward, and the sign shows that it starts from the 1st position [Fig. 267].

In the part-measure, the left foot is lifted and carried forward, and the transfer begins upon the first part of the complete measure, and finishes upon the second part by the putting down of the left foot in anterior 4th position, which leaves the right in posterior 4th. Continuing, the right foot is carried forward and put down upon the first beat in the second measure.

FIG. 267.

The signs are unnecessary for any but the part-measure, the first measure and the end, as all measures which intervene are like the first and may be indicated by the regular symbol of repetition ( ⁓ ).

**397.** Side Steps are executed in a similar manner. A whole step to the side passes from the 2d position, through the 1st and 3d to the 5th. If the foot is only carried to the 1st position, it is a half-step; if to the 3d, a three-quarters step; and if it passes beyond the 5th position, it is a large or prolonged step.

NOTE. — Never forget the distinction between a *temps* and a *pas*. If, for example, a movement is made from the 2d or 4th to the 1st position, and no transfer is made, it is a step-syllable; but if the transfer is added, it is a half-step.

**398.** Small, Medium and Large Steps. In the explanation of the positions under § 14, it was stated that the proper width of an open position is the length of the person's foot. If, therefore, a whole step consists of a movement from an open to an open position, the entire distance will be found to be equal to the length of both feet. This rule for width, however, is taken from the dancer, whose feet are, suppositiously, turned entirely outward. If the feet are turned less strongly outward, or parallel (i. e. straight forward), the steps are lengthened; for the reason that the centre of gravity is carried from the heel to the toe of the supporting foot, while the free foot is carried forward. The distance in such open positions is, therefore, from the toe of the supporting to the heel of the advancing foot. An average step directly forward in parallel foot-position is nearly 36 inches long; and with the feet turned half outward, about 30 inches. An average dancing step should, therefore, be equal to the length of both the dancer's feet; if it exceeds that limit, it is a large, and if it does not reach it, it is a small step.

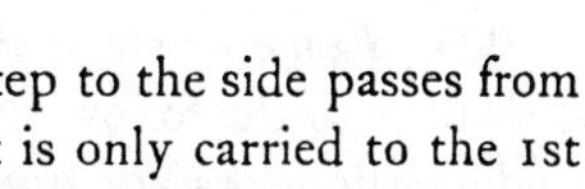

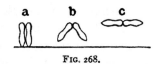

FIG. 268.

Fig. 268 shows (*a*) the parallel, (*b*) the half-outward, and (*c*) the entirely outward positions of the feet, respectively.

**399. Diminished and Prolonged Steps.** The composer of a dance prescribes either medium or small or large steps to fit the requirements of his music; but dancers are frequently compelled, by force of circumstances, to execute the steps either in greater or in smaller width. If, for instance, a small lady dances with a tall gentleman, she must prolong her steps, while he diminishes his.

**400. Simple and Compound Steps.** A simple movement cannot be divided into different movements, nor can a simple step be divided into different steps; but a simple step may consist of various movements and several *temps*, and may possess different secondary qualities. A compound step consists of a combination of simple steps.

**401. Direction.** Steps on the place require no movement from the spot, but contain an alteration of position and a transfer of weight.

If such steps are worthy of the attention of soldiers who practice them in " marking time," they must certainly be of more consequence to the dancer, who is obliged to carry his application of the word step to more minute detail.

**402.** If the objective point is reached without deviation, it is a straight step, as, for example, the marching step, which is directly forward; but if such a point is reached by a curved, a wavy or a zig-zag line, the step is diagonal.

**403.** *Temps* or step-syllable has been explained and repeated in various sections, and if we refer in the following pages to a step as of one *temps*, we mean that the entire step, including the necessary transfer, does not require more than one syllable of music. Such steps may be compared with monosyllabic words.

**404. Measure of Speed (*Tempo*).** That degree of speed which is neither slow nor rapid may be called *temperate*, and it is a degree which is natural to the organism of the body. *Quick* steps require a certain amount of impetus, and are more laborious than *temperate* steps; *slow* steps require a voluntary holding back which coincides with the duration of the music. Therefore, *slow* and *prolonged* steps are more tiresome than *temperate* steps, because one is obliged to restrain his natural impulsiveness in order to properly execute them.

**405.** Since the invention of the metronome, the degree of speed is seldom given in words, as the numbers of the metronome scale are far more definite. The metronome measures given herein, particularly those for the social dances, are for the *temperate* speed. This degree is often difficult to determine, but the following principles may be of service:

**406.** The ordinary walk of a man coincides with the beating of his pulse. Young persons walk more rapidly than older people; lymphatic persons more rapidly than phlegmatic persons; gay people more rapidly than solemn people.

**407.** This law has a natural influence upon dancing, and in the social dance, as gayety predominates, the temperate rate of speed in dancing is greater than in ordinary walking. The degree of speed in theatrical dancing varies according to the characteristics expressed.

**408.** From these explanations it is fair to assume that a person about thirty years of age steps at about the average or temperate rate of speed.

*Large* steps necessarily require more time than *small* steps, and those of the Polka require more time than those of the glide Galop, because of the leap, which demands a certain time according to natural law.

## Secondary Attributes of Steps

**409.** Unless the name of a step signifies that it is "glided," or executed in some other specific manner, it is always understood to be "carried" (that is, lifted off the floor during transit to the new position).

Unless a step is more than ordinarily bended or stretched, the common walking step which contains an agreeable and natural degree of bending and stretching of the leg, is taken as the normal type.

**410.** A secondary quality may be omitted from a step without changing it to anything less than a step; for a secondary quality is a characteristic attribute which relates exclusively to the component parts of the step; that is, to the movements and positions of which it is constructed.

## The Meaning of the Term *Pas*

**411.** The term *pas* has a more varied and a wider significance in the language of dancing than it has in ordinary usage, and while the word "step" is its equivalent in the English language, the French term *pas* is more comprehensive, for it may be used to express an entire dance of one or more persons; for example the *pas seul, pas de deux, pas de trois* or even chorus dances such as *pas de fleurs, pas de soldats* or *pas de manteaux*.

## The Names of the Steps

**412.** Every step has a technical name, usually of French origin, which may be understood by a knowledge of the meaning of the word; but time and custom, and in some cases an improper usage of the word outside of France, has evolved a different technical meaning. An incorrect application of the original word has in some instances even been so persistently made that the wrong expression has grown into technical value by its constant use. This feature renders it very difficult at times to get at the real meaning of some terms and indeed has seriously injured the value of most of the works upon dancing that have been published up to this time.

**413.** We have, therefore, no better criterion to go by than the usage of the best authors upon dancing, for determining the significance of the terms, although a dictionary of the *termes de danse*, such as might be produced by the German or the French Academy, would be of great value, provided the definitions were clear and intelligible.

**414.** In the French language, the term *pas* is often omitted and the indefinite article *un* substituted for it, and the expressions *faites un glissé, deux tortillés, un jeté et un assemblé,* etc., are used to express steps or step-syllables. The English language, however, requires the use of the word "step," for it would be improper and unsatisfactory to say "a gliding," and one must say "a gliding step" to fully convey the meaning. If, however, the French term is used in its technical sense, it is correct to speak of a *glissé,* a *tortillé,* a *coupé,* etc.

NOTE. — The reader will avoid many noticeable errors by following the suggestions of this last paragraph in the description of dances and the use of dance-script.

**415.** Wherever the participles, such as *glissé, plié, tourné,* etc., are combined with the article *un,* they become nouns, and are significant of the respective steps, with the incidental transfer thereof.

**416.** In order, therefore, to determine upon the proper name of a step, one must ascertain, besides the necessary attributes : first, the qualities of the movement of the free leg and those which follow them ; and, second, the movement of the supporting leg during the activity of the free one.

## Walking Steps — *Pas Allés*

**417.** While this step is usually spoken of as *pas marché,* there is in reality a vast difference between walking and marching ; for walking is an entirely free movement, while marching is the result of the continued application of rule to the step for the purpose of a precision of execution which is unnecessary in ordinary walking. Again, a person in walking allows the arms to swing naturally and free ; while in marching the arms must be carried in a certain prescribed manner ; and while, in walking, the free foot is put down in such a manner as to gradually receive the weight of the body, in marching the foot must fall first upon the point and then pass to the ball for the balance.

**418.** In order to walk not only gracefully but with ease and safety, the body should be held erect, and the free foot should be carried horizontally and only naturally stretched. If the feet are at right angles, as shown in § 398 *b,* they are turned sufficiently outward. If they turn more strongly outward, the gait becomes less beautiful and appears affected. In walking, a pupil should not be required to touch the floor with the extreme tips of the foot first, for such a gait could not be maintained ; besides it would appear pedantic and render the person ridiculous. The knee should be bended only enough to permit freedom of movement.

**419.** The ordinary forward walking step should be executed directly forward ; that is, the foot should be carried from the posterior to the anterior position without crossing — as in the case of artificial tripping steps, or other deviations — and the steps should not be too large. To kick with the heels betrays carelessness in walking.

**420.** The degree of speed in walking should be considered, and, as has already been stated, is in accordance with the beatings of the pulse. Growing young persons would therefore take about 80 steps per minute, to coincide with the 80 pulsations which is their average. In the Quadrilles a dancer usually takes about 90 to 100 steps per minute; more rapid tempo is unreasonable.

If a man in walking takes less than 80 steps per minute either fatigue or sluggishness is indicated; if more rapidly than 120 steps, excitement or hurry; and as both are unnatural speeds, either can be maintained but a short time. If one is conversing with an agreeable companion the gait is naturally lessened.

**421. The Movement of the Arms in Walking.** The arms move naturally, and in opposition to the legs, in walking: that is, the movement of the left arm coincides with that of the right leg, and that of the right arm with the movement of the left leg. This may be termed *natural opposition* [§ 289]. The arms are allowed a degree of freedom of movement which is consistent with and regulated by a proper carriage of the upper body.

The fingers should be rounded. Fully stretched fingers appear stiff, clenched fists indicate rage; hands supported upon the hips appear awkward and give the idea that one is at a loss as to what to do with them; and the placing of the fists at the sides (arms akimbo) gives an appearance of impudence.

**422.** For the purpose of developing refinement of gait, allow the pupils to walk, either singly or in couples, with music, and to describe such circles, squares, serpentine lines and other figures as space and circumstances permit.

For new pupils, play a simple march or polka and for those further advanced, a Polonaise; as the accentuation of 2-4 or 4-4 measure is more readily understood than that of 3-4.

In this practice the height of the pupils should always be considered, and it is unwise to require the execution of them in lines which are composed of both children and adults, for in such cases the children must enlarge their steps while the adults are forced to diminish theirs, thereby destroying the benefit of the exercise for both classes of pupils.

**423.** The difference between marching and walking has been explained in § 417, and as the term marching is understood to relate to the regular military gait, the carriage is more deliberate and the steps more precise.

The "Field Step" (*pas ordinaire*) is usually executed at the rate of 112 to 116 steps in a minute; the "quick step" (*pas accéléré*), 144, and the "parade step" (*pas de parade*) —now obsolete—about 70 steps a minute.

Exercise 48. Marching Step (*Pas marché*) [Fig. 269].

FIG. 269.

**424.** Slow marching is an exercise of great utility to pupils, and is especially to be recommended. M. M. 72 is a very suitable tempo, and 60 is adapted to the more experienced pupils, as the exercise increases in difficulty as the tempo diminishes.

In marching, the leg should be raised to half-height [§ 67], which is indicated in the script by the addition of two auxiliary lines above the carrying sign.

**425.** It is generally agreed that, in marching, one should begin with the left foot, and the teacher should pronounce the command "forward" slowly; but the word "march" must be given sharply and with a decided accent, in order that the left foot may be raised immediately to coincide with the unaccented part measure, and put down upon the accented first note of the measure succeeding.

## Changement of the Feet (*Changement de Pieds*)

**426.** It is of great importance, in marching, that every person steps an equal distance with the same foot at the same time. If one misses the step, it may be regained in the following manner [Fig. 270]:

Supposing the left foot to have been put down upon an unaccented beat — instead of carrying the right forward to the 4th position, execute only a half step and put it down in either 1st or posterior 3d position, and continue with a half step with the left foot.

FIG. 270.

**427.** This changement of step can only be executed in proper rhythm to correspond with the movement. As an exercise, these changements should be alternated and frequent and in well defined measure, as in

Exercise 49. Changement of the Feet (*Changement de Pieds*) [Fig. 271].

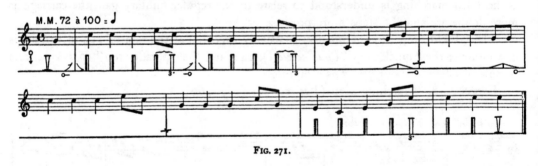

FIG. 271.

(In this exercise, the 3d position is used because it is more distinct and less liable to be misunderstood than the 1st.)

**428.** Those persons who have a proper sense of measure readily understand the commencement of the measure.

The abbreviated sign of the *changement de pieds* is as follows :

## Order of Steps in Instructing

429. Every teacher understands that he should lead gradually from what is easy to that which is difficult, but, notwithstanding this fact, teachers and books of instruction seldom agree as to the exact order in which the various steps should be taught. They usually affirm that theirs is the only correct sequence, and require all others to follow their direction.

This is of course unreasonable and impossible, and for that reason the present directors of the "German Academy of the Art of Teaching Dancing," have adopted the succession of steps which was used by the celebrated ballet-masters, Taglioni and Lauchery, and their best pupils.

This arrangement of steps for teaching has been proven to be efficient for schools of ballet and for other institutes of higher instruction, but of course, the order given in this work cannot be so completely applied in the case of persons who require instruction only in the social dances, and who desire to learn to dance in the shortest possible time, as it can in schools where the course is planned·to cover several years.

The teacher must, therefore, make his own selections from the preparatory exercises and dancing steps, according to the abilities of his pupils, and the result to be attained in the given time.

## Raising Steps (*Pas Élevés*)

430. The movement of raising has been explained in § 121. By the term, "raising" steps, there is an implied rising upon each step, which imparts a degree of elasticity to the movement and lends an added grace to the dance. Each step, therefore, to which a rising movement is applied is a "raising" step. If still other qualities are added to the raising steps they are denominated accordingly.

431. A raising-walking step is different from the step of walking upon the points; because in walking-raising, the raising and lowering occurs upon each step; while in the walk upon the points, the raising position is maintained to the end, when the lowering is made after the final step.

432. The difference between raising-walking and jumping-walking is still more important. Raising is an easy movement produced by forcibly bending down the instep; while jumping is a species of kicking movement, which requires that the knee be bent, and stretched so forcibly as to project the body into the air.

433. Straight raising steps go into the 2d or 4th position, and crossed ones into the 3d or 5th or intermediate positions. With few exceptions, the raisings occur upon the light beats and the lowerings upon the accented beats of the music.

The raising steps should be practiced gliding, after they have been executed in carrying form. The gliding will be indicated by the usual sign. The difference in the names should be noted in all cases.

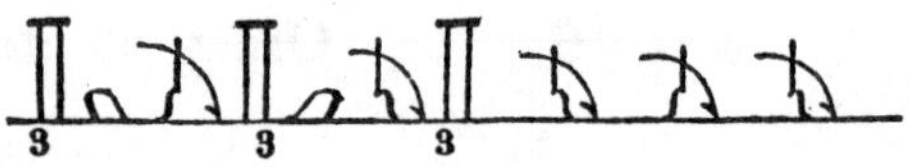

The script signs for the raising steps are shown in Fig. 272.

FIG. 272.

The music for the following exercise should be repeated, so that the movement may be executed in the opposite direction from that indicated by the keys.

Exercise 50.  Raising Steps (*Pas élevés*) [Fig. 273].

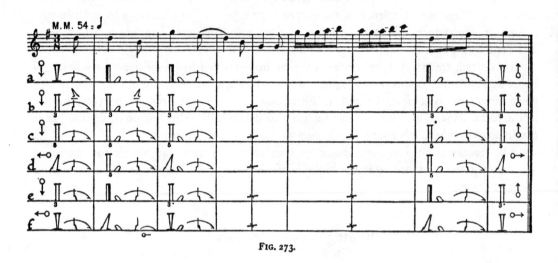

FIG. 273.

## Raising-Marching Steps (*Pas Marchés Élevés*)

434. The difference between these and the raising steps is indicated by the word "marching," which signifies that the stretching is more complete, the carriage firmer, and the appearance more seriously attentive. A signal difference is noticeable at the moment of transfer. In raising-walking, the free foot is put down to receive the weight of the body, which is already following it, while in raising-marching the free foot is placed upon the floor before the weight is carried to it from the supporting leg. Simple and lively melodies are suitable for raising-walking, but raising-marching demands slow and majestic music.

FIG. 274.

The raising is slight in raising-walking and great in raising-marching. The script of the raising-marching steps (*pas marchés élevés*) is shown in Fig. 274.

Exercise 51.  Raising-Marching Steps (*Pas marchés élevés*) [Fig. 275].

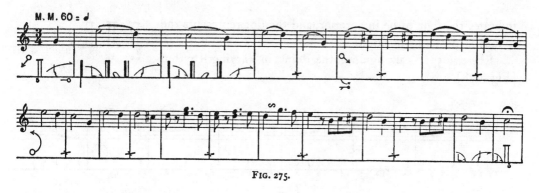

FIG. 275.

## The Steps Upon the Points (*Les Pas sur les Pointes*)

**435.** It has been already stated that in walking upon the points the raising position is maintained without lowerings, throughout the movement; the steps are therefore smaller than those upon the sole or the ball.

**436.** These steps are also called *pas emboités*, "boxed-in steps," if they are so small that they do not pass the measure of the simple open positions (the length of one of the feet).

Exercise 52. Small Steps upon the Points or Boxed-in Steps (*Petits pas sur les pointes ou pas emboités*) [Fig. 276].

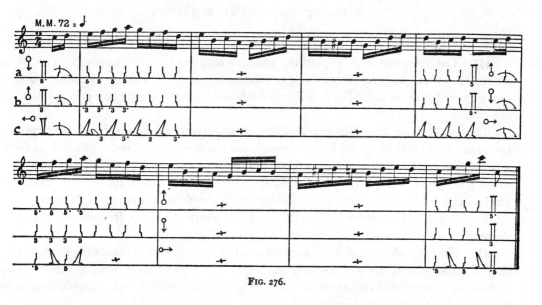

FIG. 276.

The manner of writing these steps is easily understood from the above exercise and the abbreviated form is given in Fig. 277. The number below the line of the floor always indicates the foot to be in anterior, and the dot represents the foot as in posterior position.

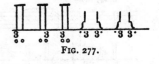

FIG. 277.

Exercise 53. Walking upon the Points in Varying Rhythm [Fig. 278].

FIG. 278.

The special aim of this exercise is to direct the pupils' attention to the rhythm, that they may learn to accommodate their movements to the requirements of the music. Too little attention is paid to this all important point.

## Running Steps (*Pas de Course*)

**437.** The difference between walking and marching has been dealt with in § 417. The difference between walking and running lies in the fact that, in running, one foot is always in the air, and that the following foot is raised while the weight is descending to the advancing one.

Thus we see that the difference between walking and running is not to be determined by speed, notwithstanding the fact that running is usually executed more rapidly. Indeed, a person may walk in more rapid tempo, and advance more quickly, than one who runs slowly; but even in the most rapid walking both feet must touch the floor at the same time once in every step. This is not done even in the slowest running movement.

Running may be executed on the soles, balls, points or heels; forward, backward or sidewise.

**438.** To carry the upper body forward and run upon the soles makes the steps longer than in walking, and requires a strong bending of the knees. As a dancing exercise, this movement appears stiff and awkward; it is only used in national and in comic dances to represent the customs and manners of the lower classes.

**439.** Running steps upon the balls are more graceful, and in these the legs are fully stretched and the upper body is held erect. These steps are often and differently used in dancing. They are usually small, and may be executed either forward, backward, sidewise or crossed.

**440.** Running upon the points occurs frequently in the serious art dances. The steps are generally very short (small) and rapid.

**441.** Running upon the heels is very unusual, occurring only in a few national dances, as the *Matelot*, etc. The steps are very small.

**442.** As a gymnastic exercise, running is of great importance and very exactly regulated. For continued running, about 150 steps may be made in a minute, and for rapid running about 210.

**443.** The running positions have been described and illustrated in § 93, and the choregraphic symbol is a serpentine line [Fig. 279]. If the symbol does not possess auxiliary marks below the line, or if it is written with a short line, it signifies running upon the soles. The other modes are shown by the regular symbols of the ball, point and heel positions.

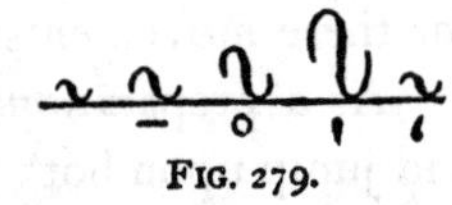

FIG. 279.

**444.** The size of the steps in running is shown by the corresponding size of the symbols; this difference is due largely to the different positions of the soles in the various modes of running.

**445.** It is often necessary to write the sign of the movement executed, to demonstrate the exact manner of transition from one position to another. If the position signs are accurately drawn, the movement is usually expressed so clearly that auxiliary symbols are not necessary.

**446.** If, however, the script is abbreviated, it may be desirable, for the sake of distinctness, to add secondary signs to the signs of movement.

**447.** As the weight of the body rests upon the foot which has executed the movement in the running steps, special attention should be given to the succeeding position sign. The sign of transfer is unnecessary in writing the running steps, as the transfer is inseparable from the movement and is contemplated by its symbol.

## Courante Step (*Temps de Courante*)

**448.** *Temps de Courante* is a slow dancing step which was taken from the *Courante*, an ancient and long since forgotten dance. The step is of some slight classical value, but is seldom used. As the step has no resemblance to running, its title is a misnomer.

**449.** There is, in the Mazurka, a so-called *pas courant* which somewhat resembles the running step. It will be completely described in connection with the Mazurka (§ 882).

## Changements of the Legs or Feet (*Changements de Jambes ou Pieds*)

**450.** There is, in every step, a changement of the position of the feet, which is consequent upon the transfer of the weight. When, however, crossed positions are changed, the movement is almost wholly done by means of changing the positions of the legs; the name *changements de jambes* has therefore been applied to this class of movements.

**451.** Section 157 refers to the *changement de jambes* as a raising exercise. We shall now consider it as a jumping exercise. The usual script for these movements is shown in Fig. 280.

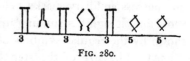

FIG. 280.

As a preparation, stand in either 3d or 5th position and jump upon both feet, changing the relative positions of the feet and falling back in such a manner that the foot which was in front will be behind after the jump.

Exercise 54. Changements of the Legs or Feet (*Changements de jambes ou pieds*) [Fig. 281].

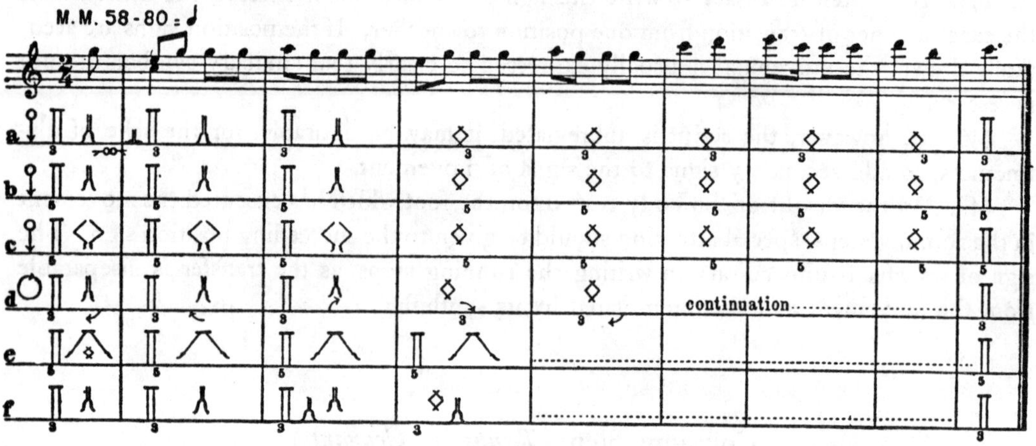

FIG. 281.

Exercise 54 *a* is known as Raising Changements of the Legs in 3d Position (*Changements de jambes élevés en troisième position*).

Exercise 54 *b* contains the Jumped Changements of the Legs in 5th Position (*Changements de jambes sautés en cinquième position*).

Exercise 54 *c* consists of the Jumped Changements of the Legs in 5th Position (*Changements de jambes sautés en cinquième position*).

This last exercise contains a high jump, while that which precedes it is executed by means of slight lifting only.

High jumps may also be expressed by the jumping sign; but in such cases, the transfer symbol is omitted.

Exercise 54 *d* shows the Jumped Changements of the Legs in Turning (*Changements de jambes sautés en tournant*).

NOTE. — The sign similar to the key, which occurs at the beginning of this exercise, shows that the turning continues throughout the entire melody. The fractional portion of the turning sign which accompanies each measure, indicates that a quarter-turn is made during each measure.

Exercise 54 *e* contains Jumped Changements of the Legs with Spreading (*Changements de jambes sautés et écartés*).

Exercise 54 *f* is composed of Jumped Changements of the Legs with Subsequent Raising (*Changements de jambes sautés et rélevés*).

These changements should also be practiced in combination with the bendings and stretchings, as they are of great benefit in the development of the muscular powers of the legs.

## Escaping Syllables (*Temps Échappés*)

**452.** The word *échapper* means to escape, or to slip; but as this movement does not contain a transfer of weight, it must be called *temps* and not *pas échappé*.

This is a compound dance movement consisting of the simultaneous lifting of both feet from a closed position and their consequent falling back and slipping to an open one.

**453.** This movement is usually executed upon the place, from a preparatory 5th position, by bending and jumping from both feet, which are separated and fall back in open position (generally the 2d) upon the balls.

## Falling Syllables (*Temps Tombés*)

**454.** When this movement (*échappé*) is accented by falling back upon the soles, as in preparation for a turn in the air, it is called *temps tombé* [§ 374].

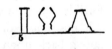

## Spreading Syllables (*Temps Écartés*)

**455.** The word *écarté* means to spread or open; this movement is also called *spagat*, which is derived from the Italian word *spalancare*, which signifies to open wide or to greatly extend.

Execution — from preparatory 5th position. Commence with high jump upon both feet, during which the feet are widely spread and fall back again in a closed position.

If, during the falling back, there is a changement of the legs, the same is noted by its corresponding symbol below the line of the floor [Fig. 282].

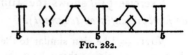

FIG. 282.

## Collecting Step or Syllable (*Pas ou Temps Assemblé*)

456. The word *assembler* means to put together or to collect, and this movement may be either a dance syllable or a dance step of one syllable, consequent upon the non-transfer or transfer of weight. *Assemblé* is generally executed at the end of a step sentence which it finishes, and it seldom occurs except in connection with other steps. Its most frequent usage is in connection with the throwing step (*pas jeté*).

457. Of the various applications of *assemblé* the most usual is chosen for example.

### EXECUTION OF THE STEP UPON THE PLACE

Preparation: Anterior 5th position of right. During the bending of the knees in the preceding part measure, slide the left foot to the 2d balancing position, stretch forcibly, jump, and bring the feet together into 5th position with the left foot in front (*dessus*), falling back upon the points. Where several *assemblés* are made consecutively, they should be executed with alternating feet [Fig. 283]. The free

FIG. 283.

foot passes from the 2d balancing position to the 5th position behind the other in the *assemblé dessous*. (*Klemm.*)

Exercise 55. Collecting Steps Before and Behind (*Assemblés dessus et dessous*) [Fig. 284].

FIG. 284.

Exercise 55*a* shows the *assemblés dessus*. Exercise 55*b* shows the *assemblés dessous*.

458. The first measure contains the complete, and the second the abbreviated script for the exercises; and in the abbreviation the open sole symbol represents the active, and the shaded symbol, the other foot.

## Throwing Steps (*Pas Jetés*)

**459.** This class of steps is very closely related to running and differs from it only in the fact that in running one foot always touches the floor; while in the throwing steps both feet are momentarily in the air at the same time [§ 372].

**460.** *Pas jeté* is a step of one syllable and contains four simple movements, viz.: bending, stretching, putting down and transferring.

To throw the body into the air, one must bend the knee of the supporting leg and then stretch it forcibly. As the weight of the body is received, in the falling back, upon the other foot, the transfer must of necessity either accompany or follow the leap.

**461.** *Jeté rélevation.* This step is frequently followed by a raising upon the foot which has received the weight; such subsequent raising is called raising again or *rélevation* [Fig. 285].

FIG. 285.

**462.** *Pas jeté* is a very common step, and while it may be variously combined with other positions and movements, in many different ways, such other positions and movements are not comprehended within the meaning of the word *jeté*; they must, therefore, be indicated by qualifying words.

The script in Fig. 286 shows the complete method of writing a simple throwing step, and the abbreviation thereof.

**463.** This abbreviation has been adopted because of the time and accuracy which is necessary when the step is written in detail.

FIG. 286.

The throwing steps might be represented by the same symbol as the running steps, but as the falling back is more strongly accented than in running, the sign of transfer would have to be made much heavier and thicker, in order to convey the distinction.

**464 a.** The symbol of this step must never rest upon the floor line, for a *jeté* is always executed into the air, and the size of the symbol varies in accordance with the rule regarding the running symbol in § 444. The terms *dessus* and *dessous* are used in connection with the throwing steps; their application is fully explained in § 176.

Exercise 56. Simple Throwing Steps into an Open Position (*Jetés simples à une position ouverte*) [Fig. 287.]

FIG. 287.

Exercise 57. Simple Throwing Steps into a Closed Position (*Jetès simples à une position close*). In these we find an inclined sole position [Fig. 288].

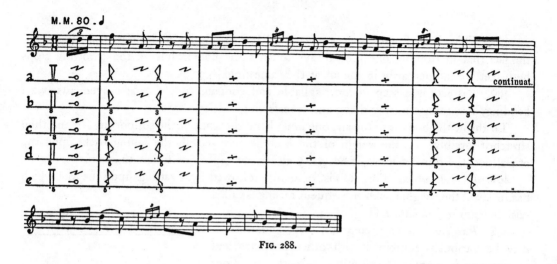

FIG. 288.

**464 b.** Exercise 58. Throwing Steps into an Open with Subsequent Raising in a Closed Position (*Jetê et relévation*) [Fig. 289].

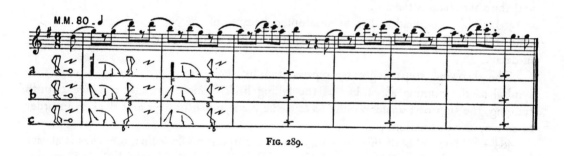

FIG. 289.

**464 c.** Exercise 59. Advancing with Small Throwing Steps [Fig. 290].

FIG. 290.

**465.** Exercise 60. Throwing Steps with Collecting (*Jetê et assemblé*) [Fig. 291].

FIG. 291.

The sign of transfer has been omitted from these exercises, because the *dégagement* is comprehended in the throwing sign. There is no *dégagement* following the *assemblé*.

Fig. 292 shows the choreography of the throwing step with turning (*jeté en tournant*).

Fig. 293 shows the choreography of the throwing step with collecting (*jeté et assemblé*)

FIG. 292.   FIG. 293.

## Scissor Syllable and Scissor Step (*Temps et Pas de Sissonne ou de Ciseaux*)

**466.** The word *Sissonne* is given as the name of a Provençal national dance of former times, and R. Voss, in his " Dictionary of Dances," mentions that dance among others as having been executed in 1565 at a festival at the French court given in honour of the then queen, but no description of the manner in which it was danced, nor of its movements and figures, has been found.

**467.** The scissor movement contains two simple movements. If, during the first syllable, the weight rests upon both feet, but in the second is supported upon only one, it is a step (*pas de Sissonne*) [Fig. 294 *b*]. But if the weight remains upon the same support during both music syllables, it is merely a movement of two syllables (*temps de Sissonne*) [Fig. 294 *a*].

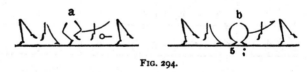

FIG. 294.

**468.** There is, in the bending and stretching of the knees in these movements, a motion which appears quite similar to the movement of the blades of a pair of scissors, and the names *temps ou pas de ciseaux* (scissor syllable or step) are therefore quite as properly applicable to these as the word *sissonne*. Nearly every other movement, as for instance, *temps levé, fouetté, pas marché* and *chassé*, may be recognized by its name, and this is as it should be; so, notwithstanding the fact that the term *sissonne* has been used for many years, it is the duty of the dancing master not alone to justify the technical terms of his art, but to invent such other more appropriate terms as may be of assistance in teaching. No title which incorrectly describes the motives or attributes of the step should be retained merely because of its ancient usage, when a more appropriate name can be assigned to it.

469. **Execution of the Scissor Step upon the Place.** From preparatory 2d balancing position of left.

First Syllable: During a light jump upon the right, in the part measure, the left foot is put down in the posterior 5th ball position, thus rendering both legs bended in the thesis of the music.

Second syllable: Jump and fall back upon one foot only, while the other foot is quickly raised into the 2d balancing position, preparatory to the next step.

If the stepping foot is put down in the thesis, into a crossed position in front of the other it forms a forward or over-crossed scissor step (*un pas de ciseaux dessus*). But if it is put down behind the other, it is a backward or under-crossed scissor step (*un pas de ciseaux dessous*).

By executing these steps, first forward, and then backward, we have the alternating scissor steps (*des pas de ciseaux alternatifs*).

All these steps may be executed with turning.

Exercise 61. Scissor Step (*Pas de Sissonne ou de ciseaux*) [Fig. 295].

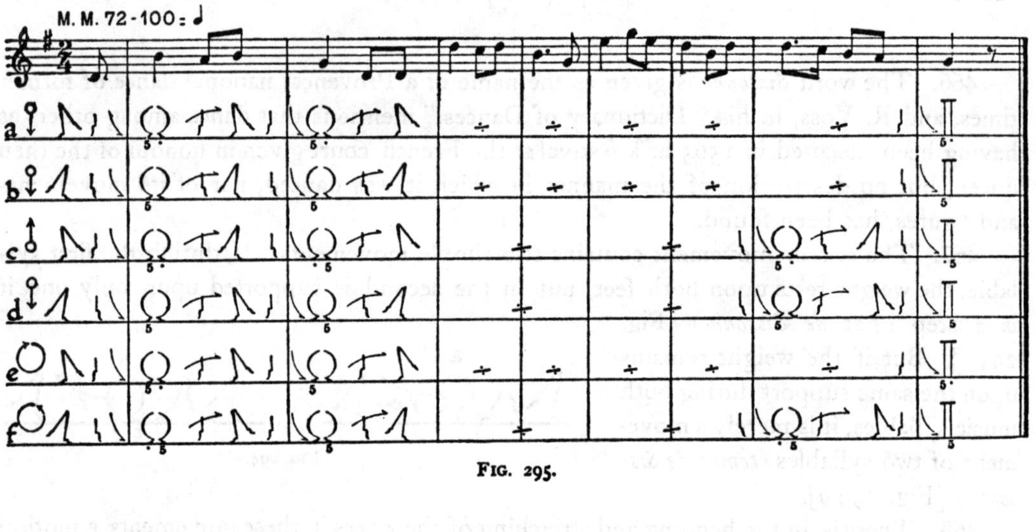

FIG. 295.

Exercise 61 *a*. Simple, Under-Crossed Scissor Steps upon the Left Foot (*Pas de ciseaux simples dessous du pied gauche*).

NOTE. — When the steps are all made with the same foot, they are called simple.

Exercise 61 *b*. Over-Crossed Scissor Step with Right Foot (*Pas de ciseaux simples dessus du pied droit*).

Exercise 61 *c*. Walking Backward by Means of Alternate Under-Crossed Scissor Steps (*Pas de ciseaux alternatifs dessous en reculant*).

Exercise 61 *d*. Walking Forward by Means of Alternate Over-Crossed Scissor Steps (*Pas de ciseaux alternatifs dessus en avançant*).

Exercise 61 *e*. Simple Under-Crossed Scissor Steps with Left Foot, with Backward Turning upon the Right.

Exercise 61 *f*. Turning Forward by Means of Alternate Over and Under-Crossed Scissor Steps.

470. Scissor Steps with Subsequent Raisings (*Pas de Sissonne ou Ciseaux Relevés*). The meaning of the word *relever* (to raise again) has been explained in § 461, and, as applied to the *pas de ciseaux*, it forms what is known as *un pas de ciseaux relevé*. It is usually executed in 2-4 measure, but may be made in either 3-8 or 3-4. In the latter measure it is often used in the Mazurka, for a finishing tour.

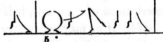

FIG. 296.

Fig. 296 shows the choregraphy of the *pas de ciseaux relevé*.

Exercise 62. Scissor Steps with Subsequent Raisings (*Pas de ciseaux relevés*) [Fig. 297].

FIG. 297.

## Double Scissor Step or Syllable (*Pas ou Temps de Sissonne Double*)

471. If the weight remains upon the same foot throughout these movements, it is called double scissor syllable, but when there is a transfer added during the execution, it becomes a regular step (*un pas de ciseaux double*).

This step is described by Bernhard Klemm, in his "Catechism of the Art of Dancing," as follows:

Upon the place.

Preparation: 5th position, right forward. During the part measure, the knees are bended, in preparation for the leap which follows upon the first beat in the full measure, and which is made upon both feet, falling back into 5th point position. Upon the second beat, there occurs a second leap, with falling back upon the left foot only, while the right is carried to the 2d position and remains there stretched and balancing, until the third beat, when it falls back again into the 5th position, either before (*dessus*) or behind (*dessous*) the left [Fig. 298].

472. This step occurs in the English national dance called the Sailor's Hornpipe.

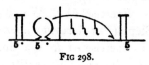

FIG 298.

473. **Pas de Rigaudon.** This step is also known as the *pas de Rigaudon* because of its use in a lively and once popular dance of that name.

The "Dictionary" of Noël and Chapsal is authority for the statement that this dance was the invention of Rigaudon, whose name it bears, and that the dance was carried to England from Provence, in the southern part of France, where it was first danced by only two persons, but afterwards became used as a social dance. The position for the *Rigaudon* was like that of the *Anglaise*, and *Ecossaise*, which later became extremely popular. The gentlemen formed in a straight line opposite and facing their ladies, and the first couple danced a figure which was afterward repeated by the others. As there are various different descriptions of the steps, it is probable that they were executed in different figures.

474. If we may believe the explanations of many competent writers, the *pas de Rigaudon* consisted of a *jeté* which was immediately followed by a *fouetté*, similar to the second half of the *enchaînement* of the so-called Rhinelander Polka.

Exercise 63. Double Scissor Step (*Pas de Sissonne double*) [Fig. 299].

FIG. 299.

## Chasing or Hunting Steps (*Pas Chassés*)

475. The word *chasser* means to chase, and is most appropriately applied to these steps, for in them, one foot "chases" the other from its position. If, as is often the case, all of these steps are executed with the same foot and in the same direction they are called simple chasing steps (*pas chassés simples*) [Fig. 300], but if they are executed alternately with one foot and then with the other, they are called alternate chasing steps (*des chassés alternatifs*).

The simple chasing steps are usually executed sidewise and the alternate steps forward, in the various figures of the Quadrilles. The alternate *chassés* also occur in many of the Waltzes.

FIG. 300.

476. **Simple Chasing Steps to the Side** (*Chassés Simples de Côté*). To execute these steps to the side, one places the left foot in 2d position, and, upon the first part measure, glides

or steps with the left foot into posterior 3d, thereby chasing the right foot from its place, whence it glides to the right into 2d position, where it immediately receives the weight, thus leaving the left free and prepared for the repetition of the movement. The step is executed to the left in countermotion.

To execute the *chassé* forward, begin with either foot, from a preparatory posterior 4th position, and close into posterior 3d, at the same time transferring the weight and gliding the advancing foot forward to anterior 4th, where it immediately receives again the weight of the body. A slight raising and lowering, combined with a corresponding bending of the knees, gives these steps a beautiful elastic appearance.

To begin from a closed position, one must make a preparatory half-step into an open one.

The *chassé* is most frequently begun from the anterior 3d position, by slightly raising the rear foot and gliding forward upon the advanced one, while the weight falls back upon the foot behind.

In the following exercise will be found the choreographic script for the step. While the script is written in full in the part measure and in the first full measure, the abbreviation only is used in the measures which succeed.

Exercise 64. Simple Chasing Steps (*Chassés simples*) [Fig. 301].

FIG. 301.

The symbol which is placed below the line of the floor, at the end of the fourth measure, indicates that a quarter-turn to the left is made upon both balls; and the key which is placed above the sign of the *chassé* shows that the last half of the exercise is to be executed in the opposite direction.

477. **Alternate Chasing Steps** (*Pas Chassés Alternatifs*). The simple chasing steps require only one music syllable, but in order to immediately execute another step with the other foot, certain movements are necessary to effect the transfer of weight. This combination of syllables is known as *pas chassé*. They may be executed any number of times, either forward, backward, sidewise or turning in 2-4 or 6-8 measure.

They occur in the Quadrilles in the *traversé*, the "chains" and various other figures.

478. The complete chasing step (*pas chassé*) consists, therefore, of one whole and two half-steps, which are executed upon two music syllables, and may be made in all directions.

**Chasing Step Forward** (*Pas Chassé en avant*). Preparation: Anterior 3d position of right.

Execution: Raise upon the left foot and glide forward upon the right, into 4th position, slightly bending and stretching the knee, and transfer; bring the left foot forward into posterior 4th position during the transition to the accented first music syllable. During the second syllable, the left foot is glided forcibly into the posterior 3d position, "chasing" the right from its place into the anterior 4th position, where the weight is trans-ferred to it; thus making it possible to begin the next *pas chassé* with the left foot.

479. Exercise 64 *a.* Alternate Chasing Steps in a Circle to the Right (*Pas chassés al-ternatifs autour de la salle*) [Fig. 302].

FIG. 302.

The key indicates a circular movement and the arrow point shows its direction.

The choregraphy of the part measure and of the first measure are written completely, but the succeeding measures contain only the abbreviated sign of the chasing steps, and the symbols of movement for the part measure.

The abbreviated sign of the *chassés alternatifs* differs from that of the *chassés simples* very slightly; the *chassés simples* being shown with one perpendicular line, and the *altern-atifs* by two perpendicular lines from the middle of the long stretching line to the line of the floor [Fig. 303].

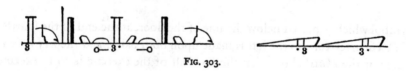

FIG. 303.

## Gliding Steps (*Pas Glissés — Glissades*)

480. The gliding steps are among the most important, as they are very frequently used in both social and theatrical dances. There are few steps which have been known by so many different names, or which have been so differently explained and interpreted.

481. For this reason, one must consider especially the proper order of words; for example, *pas élevé-glissé* (raising gliding step) and *pas glissé-élevé* (raised gliding step) mean quite different movements. In the raising gliding step the body is raised upon the supporting foot, while the free foot glides upon the floor, but, in the raised gliding step the free foot glides with the point on the floor, without reference to the occupation of the supporting

one. *Pas élevé glissant* (gliding raising step) is still different, as that term is applied to the simultaneous raising and gliding of the supporting foot.

**482.** The terms *glissade* and *pas glissé* are often interpreted to mean the combination of a raising step to the side and a subsequent gliding movement of the other foot, but this is incorrect, for such a movement is not a simple gliding step (*pas glissé simple*), but a *demi-glissé* or *pas élevé et un glissement.*

**483. Gliding Half-Steps** (*Demi-Glissés*). The definition of a half-step may be found in § 395. If, then, the foot is glided from the anterior 3d to the anterior 4th position, and the weight transferred, thus throwing the rear foot into posterior 4th position, there has been executed a gliding half-step.

FIG. 304.

This is also the case if the foot is glided from 4th to 3d, or from 1st to 2d position, with immediate transfer. Fig. 304 shows both the complete and abbreviated choregraphy for the *demi-glissé.*

**484. Whole Gliding Steps** (*Pas Glissés Entiers*). A gliding step is whole if it extends the full width of a step; as, for example, from the posterior to the anterior 4th, or from the 2d, past the 1st into the 3d, 5th or similar crossed position. The expression *pas glissé* is always understood to mean a whole gliding step; and the word "whole" is therefore only necessary in cases where the meaning is to be defined more clearly. The word "half," however, should never be omitted when a *demi-glissé* is intended, as one might be led to believe, from the similarity of the symbols, that a whole step was meant.

Exercise 65.  Gliding Half-Steps (*Demi-glissés*) [Fig. 305].

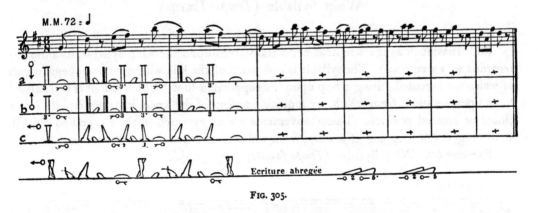

FIG. 305.

**485. Alternate Crossed Gliding Steps** (*Glissés Croisés Changés ou Glissades Croisées*). Gliding steps which pass into crossed positions are called *glissés croisés*. If executed alternately before and behind the supporting foot, they are known as *glissés croisés changés dessus et dessous ou dessous et dessus.*

Fig. 306 shows the abbreviated script of these movements. A complete description will be found in Exercise 66.

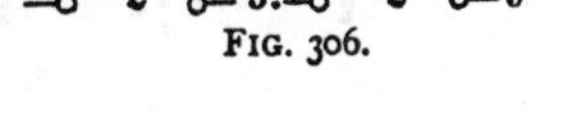

FIG. 306.

Exercise 66.  Crossed Gliding Steps to Right and Left (*Glissés changés*) [Fig. 307].

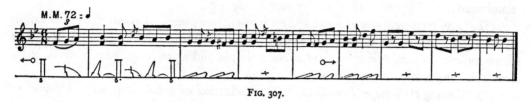

FIG. 307.

**486.** A very appropriate and sensible comparison of language and dancing may be found in Klemm's "Catechism of the Art of Dancing" in connection with his explanation of the *glissades* in which he likens an *enchainement* to a line of poetry, as in Fig. 308.

FIG. 308.

By such examples, one might properly indicate, by means of the signs of prosody, a certain rhythmic formation for the use of a composer in writing a melody.

## Whip Syllable (*Temps Fouetté*)

**487.** Inasmuch as the weight is never transferred upon the whip syllable, it cannot be regarded as a step (*pas*).  The syllable is composed of the following simple movements, all of which are executed during a hop upon the supporting foot:  The free foot is first carried to an open position, from which, by a quick bending of the knee, it passes rapidly into a closed or crossed position.  These movements are all executed in the air, and so quickly as to suggest the snapping of a whip, from which resemblance it derives its name.

Exercise 67.  Whip Syllable (*Temps fouetté*) [Fig. 309].

FIG. 309.

Exercise 67 *a* is called "Simple Whip Syllables upon the Place" of the right foot into the low crossed anterior 3d position, with inclined direction of the sole and immediate raising of the same foot into half-high balancing 2d position. (*Temps fouettés simples du pied droit, sur la place, à la 3ième position dessus en balancé avec la direction inclinée de la semelle et levée immédiate du pied droit à la 2de position jusqu'à la demi-hauteur.*)

Thus, we see again, how many words are necessary to explain a simple dance movement that can be completely described beneath a single note, by means of choreography; for the entire movement is completely expressed under the second quarter note in the exercise.

**487 *a*.** Both the first and the second measures contain the complete script, but the third has simply the abbreviated sign of the whip, below which is the number of the position and the symbol of the sole direction. The succeeding measures show merely the sign of repetition.

Exercise 67 *b* contains the whip movement into posterior 3d position, with perpendicular sole direction.

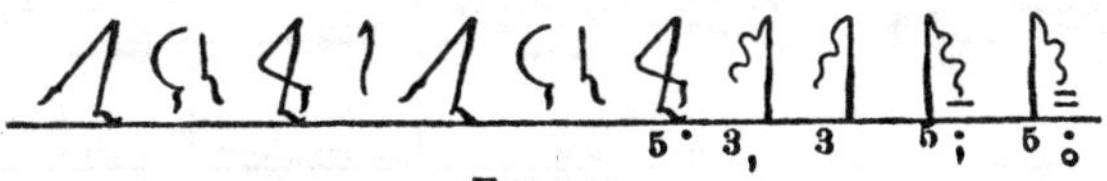

FIG. 310.

Exercise 67 *c* is composed of whip movements crossed alternately above and below.

Fig. 310 shows the different signs of the various whip syllables.

Exercise 68. Phrases of Two and Enchainment Four Measures.

FIG. 311.  FIG. 312.

Exercise 68 *a*. (*a*) Phrase of Two Measures to the Right Composed of One Raising Step with Gliding, Two Simple Chasing Steps, and One Whip Syllable (*Phrase à deux mesures, contenant: un pas levé et glissé et un temps fouetté à droite*) [Fig. 311].

(*b*) The Same Phrase Executed to the Left [Fig. 312].

(*c*) Enchainment of Both Phrases [Fig. 313].

FIG. 313.

The short perpendicular line has been omitted in the sign of the raising step with gliding because there is no striking in this step such as occurs in *pas chassé*.

This exercise may remind the student of some others which are mentioned much earlier in the book.

**488.** The phrase (§ 193) of two measures begins in the part measure, and ends, therefore, with the third eighth-note of the second measure — that is, upon the completion of the first *cæsura* (§ 197) — and the final eighth-note of that measure belongs to the second *cæsura*, or phrase of the melody. The preparatory raising steps belong, in like manner, to the second dance phrase.

**489.** The second phrase contains the same combination of steps as the first, but is executed in countermotion, in order to bring the dancer into the original position.

**490.** By such a repetition, with a suitable cadence (§ 192), the melody of the music and the period of the dance are completed (§ 194).

Exercise 69. Sentence of Eight Measures (*Enchaînement à huit mesures*) [Fig. 314].

FIG. 314.

The steps are indicated by abbreviated signs, and the music which has been selected is the second part (*clausula*) of the Galop, to which composition the preceding exercises belong. In this exercise the number of steps in each direction is doubled.

## Cutting Step (*Pas Coupé*)

**491.** A cutting step extends from an open through a closed and into an open position. A cutting step with the right foot from the posterior 4th position, passing through the 3d position, is executed as follows:

The right foot is carried from the posterior 4th to the posterior 3d position, touching the heel of the left foot, where it receives the weight, and the left foot, now free, is raised into the anterior 4th balancing position [Fig. 315].

These movements, if they are all executed upon one music syllable, constitute what is known as *pas coupé dessous* (cutting step behind).

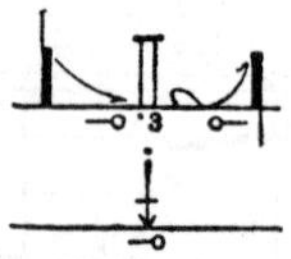

FIG. 315. 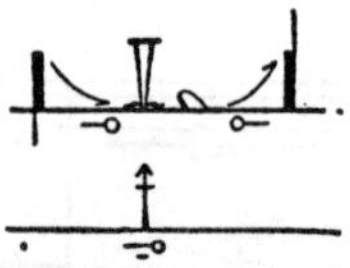　　　FIG. 316. 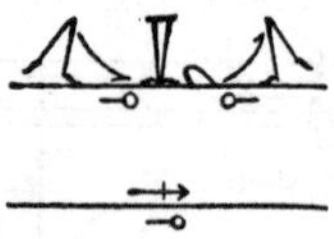　　　FIG. 317.

**492.** If the step commences from the anterior 4th and passes through the anterior 3d to the posterior 4th position, it is a *pas coupé dessus* (cutting step before) [Fig. 316].

**493.** If the step commences in the 2d position and passes through the 1st (or another closed position) carrying the other foot into 2d position, it is called a *pas coupé latéral* (cutting step sidewise) [Fig. 317].

In these diagrams the symbol upon the lower line is the abbreviated sign of the corresponding step.

A point above signifies *dessous* (behind); a short horizontal line below means *dessus* (before). This direction is also indicated by the arrow point.

**494.** If, as occurs in the step of the Mazurka, there is a strongly perceptible knocking, the step is called a *coupé poussé* (pushed cutting step— § 893).

**495.** If the foot is put down in an audible manner, it is called a *coupé frappé.*

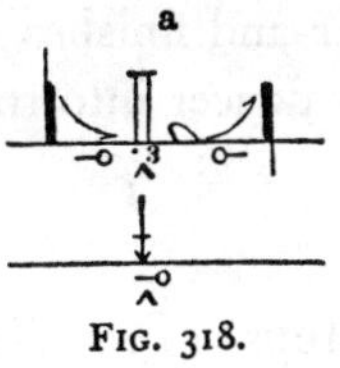

FIG. 318. 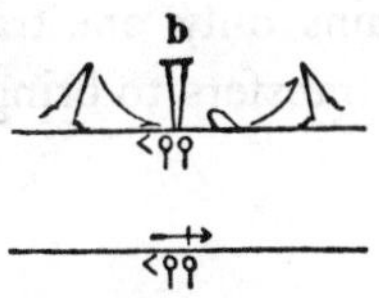   FIG. 319. 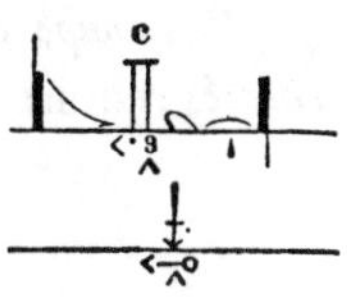   FIG. 320.

The *coupés frappé et coupés poussé* often occur in Russian dances, with the points of the feet turned upward and the heels gliding upon the floor as shown in Fig. 48.

The choregraphic symbols of the steps are as follows:

Beaten cutting step forward (*coupé dessus frappé*) [Fig. 318].

Pushed cutting step, to the side, with parallel feet (*coupé latéral poussé parallèlement*) [Fig. 319].

Pushed, beaten, under-crossed cutting step, followed by gliding on the heel (*coupé dessous poussé et frappé suivé d'un glissement sur le talon*) [Fig. 320].


## Cutting Half-Step (*Demi-Coupé*)

**496.** If only the first half of the step and the transfer is executed, the movement is called *un demi-coupé.* In such cases the remainder of the step does not, in itself, constitute a step, as it lacks the *dégagement.* That portion of the step must therefore be known as *temps glissé, temps levé, temps baissé,* etc., as the case may be.

In the abbreviated script, the point is omitted from the arrow which represents the *demi-coupé.*

### DIFFERENCE BETWEEN COUPÉ AND CHASSÉ

**497.** *Pas Coupé,* to the right, from 2d balancing position of left, and passing through the 3d to the 2d balancing position of the right, is represented by Fig. 321 *a.*

*Pas Chassé,* to the right, from 2d ball position of left, and passing through the 3d to the 2d ball position of the right, with immediate transfer to right, leaving left foot in 2d position, is represented by Fig. 321 *b.*

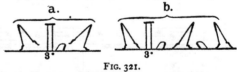

FIG. 321.

The *pas coupé* forward finishes in anterior 4th balancing position of the right.

The *pas chassé* forward finishes in posterior 4th ball position of the left.

The positions in the *pas coupés* are usually " balancing," while those of the *pas chassés* (almost without exception) touch the floor.

In the execution of the *coupés* the feet are " carried," while the *chassés* are generally made by a light gliding upon the floor.

*Pas coupé* contains only one transfer and finishes upon the supporting foot, but *pas chassés* require two transfers to bring the dancer into readiness for a repetition of the step.

## Tossing Steps (*Pas Ballotés*)

498. The French word *balloter* means to toss in various directions, and may be applied to tossing a ball, a package, or the movement of a ship in a storm.

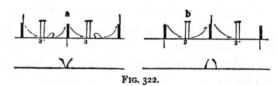

FIG. 322.

499. A tossing step consists of two consecutive and opposite *pas coupés*.

Fig. 322 *a* shows the tossing step crossed behind and before (*balloté dessous et dessus*).

Fig. 322 *b* represents the tossing step crossed before and behind (*balloté dessus et dessous*). (The signs on the lower line are abbreviations.)

500. While *pas balloté* never contains less, it may contain more than two syllables. Note the following examples [Fig. 323]:

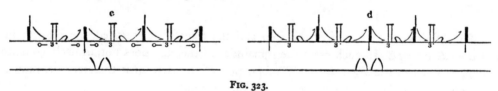

FIG. 323.

*c. Pas balloté* of three syllables.    *d. Pas balloté* of four syllables.

Exercise 70. English Sailor Step (*Pas de matelot anglais*) [Fig. 324].

FIG. 324.

This *enchainement* is composed of a triple tossing step (*pas balloté*) and a whip syllable (*temps fouetté*) in anterior 3d balancing position. The whole is repeated alternately six times and finished with three alternate stamping steps in 3d position.

The same *enchainement* is repeated upon the succeeding eight measures, commencing with the other foot.

## Stuffing Steps (*Pas de Bourrée*)

**501.** *La Bourrée* is the name of a now obsolete dance which was once very popular in the province of Auvergne, France; this movement takes its name from that dance.

The word *bourré* is an adjective, meaning "stuffing," and is most appropriately applied to the movements which go to make up this step. Indeed, it is not at all unlikely that the dance itself derived its title from this quality of the movement.

**502.** As the name of this step should indicate its peculiar quality of movement (in the same manner as do the titles of the *chassés* and *glissés*) the name *pas bourré* would, in the opinion of the author, be more correct than that of *pas de Bourrée*.

The practice of naming steps for dances is extremely impracticable. It almost invariably leads to ambiguity, because many dances, though similarly named, are differently executed; while others differently named are executed in much the same manner. Is there one of our dancing masters who can state definitely the exact manner in which *La Bourrée* was danced, or who would claim indeed that it was danced everywhere in the same manner? This element of doubt is eliminated by the use of an adjective which explains the quality of the movement, for this kind of a description is not subject to subsequent change of meaning.

This reason, therefore, is offered for the author's preference for the term *pas bourré* as a name for this step.

**503.** While there is a marked similarity between the stuffing and the chasing steps, there is in reality a considerable difference, which is indicated in some degree by their names. That which is "stuffed" is usually stationary, while that which is "chased" is forced from its place, and these characteristics apply to the *pas bourrés* and *pas chassés*. In the *pas bourré* forward, the free foot is brought against the supporting one, which is momentarily held in position before it glides forward; and in the *pas chassé* forward, the rear foot drives or chases the supporting foot from its place before receiving the weight, as is indicated by the name *chassé*.

**504.** *Pas Bourré* may be executed in either 2-4 or 6-8 time.

At the period when it was fashionable to dance Quadrilles, Contra-Dances, Ecossaises, Anglaises, etc., with slow and precise steps, such steps were known as *pas de Bourrées*, and these really were stuffed steps, that quality being necessary to fill out the slow tempo. Since that time, however, fashion has changed, and in place of the slow stuffing steps, we have quick chasing ones to correspond with the more rapid tempo now in vogue.

**505. Ancient Stuffing Steps** (*Pas de Bourrée Anciens*). The word "ancient" is used, in this case, to distinguish between this step and the sidewise stuffing step which occurs in several of the more recent dances. To these latter steps we shall apply the name "modern" stuffing steps (*pas de Bourrée moderne*).

Exercise 71. Ancient Stuffing Steps Forward and Backward (*Pas de Bourrée anciens en avant et en arrière*) [Fig. 325].

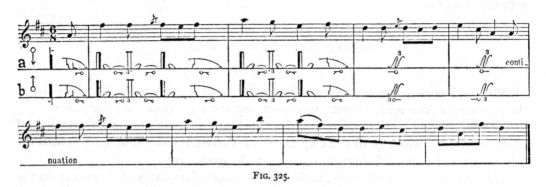

FIG. 325.

Exercise 71 *a*. Forward (*En avant*).

Preparation: Posterior low balancing 4th position of right.

Execution: First syllable: — Bend the supporting knee slightly and glide right foot forward to 4th position, where it receives the weight of the body upon the *thesis* of the music, thus completing a whole step.

Second Syllable: — Glide left foot into posterior 3d position and transfer (half-step), and advance right to 4th position and transfer (half-step.) The succeeding movement commences with the left foot [Fig. 326].

FIG. 326.

Exercise 71 *b*. The Same Movement Backward. Executed in the countermotion.

506. In Quadrilles and dances of similar nature, the first *pas bourré* forward usually starts from the anterior 3d position, which makes it only a half-step; the first one backward usually starts from a posterior 3d. At the end of a step, phrase, or sentence, the dancer usually stands in 3d position.

507. The choregraphic symbols in Exercise 71 contain no features that have not already been explained, with the exception of the abbreviation, which is new to the reader. The number above the symbol indicates a posterior and the number below it an anterior position.

508. Modern Stuffing Steps (*Pas de Bourrée Moderne*). The *pas bourré latéral* has been applied, in some of the modern dances, in such a way that all three step movements are executed upon a single music syllable, or *triole*, or so that the first and second step movements coincide with the part measure, the third falling upon the first syllable of the full measure, as shown in the following exercise:

509. Exercise 72. Over and Under Crossed Stuffing Steps to the Side (*Pas de Bourrée latéraux dessus et dessous*) [Fig. 327].

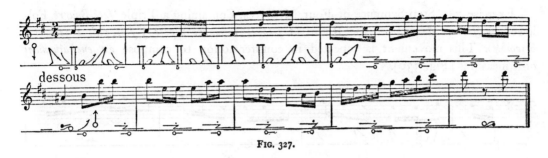

dessous

FIG. 327.

During the first half of this exercise, the steps are crossed in front or above, which carries the dancer forward as indicated by the key. During the second half, they are crossed behind or below, by which the dancer goes backward.

**510.** Exercise 73. Stuffing Steps to the Side in Triole Rhythm (*Pas de Bourrée en rhythme de trioles dessus et dessous*) [Fig. 328].

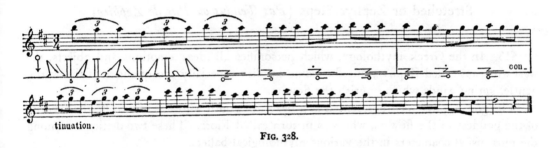

con-

tinuation.

FIG. 328.

In executing the stuffing steps to the side, for example, to the right — the dancer raises the left leg into the half-high 2d position, as preparation, and from this carries the left foot either before or behind the right into 3d or 5th position, upon the first music syllable belonging to the step. Upon the second music syllable, the right foot is carried to 2d position and receives the weight; and upon the third music syllable, the left foot is again carried to its former crossed position and the weight transferred, while the right is immediately lifted to half-high 2d position, so as to be in readiness for the succeeding step [Fig. 329].

FIG. 329.

**511.** In Spanish and Italian dances, the stuffing steps are usually made in the 5th position; in French dances, they fall in the 3d; and in different Hungarian, Polish and Russian dances, in 1st position, with the feet nearly parallel.

**512.** The abbreviated signs are easily understood. The symbol of the "ancient" step is rounded and nearly perpendicular, while that of the "modern" is angular and horizontal. The same signs are added to indicate the forward and backward crossing (*dessus et dessous*) as are applied to the other symbols.

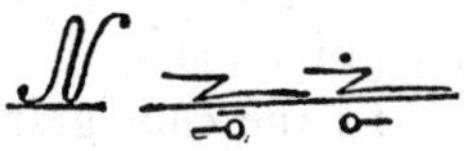

Exercise 74. Step Sentence of Four ·Measures, Containing a Triple *Jeté Bourré* Followed by *Jeté et Assemblé* to the Right (1 *jeté et* 1 *bourré répété* 3 *fois, puis* 1 *jeté et* 1 *assemblé*). This movement is repeated in countermotion to compose an *enchaînement* of 8 measures [Fig. 330].

FIG. 330.

## Stretched or Zephyr Steps (*Pas Tendus ou Pas de Zéphire*)

**513.** In the Greek mythology, which personifies all ideas, emotions and objects, the west wind was called Zephyr, and the name implies especially the qualities of the warm, gentle, spring winds which nourish the flowers.

The god Zephyr was represented as a beautiful youth who was said to be the favorite of the goddess of the flowers, who was in turn called Flora. These two deities are among the most usual characters in the various mythological ballets.

It is, therefore, natural to suppose that the dancing step to which this name has been applied contains movements of a peculiarly dainty and attractive quality.

**514.** The expression *pas tendu*, which means a stretched step, might properly be applied to any step in which the legs are stretched, but it is usually applied, in its technical sense, to the following movement of two syllables, which may be executed in all directions, either upon the spot or turning:

**515.** *Pas Tendu.* First syllable: The movement commences with the right foot, from the preparatory anterior 4th balancing position, with the execution of a cutting step into 1st position, by means of which the left goes backward into the 4th position.

The second syllable begins with a jump upon the right foot while the left is stretched forward into the 4th position, touching the floor lightly in transit through the 1st [Fig. 331].

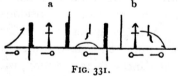

FIG. 331.

In the choreographic script, division "a" shows the complete, and division "b" the abbreviated form of writing.

**516.** The word *tendu* has been applied to this step because of the fact that the active leg is stretched during transition, notwithstanding the fact that the supporting leg necessarily has to be bended, in order to execute the jump. Indeed, the active leg must be slightly bended during transition, or the movement appears extremely stiff, and only the tip of the foot should touch the floor in passing through the 1st position.

517. The whole movement, if executed in this manner, is more agreeable to the eye, and corresponds more closely to the meaning of the name *pas de zéphire*. The term is entirely justified if the active leg beats gently backward and forward in 3d position during transit, which movement furnishes the requisite shading to complete the sentiment of the name. *Pas de zéphire*, then, is a beating step [§ 583].

518. Although this step may be executed in the 2d position, it is more beautiful in the 2–4 intermediate, and by the addition of the corresponding movements of the upper body and arms, which are very easily determined, one may improvise many very agreeable exercises [Fig. 332].

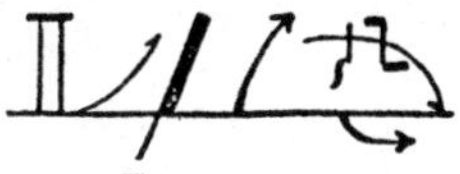

FIG. 332.

519. *Pas de Zéphire* may also be composed of a *coupé dessus* and a *temps balloné* [§ 528] and it is often used in this form in that exquisite composition, the *Gavotte de Vestris*.

520. Exercise 75. Gliding Zephyr Step in 4th Position upon the Place (*Pas de zéphire sur la place*) [Fig. 333].

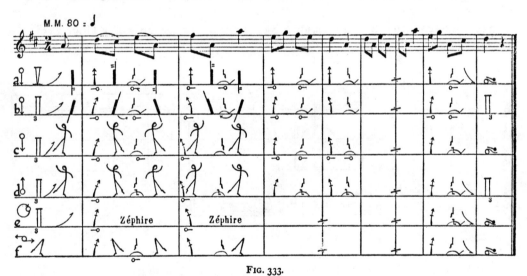

FIG. 333.

If the transition which occurs upon the 2d syllable is to be glided, the gliding symbol must be written upon the line of the floor; if executed in half-height, the movement sign cuts the line of the leg; and if transition occurs at full height, the sign is placed above the sign of the supporting leg [Fig. 334].

FIG. 334.

Exercise 75 b. Zephyr Step in 2–4 Position upon the Spot, with Quarter-Turns (indicated by the turning sign below the line of the floor) [§ 546].

Exercises 75 c and 75 d are completely drawn for the purpose of acquainting the reader with the signs, and in order to demonstrate the proper corresponding movements of the head and the arms.

Exercise 75 e shows the movement in a circular form, as indicated by the key. In various places the word *zéphire* has been substituted for the script.

Exercise 75 f is composed of zephyr steps sidewise, going first to the right and then to the left, as indicated by the key.


## Basque Steps (*Pas de Basques*)


521. The Basques are a people who live around the Bay of Biscay, among whom there have always been many good dancers, and this movement forms the most important portion of their national dances. The same combination is also to be found in the Spanish dances, such as the Aragonesa, the Gitana and the Cachucha, in which it is executed either in 3–4 or 3–8 time. It also exists in various French dances, where it is danced in 2–4 or 6–8 time.

522. Exercise 76. Spanish Basque Step (*Pas de basque espagnol*) [Fig. 335].— *a* forward, *b* backward.

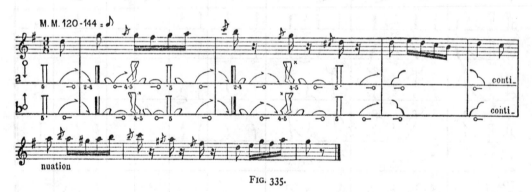

FIG. 335.

In this step all three syllables are distinctly accented. The music is that of the famous Cachucha.

### EXECUTION OF THE BASQUE STEPS

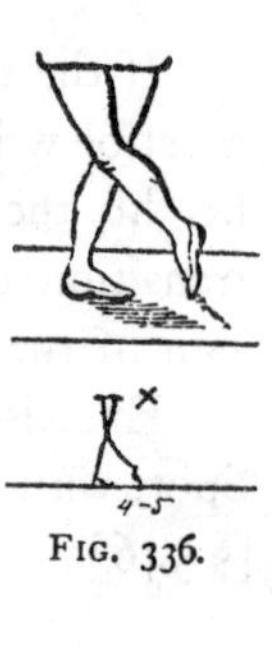

523. Exercise 76 a. In 3-4 Measure, Forward.
Preparation: Anterior 5th position of right.
First syllable: Easy *jeté* in anterior 2-4 position. Second syllable: Glide or carry left to double crossed anterior 4-5 position and transfer [Fig. 336]. Third syllable: Glide right foot into posterior 5th and transfer [Fig. 337.]

FIG. 336.

Exercise 76 *b*. Backward. Preparation: Posterior 5th position of left.

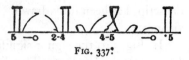

FIG. 337.

First syllable: Light *jeté* into posterior 4th position. Second syllable: Carry right lightly into 4-5 position and transfer. Third syllable: Glide left into anterior 5th position and transfer, thus leaving right foot free and prepared to commence the succeeding step.

Exercise 77. Basque Step Sidewise (*Pas de basque latéral*) [Fig. 338].

FIG. 338.

This step is executed first to right and then to left, as indicated by the key.

524. The first and second syllables are so executed, in 2-4 and 6-8 time, that they coincide with only one music syllable; and the preparation, which begins in the part measure, is so closely joined to the accented movement as to form a syncopation. The steps are the same as in the forward movement, but go to the side, and the transition from one to another Basque step to the side is accomplished by the addition of half an outward foot-circle [§ 262].

Exercise 78. Basque Step with Turning (*Pas de basque en tournant*)—*a* forward, *b* backward [Fig. 339].

FIG. 339.

525. Exercise 78 *a*. Basque Steps Forward in Turning, to the Right (6-8 Time) (*Pas de basque en avant en tournant à droite*).

The legs must be crossed in the first half of the step, sufficiently to produce a half-turn; the second half contains a half-turn to the right upon the toes of both feet, which restores the right foot to the anterior 5th position.

Exercise 78 *b*. Basque Steps Backward in Turning, to the Left (*Pas de basque en arrière en tournant à gauche*).

This movement is exactly similar to the preceding, but in countermotion.

526. Abbreviated Script. In the first two measures in each of the foregoing exercises,

the script has been fully drawn. In the remaining measures it has been indicated by abbreviations.

In Fig. 340 the sign *a* signifies an entire Basque step with the right foot, and the sign *b* one with the left foot. The direction is indicated by the key. The tip of the free foot

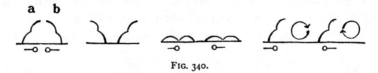

FIG. 340.

should always be directed strongly down. The symbol of the lateral Basque step is drawn horizontally; in cases where there could be doubt, the sole direction is added below the line.

The turnings are indicated by the regular turning signs [§ 548].

## Ball Step (*Pas Ballonné*)

527. This step derives its name from the circular movement of the free foot, which has the appearance of stepping over a ball. It is usually executed to the side, but it may also be made forward or backward. Although it may be practiced alternately, it is usually applied in "simple" form, that is, without change of direction.

## Ball Syllable (*Temps Ballonné*)

528. If the circular movement of the free foot is unaccompanied by transfer, as in the second syllable of the zephyr step, it is called *temps ballonné*.

### EXECUTION OF THE BALL STEP

529. Preparation: 3d or 5th position of right. The first syllable commences in the part measure, with a jump on the left foot, during which the right is carried in a circular direction to the 2d position, where it immediately receives the weight.

In the second syllable, the left foot glides into posterior 5th position [Fig. 341]. In order to maintain the same direction, it is necessary to add

FIG. 341.

a transfer to the second syllable, but such is not necessary in the case of alternate ball steps.

Exercise 79. Ball Steps (*Pas ballonnés*) [Fig. 342].

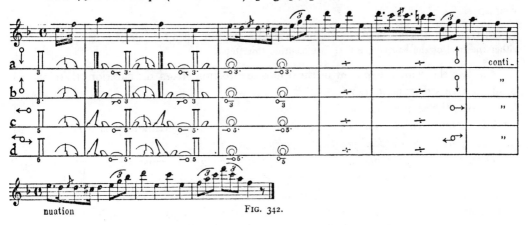

FIG. 342.

*a.* Simple Ball Steps Forward (*Pas ballonnés simples en avant*).
*b.* Simple Ball Steps Backward (*Pas ballonnés simples en arrière*).
*c.* Simple Ball Steps to the Right (*Pas ballonnés simples à droite*).
*d.* Alternate Ball Steps to the Side (*Pas ballonnés alternatifs de côté*).
The abbreviation needs no explanation.

## Twisting Steps (*Pas Tortillés*)

**530.** The simple turning movements are explained in §§ 246 to 250 and the compound movement *tortillé*, and its choregraphic symbol ($w$), are dealt with in § 251.

The word *tortillé* occurs very frequently in the descriptions of dances, particularly in describing dances of Slavic and Hungarian origin. A twisting step (*pas tortillé*) contains at least two turns and a transfer, all of which must of course be written beneath the notes with which the steps coincide. For the purpose of abbreviation, the letter $w$ has been chosen as a symbol, being composed of two $v$'s, which letter is the symbol of a turn [§ 251].

**531.** These steps may be executed upon the sole, ball, point or heel, or in balancing position, with either or both feet, and in all directions.

While they may be made independently of all other steps, they are often executed in connection with other steps, and thus either form enchainments or complete them.

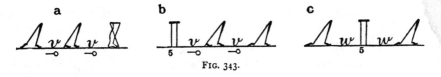

FIG. 343.

**532.** In Fig. 343, *a* shows a twisting step on the sole of the right foot, from the 2d to the anterior 5th position (*un pas tortillé du pied droit sur la semelle*), consisting of an inward and an outward turn of the right foot, made upon the sole and followed by a transfer of weight.

Note. — As it is practically impossible to make a real turn upon the sole, it is necessary to raise either the heel or the ball of the foot in executing this step.

*b* shows the same movement in the opposite direction (from the anterior 5th to the 2d position with subsequent transfer).

*c* shows the abbreviated script.

533. Low twisting step of the right foot going upon the ball and heel from 1st to 2d position (*tortillé sur la demi-pointe et le talon du pied*).

*Demi-pointe* means the ball of the foot, and the sign of transfer is placed above the symbol of *tortillé* to indicate that the *dégagé* occurs during the turning. The signs below the turning sign show that the first turning movement is made upon the ball, and the second upon the heel.

534. Twisting Steps upon the Heels and the Balls (*Tortillé sur les Talons et les Demi-Pointes*). This step is combined with a *frappé* in the 2d position, and a *pas de basque* in the Spanish dances.

535. Twisting Step upon Both Feet in Opposite Directions (*Tortillé Bipède Contraire*) [Fig. 344]. In this step there is a simultaneous turning of both feet, but the right foot makes first a turn upon the heel, and then one upon the ball; while the left foot makes a turn on the ball, followed by one on the heel. This movement contains the step of the *Tour tortillé*, which will be explained in § 538.

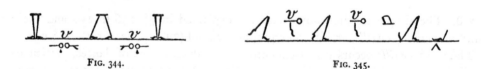

FIG. 344.                                    FIG. 345.

536. Twisting Step upon Both Feet in the Same Direction (*Tortillé Bipède Simultane*) [Fig. 345]. This step is composed of a simultaneous turning of both feet in the same direction, either upon the balls or the heels. It is very seldom used, while the *tortillé bipède contraire* occurs very frequently in the Russian dances.

537. Leaping Twisting Step upon the Point and Heel, with Audible Lowering of the Ball of the Foot (*Tortillé Sautillé sur la Pointe et le Talon et Terminé par un Tapé*) [Fig. 345]. This movement starts from the 2d balancing position of the right, by throwing the heel outward, after which the leg is put down forcibly and audibly upon the ball of the foot. The transfer of weight occurs before the putting down, and the whole movement is simultaneous with the leap, which is made upon the left foot.

538. Movement from the Place by Means of Twisting (*Tour Tortillé*). The twisting step upon both feet in opposite directions, which has been referred to in § 535, carries the dancer from the place, toward the left, and may be executed either in a straight or a curved line. It may, of course, be executed in the opposite direction. If, however, the move-

ment is upon a curved line, it is called a circle of turning steps to the right or left (*un tour tortillé à droite*, or *un tour tortillé à gauche*). This is also a part of nearly all the Russian dances.

## Body Turns (*Tours de Corps*)

**539.** The various turns and their differences have been explained in §§ 126 and 127, and some reference to the turning of the rump has been made in §§ 322 to 325.

The term "rump turn" (*tour de torse*) applies only to the turning of that portion of the body and the movement is executed mainly in the hips, without the assistance of the feet. The term *tour de corps* (body turn) refers to the movement of the entire body.

These movements are usually executed upon the points, or balls, of both or either of the feet, and they occasionally take place in the air. Only in very rare instances are they made upon the heels.

**540. Whole or Part Turns.** The dancer who stands directly facing the spectators and turns in one direction until he has resumed his original position describes a "whole turn." If he stops the turning with his back to them he executes a "half-turn." If he turns to the right only so far as to stand with the left shoulder toward the spectators, he has made a "quarter-turn," and one half-way between this and the original position is an "eighth-turn."

**541. Body Turns upon Both Feet.** To make an eighth-turn to the right upon the points from the first (sole) position, carries the dancer into the intermediate 3–4 position of the right [Fig. 346].

NOTE. — If the weight is upon the left foot during this turn, it finishes in anterior 3-4 position of the right ; if it is on the right foot it ends in posterior 3-4 position of the left.

A quarter-turn to the right upon the points, starting from the 1st (sole) position, brings the dancer into 4th position. If the weight during this movement rests upon the

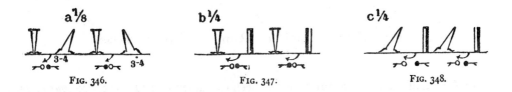

FIG. 346.        FIG. 347.        FIG. 348.

left foot, the result is an anterior 4th position of the right ; if upon the right foot, it produces a posterior 4th position of the left [Fig. 347].

A quarter-turn to the right, from the 2d position, carries the right foot into anterior 4th [Fig. 348] ; while a similar movement to the left, backward, has the opposite effect.

An eighth-turn upon the points in 3d position [Fig. 349] reverses the position. (Do not confound this movement with that of the crossed alternate raisings — *élévations croisées alternatives* — mentioned in §§ 157 and 158.)

A quarter-turn to the left, from the anterior 4th position, brings the right into posterior 4th [Fig. 350 *e*], and a half-turn to the left upon the points carries the right foot from the anterior to the posterior 4-5 position [Fig. 350*f*].

NOTE. — Bear in mind the distinction between the 4th and the 4-5 position, as explained in the note to § 16.

A half-turn to the right forward, from posterior 4-5 position, brings the right foot into anterior 4-5 position [Fig. 351].

The 5th position is changed in the same manner as the 3d.

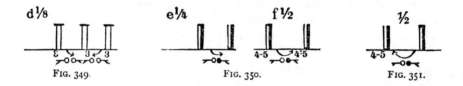

FIG. 349.                    FIG. 350.                    FIG. 351.

## Body Turns Upon One Foot

542. In order to artistically execute a complete turn upon one foot, the body must be securely balanced and held firm. This is greatly facilitated by a preparatory bending of . the supporting knee. From this bended position the dancer should stretch the supporting leg and raise the body in the first half-turn, and lower it in the second half-turn.

543. A turn to the right is one in which the dancer faces from the front position toward his right; and a turn to the left goes from the front toward his left. By turning to the right upon the right foot, the body moves forward; and by turning to the left upon the right foot it moves backward.

## Turn of the Trunk or Rump (*Tour de Torse*)

544. A turn of the trunk or rump, as has been explained in § 322, is called *tour de torse;* and a turn of the entire body is called *tour de corps.*

545. In marching, and in the figure dances, and even in the round dances of the Waltz class, there are various turns which, however, cannot be called pirouettes. If, therefore, a dancer executes, as some persons do, real pirouettes in dancing Quadrille solos and Mazurka figures, they exhibit more skill than is essential to the ordinary social dance.

## Choregraphy of Turning

**546. Quarter-Turns upon One Foot** (*Quart de Tours de Corps sur l'un Pied*) [Fig. 352].

*a.* Quarter-Turn to the Right upon the Right Foot (*Un quart de tour à droite sur le pied droit*).

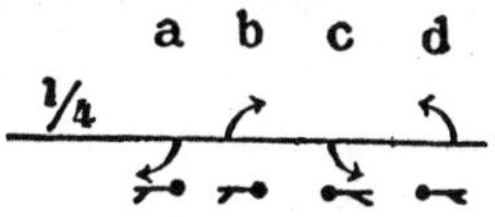

*b.* Quarter-Turn to the Left upon the Right Foot (*Un quart de tour à gauche sur le pied droit*).

*c.* Quarter-Turn to the Left upon the Left Foot (*Un quart de tour à gauche sur le pied gauche*).

*d.* Quarter-Turn to the Right upon the Left Foot (*Un quart de tour à droite sur le pied gauche*).

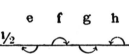

FIG. 352.

**547.** While this system of describing the quarter-turns is very simple, the symbols must be perfectly memorized before proceeding further, in order to clearly distinguish them from the symbols of the half-turns.

**548. Half-Turns upon One Foot** (*Demi-Tours de Corps sur l'un Pied*) [Fig. 353].

*e.* Half-Turn to the Right upon the Right Foot (*Demi-tour à droite sur le pied droit*).

*f.* Half-Turn to the Left upon the Right Foot (*Demi-tour à gauche sur le pied droit*).

*g.* Half-Turn to the Left upon the Left Foot (*Demi-tour à gauche sur le pied gauche*).

*h.* Half-Turn to the Right upon the Left Foot (*Demi-tour à droite sur le pied gauche*).

**549. Whole Turns upon One Foot** (*Tours de Corps Entiers sur l'un Pied*) [Fig. 354].

*i.* Whole Turn to the Right upon the Right Foot (*Tour à droite sur le pied droit*).

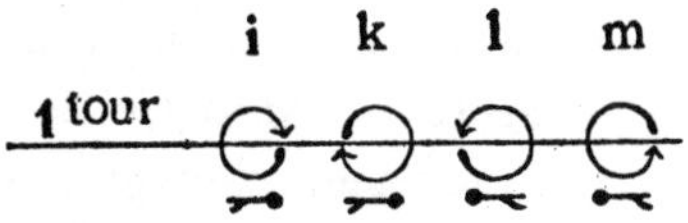

*k.* Whole Turn to the Left upon the Right Foot (*Tour à gauche sur le pied droit*).

*l.* Whole Turn to the Left upon the Left Foot (*Tour à gauche sur le pied gauche*).

*m.* Whole Turn to the Right upon the Left Foot (*Tour à droite sur le pied gauche*).

**550. One and a Half Turns upon One Foot** (*Tour de Corps et Demi sur l'un Pied*) [Fig. 355].

*n.* One and a Half Turns to the Right upon the Right Foot (*Tour et demi à droite sur le pied droit*).

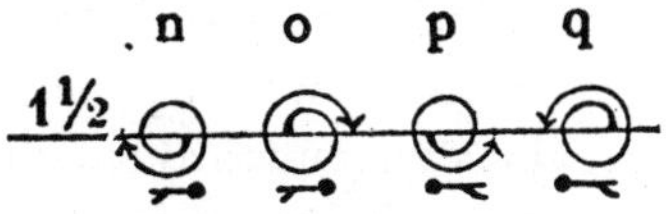

*o.* One and a Half Turns to the Left upon the Right Foot (*Tour et demi à gauche sur le pied droit*).

*p.* One and a Half Turns to the Left upon the Left Foot (*Tour et demi à gauche sur le pied gauche*).

*q.* One and a Half Turns to the Right upon the Left Foot (*Tour et demi à droite sur le pied gauche*).

## Occupation of the Free Leg in Turning

**551.** In all of the above mentioned turns, the movement of the supporting leg has been shown without reference to the occupation of the free one, which may be carried into any possible position, and which may execute any possible movement either before, after or during the continuance of the turn, as will be demonstrated in the application of the turns to the various exercises and *enchaînements* which are to follow.

## Turns in the Air (*Tours en l'Air*)

**552.** Turns are sometimes executed during the continuance of a jumping or throwing movement, or a vigorous turn in the air, which will be explained in § 574.

## The Pirouette (*La Pirouette*)

**553.** The French word *pirouette* is derived from the Low Latin word *gyruetta*, which, in turn, comes from *gyrus*, a turn.

In the "Dictionary" of Noël and Chapsal, such a turn is described as follows: "*Un tour entier du corps, qu'on fait en se tenant sur le pointe d'un seul pied*" (a complete turn of the body, which is executed while the body is held upon the point of one foot).

The Italian word *piroetta* also means a complete turn upon the spot.

In the "Stenochoregraphy" of Arthur de St. Léon, he says: "*Pirouette se dit en danse de l'action d'un tour entier * * *"* (the performance of a complete turn in dancing is called a pirouette).

From these quotations it is clearly demonstrated that the word *pirouette* means, technically, a turn.

**554.** The French word is composed of two words, viz.: *pied*, foot, and *rouette*, a small wheel, and thus most happily describes this wheel-like rotation of the body upon the point of one foot containing one or more complete turns. Certain other authors besides those previously mentioned maintain that a pirouette must contain not less than three complete turns, but the Academy of the German Art of Teaching Dancing have agreed to call a single, artistic, complete turn a "simple pirouette."

**555.** Pirouettes relate exclusively to theatrical dancing; if, therefore, one or more complete turns are artistically executed in theatrical dancing, they may be called pirouettes, whereas, quarter, half, or even entire or simple turns cannot be considered pirouettes if they occur in social dances.

556. Pirouettes may be executed in two directions: outward (*en dehors*) or inward (*en dedans*).

The backward turns are usually called outward; and the forward turns, inward.

## Simple Pirouettes

557. The Principal Forms of the Pirouette are:
> *Sur le cou-de-pied* (on the ankle) [Fig. 356].
> *A la seconde* (in 2d position) [Fig. 357].
> *En attitude* (in attitude, in various forms) [Fig. 358].

FIG. 356.    FIG. 357.    FIG. 358.

## Composite Pirouettes (*Pirouettes Composées*)

558. Various combinations of movements, which are known as *pirouettes composées*, may be formed by means of varying the carriage of the upper body and arms (*des attitudes et arabesques*), by changing the occupation of the free leg in transit, and by ending the pirouette in different form. Nearly every great dancer has his own peculiar method of executing pirouettes, and the following treatise upon them has been kindly and unselfishly prepared for this work by Herr Otto Stoige, ballet master and dancing teacher at the University in Koenigsberg in Prussia.

### EXECUTION OF THE PIROUETTES

559. Outward Pirouette (*Pirouette en Dehors*). The *pirouette en dehors* commences from the 3d position and is executed upon three *tempi* or music syllables. If executed upon

the left foot, the right is placed in anterior 3d position as preparation. Upon the first syllable, the body is raised upon the ball of the left foot, simultaneously with the extension of the right foot into half-high 2d position, and the raising of the arms at the sides to a position almost shoulder-high.

FIG. 359.

Upon the second syllable, the body is lowered upon both feet into the bended 2d position, during which the left foot is turned outward upon the point, thus thrusting the right side slightly forward, and the right arm is rounded and carried forward in nearly horizontal position [Fig. 360].

Upon the third syllable, the right foot is quickly lifted from the floor and the body raised to a point position upon the left, in which the turn is executed by the aid of the arms [Fig. 359].

FIG. 360.   FIG. 361.   FIG. 362.

**560.** If the pirouette is executed upon the ankle (*sur le cou-de-pied*) the arms are held equidistant from the body [Fig. 361].

In the pirouette in second position (*à la seconde*), the arms are held in horizontal position sidewise as in Fig. 362 and may be carried to a higher position at the end [Fig. 363].

**561.** In this example [Fig. 363] the turn is made to the right, and the right side is thereby carried backward.

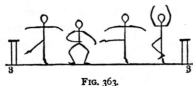

FIG. 363.

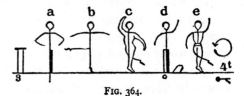

FIG. 364.

If the pirouette is made upon the right foot, the movements are executed in counter-motion.

**562.** Inward Pirouette (*Pirouette en Dedans*). This also starts from 3d position and is executed upon two music syllables.

In order to render the first syllable more intelligible to the reader, it has been divided into four movements which have been marked *a*, *b*, *c*, and *d* [Fig. 364].

As this pirouette is executed upon the left foot, it starts from the anterior 3d position of the right.

*a* shows the lifting of the right foot forward into the stretched 4th position, with simultaneous raising of both arms into the rounded horizontal position.

*b* indicates the opening of the arms, with simultaneous movement of the right foot backward into the high 2d position.

*c* shows the carriage of the right foot backward into the 4th position, accompanied by a quarter-turn to the right, with raising upon the left; during which the right arm is raised and the left lowered as in Fig. 365, but with the right foot in high posterior 4th position.

FIG. 365.

*d* shows the putting down of the right foot in posterior 4th position and immediate transfer. As soon as the tip of the right foot reaches the floor, the positions of the arms are changed before the body, by which *changement* (which is simultaneous with the transfer of weight) the right arm is lowered and carried to a half-stretched posterior position, slightly below the shoulder height, and the left arm is raised to a corresponding position in front [Fig. 367].

All these movements must be executed in unbroken continuity, after which occurs the first opportunity for rest.

In order to execute the pirouette, the weight must be once more transferred to the left foot, the heel of which is momentarily lowered to the floor and immediately re-raised into ball or point position, while the left arm is lowered and the right side advanced; in order, by the assistance of the right arm and leg, to execute the turns to the left.

NOTE. — If this pirouette is executed *sur le cou-de-pied*, the arms are not raised, and the right foot is carried through the 2d balancing position before it touches the ankle.

The carriage of the arms in the *pirouettes en attitude*, *tire-bouchon* (cork-screw*), etc., should be such as are appropriate to the movement.

563. In the *pirouette sur le cou-de-pied* which begins with the right foot, the turn is chiefly accomplished by means of the left arm, and vice versa.

564. In the *pirouette à la seconde*, beginning with the right foot, the turning is principally aided by the right arm, and vice versa.

In commencing the *pirouette en dehors*, that side of the body from which it is executed is slightly advanced [Fig. 360].

565. Outward pirouettes usually end *sur le cou-de-pied*, and the inward, either *en attitude*, *en arabesque*, or with a *pas de basque*.

566. The most common of the *pirouettes composées* (composite pirouettes), which may also be called " deviating " or " mixed," are the following:

---

* So called from the screw-like movement of the free foot during the turning.

*En dehors:*

> *Pirouette à la seconde et sur le cou-de-pied.*
> *Pirouette à la seconde et grand rond de jambe.*
> *Pirouette à la seconde et en attitude et pas de Bourrée.*
> *Pirouette à petits battements sur le cou-de pied.*

*En dedans:*

> *Pirouette sur le cou-de-pied en tire-bouchon* and a *pirouette renversée* (usually of two turns).

NOTE. — This pirouette generally precedes *coupé*, *jeté* and a sharply accented step into posterior 4th position, and, as it ends in an open position, its principal use is in the middle of a dance to bring the dancer back to the commencement of a step or an *enchaînement*.

Figs. 366, 367, 368 and 369 represent positions which are frequently found in the *pirouettes composées.*

FIG. 366.　　　　FIG. 367.　　　　FIG. 368.　　　　FIG. 369.

**567. Pure Pirouette.** A pure pirouette which consists of four or five turns without lowering the heel is most artistic.

NOTE. — Stullmueller, formerly royal solo dancer of Prussia, brought the *pirouette sur le cou-de-pied* to seven rotations.

**568.** A mixed pirouette, in which the turns may be made alternately upon the heel and ball, may be carried to fifteen or even more complete turns, with various changes of positions and movements.

**569.** The dancer should be precise in measuring the duration of his pirouettes, that they may end with the music; as it has an extremely disturbing effect upon what follows if the pirouette is not finished upon the last music syllable allotted to it. For a *pirouette* to be finished too late is more annoying than when it is finished too soon, for in the latter event the time may be filled in by one or two *tours en l'air.*

**570.** The *pirouette sur le cou-de-pied* effects a changement of the feet; that is, if the turn is upon the left foot, it starts with the right foot in front, and ends with the right foot behind the supporting left; and it is proof of great skill and precision if the dancer ends in a position exactly opposite to that from which he has started. A spring or jump, accompanied by a quick raising of the arms, is usually only made for the purpose of aiding a poorly executed pirouette.*

571. The free leg may, during the turns of the pirouette, execute different embellishments, such as *battements*, *ronds de jambe*, *fouettés*, etc., but these are left to the taste and discretion of the dancer.

572. The pirouette is most frequently used to lend a brilliant finish to *enchaînements* of dancing steps, but it may also be used as a preparation for a succeeding step.

573. The execution of beautiful pirouettes is an indication of the highest ability in dancing, but their frequent use is ridiculous and always appears pedantic.

574. Pirouettes in the Air (*Pirouettes en l'Air*). Sect. 552 refers the reader to this number for the turns in the air. While a *jeté en tournant* is of course a turn in the air, the expression *pirouette en l'air* is usually understood to mean those turns which are executed while the body is lifted in the air as the result of a strong jump upon both feet.

575. This movement is sometimes called *volta* or *rivolta*, Italian words which mean, respectively, a turn, and a repeated or an opposite turn.

This kind of turn requires greater muscular exertion than is necessary in social dancing. They occur in various national dances, and frequently persons who are not trained dancers have acquired so much perfection in them as to be able to execute them in an oblique position of the upper body. They are oftenest employed by circus riders.

They are usually executed after a preparatory *temps tombé*, and may be represented in the script as follows:

*a*, Échappe; *b*, strong jump upon both feet; *c*, single (simple) turn in the air; *d*, double turn in the air; *e*, finishing position [Fig. 370].

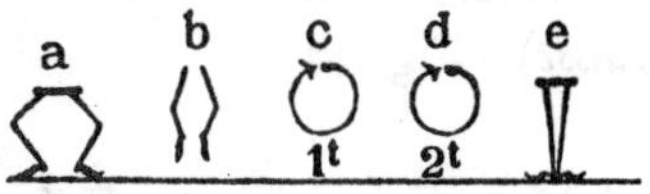

576. Choregraphy of the Pirouettes. The pirouettes are written in the same manner as the complete turns, but in addition to the turning symbol, the letter *t*, meaning *tours*, with the corresponding number, is placed below.

Fig. 371 shows: *a*, simple inward pirouette upon the right foot; *b*, double inward pirouette upon the left foot; *c*, triple outward pirouette upon the right foot; *d*, quadruple outward pirouette upon the left foot.

The symbol of the pirouette is written above the line, to distinguish it from the symbol of the complete turn.

FIG. 370.

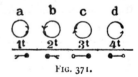

FIG. 371.

---

* Herr Stoige's explanation of the pirouettes ends here. It will be evident to those who have devoted much time to the study of these movements, that the description that he has given is the result of thorough knowledge of his subject, combined with many years of practice and the most exact observation of every movement.

## Thigh Beating Syllables (*Temps de Cuisse*)

**577.** The word *cuisse*, which means the thigh, as used in connection with this movement, implies that that portion of the leg is particularly active therein.

In this movement the leg is entirely stretched and the thigh (*cuisse*) is so moved as to describe two lines upon the floor with the tip of the foot. On account of this unusual activity of the thigh, the movement is called *temps* or *pas de cuisse*, differing in accordance with the non-transfer or transfer of the weight.

**578.** Execution to the right [Fig. 372]. Preparation: 2d balancing position of left.

In the part measure, the supporting leg is bended, and the left leg, entirely stretched, beats audibly with the tip in 2d position, after which movements the dancer hops to the right upon the supporting right foot, and the left is put down again in the 2d and drawn audibly into 5th position, either *dessus* or *dessous*.

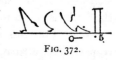

FIG. 372.

**579.** If several such movements are executed consecutively with the same foot, no transfer is made, and they are therefore merely *temps* or syllables. But if executed alternately, a transfer must be added to each, thus constituting them steps which are known as *pas de traits de cuisse*. They may be executed forward, backward or to the side.

**580.** These steps are very similar to beating steps, although no actual *battement* is made.

Exercise 80. Thigh Beating Syllables and Steps (*Temps de cuisse et pas de traits de cuisse*) [Fig. 373].

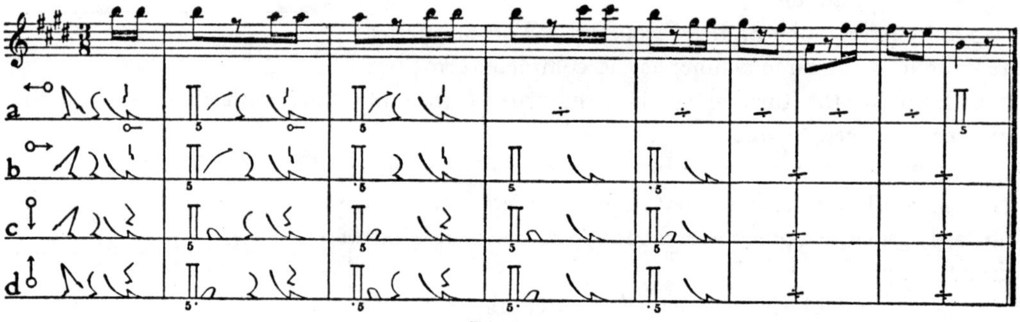

FIG. 373.

*a.* Simple Over-Crossed Thigh Syllables to the Right (*Temps de cuisse simples dessus à droite*).

*b.* Alternate Over and Under-Crossed Thigh Syllables to the Left (*Temps de cuisse changés dessus et dessous à gauche*).

*c.* Alternate Thigh Step Forward (*Pas de traits de cuisse alternatifs en avançant*).

*d.* Alternate Thigh Steps Backward (*Pas de traits de cuisse alternatifs en reculant*).

## The Beating Steps (*Les Pas Battus*)

**581.** The definition, explanation and execution of the term *battre* and its choregraphic script have been given in §§ 160 and 267. This movement may be made with either or with both feet.

**582.** Beatings are not steps, in themselves; they should rather be considered as embellishments which are added to other movements, in much the same manner as grace notes or trills are added to a note of music; for beatings must be so much a part of the steps which they ornament, that they will consume no more time than if they had been omitted and the step or movement rendered in simple form.

**583.** Practice, skill, muscle, elasticity and endurance are all necessary to the proper execution of the beating steps, and they belong to the theatrical dance exclusively.

NOTE. — The Zephyr step, with over and under beatings in the 3d position, referred to in § 517, may be regarded as a beating step.

**584. Changement of the Legs (*Changements de Jambes*).** The most common *pas battus* are what is known as the *changements de jambes*.

In Fig. 374 * the beatings are numbered, to demonstrate the method of counting them.

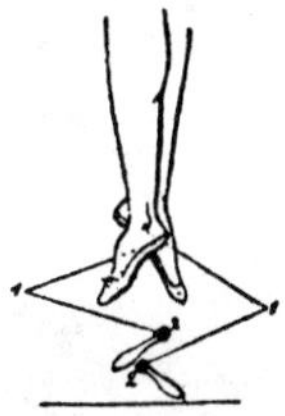

**585.** At this point let us consider the difference between the terms *battu* and *battement*. The former (*battu*) relates to the actual contact which is produced by the movement; while the latter (*battement*) is the technical name for the entire movement of which the beating is the result. In the *battements* the simple beatings (*battus*) are counted.

FIG. 374.

**586.** There are, therefore, two beatings, in a single changement of the legs, in which the change is effected in balancing position, and upon one music syllable; of which the first is the separation from a closed to an open position; and the second is the resumption of the closed from the open position.

**587.** In the cuts, the beatings are shown commencing from the heels, and extending to the finishing positions, which are indicated by means of perpendicular dotted lines.

**588.** A simple *changement de jambes* is not technically regarded as a *pas battu*, unless another beating is added to it.

In the beating steps, the falling back may be upon either or upon both feet; if upon only one the other may be carried to any of the balancing positions.

**589. Crossed Jump (*Capriole ou Entrechat*).** This name is applied to the repeated crossing of the feet during the continuance of a single strong jump, and the name is derived from the Italian word *intrecciare*, which means to weave or braid. For instance, *colle mani intrecciate* means with braided hands.

---

* This and many other examples and explanations have been taken, by permission, from Klemm's "Catechism."

The repeated beating together of the feet or legs with crossing called *capriola*, and the crossed or braided beatings, are known as *capriola intrecciata*.

590. Both legs must coöperate in the execution of the *entrechat*, which may be made from a preparatory bending in any position, followed by a strong jump.

The *trioles*, or triple crossings, should be executed during the jump; as that movement is of greater duration than the falling back.

The falling back occurs either in open or in closed position, according to the number of the beatings and the original position.

591. Fig. 374 shows a simple *changement de jambes* from the anterior to the posterior 3d position.

Fig. 375 represents an *entrechat clos à trois* (a closed crossed jump of three beatings) which goes from a closed to an open position.

Fig. 376 shows an *entrechat ouvert à trois* (a crossed jump of three beatings) going from an open to a closed position.

Fig. 377 shows an *entrechat à trois* (Royal) beginning from a closed and ending in a closed position.

NOTE. — The term "Royal" is understood by some authorities to mean the triple beating in 3d position without changement, but that movement is really the *capriole à trois*.

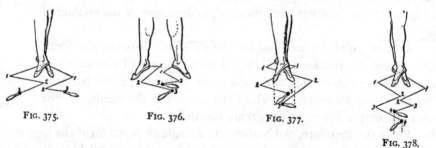

FIG. 375.      FIG. 376.      FIG. 377.      FIG. 378.

Fig. 378 shows the *entrechat à quatre*, a crossed jump of four beatings.

The *entrechats à cinq, six, sept, huit*, etc. (of five, six, seven, eight beatings, etc.) are easily understood by means of the above examples.

592. Turning in the cross jumps (*entrechats*) will be aided by placing the foot toward which the body is to turn in a preparatory posterior 5th position.

593. Abbreviated Script. The symbol of the *entrechat* is composed of an appropriate sign, to be written in place of the complete choregraphy. Below it the number of the position in which it ends is added. Fig. 379 represents:

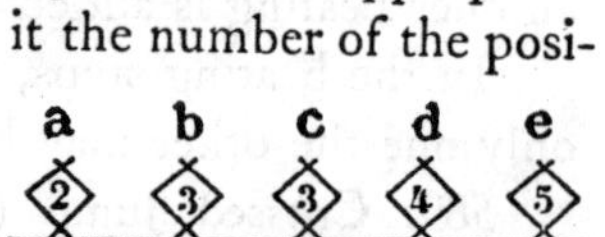

*a. Changement de jambes*, ending in anterior 3d position of right.

*b. Entrechat ouvert à trois*, ending in 2-1 position.

*c. Entrechat clos à trois*, ending in posterior 5th position of the right.

*d. Entrechat quatre*, ending in anterior 5th position of right.

*e. Entrechat cinq*, ending in double 2-1 position.

The number of beatings is placed inside the sign.

FIG. 379.

**594. Half Counter Beating (*Demi-Contretemps*).** The word *contretemps* means something which is unexpected and apparently out of measure, and is used as a term for those movements in dancing which appear unexpectedly, and which seem to be contrary to the measure.

Fig. 380 shows the movements very clearly. They are executed as follows: Starting from a preparatory balancing 2d position, the free leg is carried into a closed position, then to an open one, and touches the supporting leg either behind and before, or before and behind, in 3d or 5th position in passing, but does not receive the weight. It is executed entirely upon one music syllable during a light jump upon the supporting foot. Thus the beating which begins while the body is in the air appears to occur too late and is contrary to the measure. It is probable that the name *contretemps* was applied on account of this

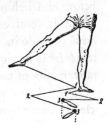

FIG. 380.

feature. The movement corresponds to the double beat in music which is called *spondee*.

**595. Whole Counter Beating (*Contretemps Entier*).** This is a step of two syllables, and it may be executed forward, backward, sidewise, or in turning, for example, to the right.

Preparation: Right foot in posterior 5th position.

In the part measure, execute a hop upon the left foot, and lift the right to the side.

Upon the first syllable the right foot is put down and glided to 2d position, where the weight is transferred to it; and the second syllable contains the *demi-contretemps*, which was described in § 594 [Fig. 381].

FIG. 381.

If the succeeding step is to be made in the same direction, a transfer is added to the second syllable.

The whole step appears almost to consist of an *enchaînement* of *pas glissé* and *pas bourré*, if the point of the active foot lightly touches the floor during the beating with immediate *dégagé*.

*Pas jeté, pas tombé,* or any similar step, may be executed as a first syllable, if desired.

Exercise 81. Whole Counter-Beating Steps (*Pas contretemps entiers*) [Fig. 382].

M. M. 60-80 = ♩

FIG. 382.

The first two measures contain the complete, and the third the abbreviated script, and the musical symbol appears in the fourth measure.

**596. Broken Syllables and Steps (*Temps et Pas Brisés*).** It was explained in § 491 that *pas*

*coupé* meant a cut or divided step. *Un pas brisé* is also a step of one syllable. It consists
of a jump, during which the free foot is carried from one
open position to another, executing, in transit, a beating
before and behind (*dessus et dessous*), or vice versa; after
which it receives the weight of the body. While the
*coupé* is made in a straight line and divided in the middle,
the *brisé* is in zig-zag form. Figs. 383 and 384 show the
movements of the feet very clearly.

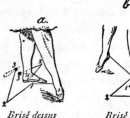

Brisé dessus        Brisé dessous
FIG. 383.              FIG. 384.

597. The distinction between *contretemps* and *brisé* is
clearly demonstrated in Figs. 385 and 386.

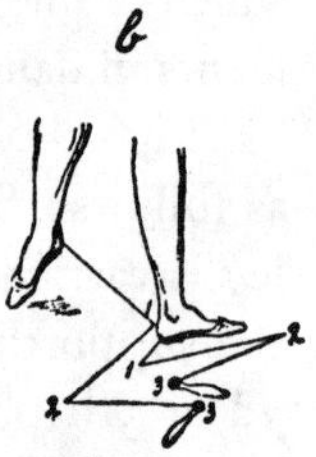

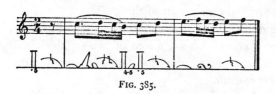

FIG. 385.

FIG. 386.

In the *contretemps* the beating is usually added to the final movement as an embellish-
ment, and in the *brisé* the step begins by beating.

598. If, after the beating, there is no transfer of weight, it is called *un temps brisé* —
a broken syllable. Two or more such syllables, following one another upon the same foot,
will finish in an open position; but if they are executed alternately, there is an unavoidable
transfer after each movement, constituting what are known as *des pas brisés alternatifs* —
the alternating broken steps.

599. Although the beating in the *brisé* is similar to that in the *entrechat*, there is this
difference: In the *entrechat* both feet are equally
active, while in the *brisé* only one actually beats,
while the other assists the movement. This movement finds its musical prototype in the *arpeggio*.

FIG. 387.

Fig. 387 shows the script of the *brisé dessus, dessous* in the full and the abbreviated
forms.

Exercise 82. Broken Syllables (*Temps brisés*) [Fig. 388].

*a.* Six over and under-crossed broken syllables to the right, one collecting syllable
and one transfer, followed by the same movements to the left (*Six temps brisés dessous et
dessus à droite, 1 assemblé et 1 dégagé, en suite les mêmes mouvements à gauche*).

In the part measure and the first full measure, the complete choregraphy is given, and
the abbreviated sign is used for *assemblé*. The key at the end of the first half of the
melody indicates that the remainder of the enchainment goes toward the left.

*b* contains the same *brisé* syllables as *a*, but they are executed *dessous et dessus*.

*c.* Alternate broken steps forward (*pas brisés alternatifs en avant*), followed in the
second half by the same movements backward.

*d.* Alternate broken steps backward (*pas brisés alternatifs en arrière*), followed by the same movements forward.

FIG. 388.

## Pigeon Wing Steps (*Ailes de Pigeons—Pistolets*)

**600.** The name "pigeon wing," which is applied to this step, doubtless arose from the similarity of the movement to the beating of the wings of pigeons, but the derivation of its other name (*pistolets*) seems to be unknown.

**601.** This step consists of the combination of *brisé dessous* and *jeté*, and may be executed alternately, forward or backward, upon the place, or in turning.

**602.** A single pigeon wing step may be compared to striking a harp from low to high (*arpeggio*), and the alternate steps may be compared to a continued trill (*trillo*).

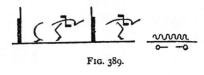

FIG. 389.

**603. Execution (to the left).** Preparation: Raise the left foot into posterior 2-4 balancing position, and bend the right leg in readiness for a strong jump, during which the left leg beats against the calf of the right, after which the legs are crossed in the air as in the *brisé*. In falling back, the weight is caught upon the left leg, and the right is immediately carried into the posterior 2-4 balancing position, in readiness for a repetition of the step upon the other foot [Fig. 389].

These movements are clearly demonstrated in Fig. 390.

FIG. 390.

Exercise 83. Pigeon Wing Steps (*Ailes de Pigeons — Pistolets*) [Fig. 391].

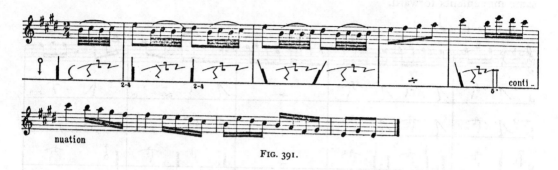

FIG. 391.

The first two measures contain the complete choreography, and the third the musical sign of *répétition*.

# Chapter XI

## PERIODICAL ENCHAINMENT OF DANCE STEPS
## AND SYLLABLES

AMONG other things, § 7 likens dancing steps to words, combinations of steps to phrases and sentences, and combinations of *enchainements* to paragraphs. Simple figures are likened to verse lines, compound figures to stanzas, and the combination of several compound figures or strophes (as in the Quadrilles) to an entire poem.

In the art of dancing, French terms are generally used, and step combinations are called *phrases; phrase* combinations are known as *enchainements;* and combinations of *enchainements* are called "strophes" or "couplets" (§§ 193 and 194). If the same *phrases* or *enchainements* are repeated, in like sequence, upon a certain number of measures of music, the whole is called a " periodical *enchainement*," and several such periodical *enchainements*, composed of the steps and syllables which have been described, will be given in this chapter, to promote skill in execution and to demonstrate their application in various social and theatrical dances. They are among the most helpful of all the exercises.

605. We will commence with a combination of *pas chassés* and *pas élevés*, such as occurs in several of the Quadrilles.

606. These exercises are ordered so as to be best fitted for practical instruction, in preference to the common method of combining the *balancés, traversés, solos,* etc., while recognizing that the old method contains certain advantages.

607. This book, however, is intended merely as a guide for the teacher, and it is left to his judgment to select proper combinations and to substitute other music. In the latter case, however, care must be exercised that the rhythm exactly coincides with the step movements.

FIG. 392.

Exercise 84 *a*. One Chasing and Two Raising Steps Forward (*Une pas chassé et deux pas élevés en avant*) [Fig. 392].

The abbreviated script is used because the *pas chassés* have been described and explained in §§ 475 to 479, and the *pas élevés* in §§ 430 to 433. The key always represents the direction upon the floor; that is, the figure.

One Chasing and Two Raising Steps Backward (*Une pas chassé et deux pas élevés en arrière*) [Fig. 393].

Exercise 84 *b*. One Chasing and Two Raising Steps to the Right with Quarter-Turn to the Left (*Une pas chassé et deux pas élevés à droite et se tourner*) [Fig. 394].

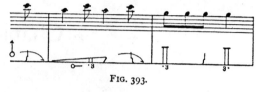

FIG. 393.

One Chasing and Two Raising Steps to the Left with Quarter-Turn to the Right (*Une pas chassé et deux pas élevés à gauche et se tourner*) [Fig. 395].

The turns upon both feet have been explained in § 541.

Exercise 84 *c*. Crossing: Three Chasing Steps and a Half-Turn to the Right (*Traversé: Trois chassés et demi-tour à droite*) [Fig. 396].

The key indicates the degree of turning.

Recrossing with Three Chasing Steps

FIG. 394.

and a Half-Turn to the Right (*Retraversé: Trois chassés et demi-tour à droite*) [Fig. 397].

Exercise 84 *d*. Balance and Transfer (*Balancé-dégagé*) [Fig. 398].

Balance with four balancing steps.

The meaning of the words *en balancé* is explained in § 56 in their relation to positions. In their application to movements, they imply a certain buoyancy of carriage upon the place. In this exercise, various different syllables may be introduced, as, for instance, a small *pas de basque, pas tendu ou zéphire*, etc.

FIG. 395.

**608.** In this movement, the *balancé* consists of four transfers into 2d position, while the free foot glides backward into 3d position during the raising of the supporting foot, and then passes immediately into 2d position. The full choregraphy is given in the first two measures, but the subsequent measures contain only the sign of transfer.

FIG. 396.

Turning by the hand (*tour de main*) with three *pas chassés* and a quarter-turn to the right. Four measures [Fig. 399].

**609.** The expression *balancé* is very frequently interpreted to mean one *chassé* and two *pas élevés* to the right, with repetition to the left; but this is not technically correct, as such movements do not contain the buoyant movement upon the place, which is usually inferred from the term *balancé*. As a compromise, however, in favor of

FIG. 397.

those who have learned the figure in that manner, we will term that combination *balancé-chassé*.

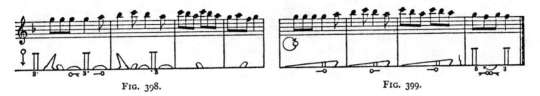

FIG. 398.  FIG. 399.

Exercise 85. Chasing Steps Forward and Back, to Right and Left Across; to Right and Left to Centre, *Balancé Chassé*, and Circular Chasing Steps Forward and Back (*Chassé en avant et en arrière, à droite et à gauche, traversé, chassé à droite et à gauche, au milieu, balancé-chassé, chassé tourné en avant et de retour*) [Fig. 400].

NOTE. — This exercise is similar to the preceding, but there is a difference in the music, the present one being in 2-4 measure. Again, the movement goes either to right or left to centre, instead of backward, and *balancé chassé* is substituted for *balancé dégagé*. Instead of the transfer there is a *chassé-tourné* forward and backward.

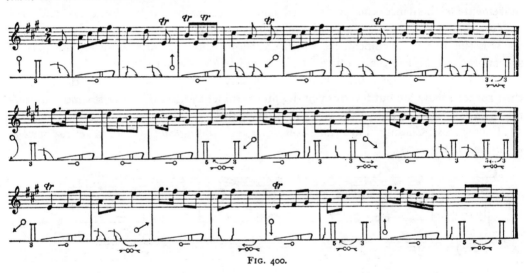

FIG. 400.

Exercise 86. Balance with One Thrown Stuffing Step, One Zephyr Step and One Thrown Stuffing Step (*Balancé par un jeté-bourré et un pas de zéphire et un jeté-bourré*) [Fig. 401].

FIG. 401.

Exercise 87.  Balance with One Zephyr Step and One Thrown Stuffing Step (*Balancé par un pas de zéphire et un jeté-bourré*) [Fig. 402].

FIG. 402.

The two last-mentioned exercises are examples of the different effects of phrasing and interpreting music.  The same piece of music is used in both, but in Exercise 86 the first measure is rendered *staccato*, and in the second, *legato*, and so on to the end.  The *staccato* movement is best fitted for the *jeté bourré*, and the *legato* for the *pas de zéphire*.  One may therefore decide, from the music, the nature of the step to be danced; indeed, the rule can be applied to the musician who can see, from the steps, how the music should be rendered.

610.  In theatrical dancing, unless the composer writes his music to coincide with the movements of the dance, the dancer must consider each note with minuteness, and execute each movement in exact coincidence with the music.

It is this feature of coincidence which creates involuntary enthusiasm on the part of spectators, and the fact that so little attention is bestowed upon it by most ballet masters is beyond comprehension; for, although this quality of coincidence is really the mark of their success, there are but few of even the most eminent artists of either sex, now appearing in the ballet, who follow the exact rhythm of the music.

Exercise 88.  Chasing, Throwing, Collecting and Gliding Steps (*Chassés, jetés, assemblés et glissades*) [Fig. 403].

FIG. 403.

611.  The old custom of executing the Quadrille steps with *jeté* and *assemblé* is retained by some conscientious teachers, for the reason that they are far more artistic and beautiful than the walking or raising steps now in vogue.

This custom cannot, however, be extended to social entertainments, because it is no longer fashionable to dance correctly, and a dancer who executes his steps in exact rhythm is regarded as ridiculous. Let us hope that fashion will, before long, change for the better in this respect, even though we realize that such a change is not probable unless a taste for correct and artistic dancing is manifested by one of the leading courts.

Exercise 89. This Exercise contains exactly the same movements as the preceding one, but it is in 2-4 measure [Fig. 404].

FIG. 404.

Exercise 90. Combinations of Chasing, Raising, Gliding and Zephyr Steps (*Phrases: Chassés, élevés, glissades et zéphires*) [Fig. 405].

FIG. 405.

Forward, one chasing, one throwing and one collecting step (*En avant: chassé, jeté et assemblé*).

Backward, eight small crossed, raising steps (boxed in) (*En arrière: 8 pas élevés emboités*.

To right, two gliding and one zephyr step; to left, two gliding and one zephyr step (*À droite: 2 glissades et 1 pas de zéphire et à gauche; les mêmes pas*).

Crossing, two chasing and two zephyr steps; recrossing, two chasing and two zephyr steps (*Traversé et retraversé par 2 chassés et 2 pas de zéphires*).

Exercise 91. This contains the same movements as the preceding, in 2-4 time [Fig. 406].

FIG. 406.

Exercise 92. Combination of Chasing Step, Changement of the Legs, Cutting and Collecting Steps (*Phrases: Chassés, changements de jambes, coupés-assemblés*).

Forward, one chasing step and two changements of the legs. Backward, the same steps; upon the place, one cutting and one collecting step, alternating to right and left, and executed four times (*En avant; 1 chassé et 2 changements de jambes; en arrière, les mêmes pas sur la place, 1 coupé, et 1 assemblé, 4 fois alternativement*) [Fig. 407].

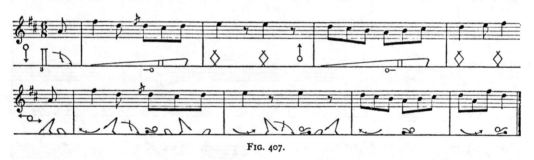

FIG. 407.

Exercise 93. The same steps as in the preceding, executed in 2-4 time [Fig. 408].

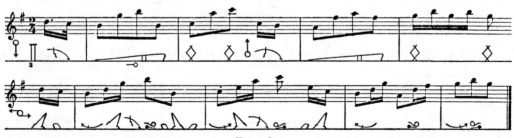

FIG. 408.

Exercise 94. Exercises in Body Turns and Pirouettes (*Exercices des tours de corps et pirouettes*) [Fig. 409].

FIG. 409.

*a. Traversé.* In the first half of the transition, execute one chasing step and one complete turn to the right, and for the second half, one chasing step and a half-turn to the right. This occupies four measures of music, and the "retransition" (*retraversé*), which contains the same movements, fills the remaining four measures.

*b.* This differs from *a* in direction only, the chasing steps beginning with the left foot and the turns and progress of the entire movement going to the left.

*c.* Midway of the *traverse* and *retraversé* two turns are made and at the end there are one and one-half; in the repetition the movement goes to the left.

This exercise is similar to the preceding one, as it contains first three and then two and a half turns.

NOTE.— If the reader has carefully studied the explanations and choregraphy of the turns and pirouettes, in §§ 546 to 549, further explanation of them is unnecessary.

Exercise 95. Combination of Four Simple Zephyr Steps, One Chasing Step in Turning, and Two Alternate Cutting and Collecting Steps (*Enchainement par 4 pas de zéphire simples, chassé tourné et 2 coupés-assemblés*) [Fig. 410].

FIG. 410.

Forward, four simple zephyr steps (*pas tendus*). Backward, one chasing step and two jumped changements of the legs in turning, followed by one cutting step with collecting first to the right and then to the left.

Exercise 96. Forward, Four Beaten Zephyr Steps. Backward, One Chasing and Two

Crossed Jumps of Four Beatings (*entrechats-quatre*); Followed by a Cutting Step to Right and Left upon the Place, and One Over-Crossed Collecting Step (*brisé*) [Fig. 411].

FIG. 411.

The last two exercises are quite similar, the only difference being that in Exercise 95 the steps are simple, and in Exercise 96 they are beaten.

Exercise 97. Combination to the Right: a Throwing and a Stuffing Step Twice Executed, Followed by a Turning Chasing Step, and the Whole Repeated to the Left (*Phrase: 2 jetés-bourrés et un chassé-tourné à droite et répétition de la phrase à gauche*) [Fig. 412].

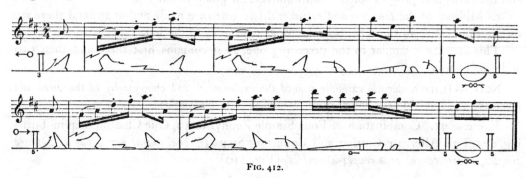

FIG. 412.

Exercise 98. Combination to the Right: One Throwing and One Stuffing Step Twice Executed, Followed by a Turning Basque Step and a Zephyr Step, and the Same Steps to the Left (*Enchaînement à droite; 2 jetés-bourrés, 1 pirouette basque et 1 pas de zéphire; à gauche; les mêmes pas*) [Fig. 413].

FIG. 413.

**612.** Exercise 99. Combination: One Gliding Step, Two Whip Syllables, and One Throwing and Collecting Step (*Phrase: 1 glissé, 2 fouettés, 1 jeté-assemblé*) [Fig. 414].

FIG. 414.

This combination is usually known as " Flig-Flag," the name being derived from the whipping movements, which follow one another in quick time. The same name is sometimes applied to another combination.

The movement consists of an accented gliding step, an over and under-crossed whip syllable in rapid succession, one throwing and one collecting step.

*a.* Beginning with the right, two measures forward; with the left, two measures backward; repeat the whole exercise. *b.* The same combination, with turning upon the whip syllables. *c.* Crossing and re-crossing with the same combination in turning.

Exercise 100. Combination: Basque and Stuffing Steps, and Basque Steps in Turning (*Enchaînement: Pas de basque, bourrée et pirouette basque*) [Fig. 415].

FIG. 415.

Forward, two Basque steps; backward, three stuffing and one collecting step; forward, two Basque steps; backward, two Basque steps in turning (*En avant, 2 pas de basques; en arrière; 3 pas de bourrées et 1 assemblé; en avant; 2 pas de basques; en arrière; 2 pas de basques en tournant*).

**613.** This combination is found in the Gavotte of Gaetano Vestris, and the study of this *enchaînement* calls that beautiful classic to mind. It is universally recognized as a model by all competent teachers of dancing, and merits all the honor it has received, for the choice and sequence of its various movements are all truly artistic.

This entire dance may be divided into its various *enchaînements*, which can be used as exercises, and he who masters them will have received a thorough course in dancing.

# Chapter XII

## THE CHOREGRAPHY OF THE FIGURE

THE word "figure," in dancing (§ 5), signifies the direction in which the dancers move upon the floor, and may be drawn as a plan. The possibility of representing the figures has been of great assistance to dance authors in writing descriptions of dances. As instructions for drawing such plans come within the province of this Grammar, the Author has examined many of the systems of writing that have appeared, and in order to obtain a method of representation that may be universally reliable and intelligible, has deduced and devised from them the symbolism described in the following pages, which appears to him to be an adequate solution of the problem.

In the following table are given symbols of the dancers and the figure which each describes, the gentleman being represented under the letter *A*, the lady under the letter *B*, the figure of the gentleman under *C*, the figure of the lady under *D*, and the symbol of the end of the figure under *E*.

| Author | Place | Date | A | B | C | D | E |
|---|---|---|---|---|---|---|---|
| Noverre . . . . . . | Paris | 1761 | ⌒ | ⌒ | ——— | --------- | —< |
| Mädel . . . . . . . | Erfurt | 1805 | 𝔄𝔏𝔏 | 𝒜ℬ𝒞 | ——— | ........ | v |
| Dancing Teachers' Society . | Vienna | 1844 | *l.* | *l* | ——— | -------- | • ∘ |
| B. Klemm . . . . . . | Leipzig | 1855 | ♙ | ♛ | ——— | --------• | { |
| Bazaar (p. 333) . . . . | Berlin | 1861 | ♦ | ◌ | ———• | -------- | ≅ |
| Bazaar (p. 347) . . . . | Berlin | 1864 | ⌓ | ⌓ | ———∘ | -------- | ≅ |
| L. Manzotti . . . . . | Milan | 1885 | ⊙ | ∘ | ———→ | --------→ | → |
| A. Freising . . . . . | Berlin | 1885 | ℋ *H* | 𝒟 *D* | ———→ | --------→ | → |
| F. A. Zorn . . . . . . | Odessa | 1887 | ● | ∘ | ———→ | --------→ | ♪ |

**615.** By referring to this table, it will be seen that the choregraphs quoted practically agree as to the symbol of the figure of the gentleman and lady, by using a continuous line to represent the former and a broken or dotted one for the latter; but each applies his own peculiar sign to indicate the persons of the dancers. Even these symbols have been changed in Berlin, as is indicated by comparing the signs published in the " Journal of Fashions " ("Bazaar"), page 333, for 1861, and page 347, for 1864.

It will also be seen from the table that Balz, the inspector of the ballet in Berlin, used the same signs in 1864 as did Noverre in Paris in 1761, but in the opposite application.

616. It is plain that the use of different symbols by individual choregraphs leads to unavoidable ambiguity, and that the only manner in which a script may become universally intelligible and definite is to adopt universal and arbitrary symbols which will not be subject to change, but which will remain the same during all time.

After carefully considering each one of the systems referred to, the Author has selected for the purpose a sign of the person which corresponds to the anatomical structure of the body. Working upon the principle that this kind of a symbol would be intelligible to all nations and would need no translation in any language (as would be the case if letters were used), he has, therefore, evolved a sign that he believes will be perfectly clear.

617. As respects the person of the dancer in connection with the drawing of the figure, one must imagine that he sees it from a point directly above; that he has a bird's-eye view, using the term in the same manner as we apply it to an imaginary view of a building or a park.

From such a position, an observer would only see the top of the head, which is covered with hair, the tip of the nose, the shoulders, and the horizontal movements of the arms. The activity of the feet would be only partly visible.

618. In drawing the symbol of the person, therefore, there has been taken the outline of the top of the head, the bone lines of the arms, and the soles of the feet. In these outlines, the direction of the face may be known by the tip of the nose, the positions of the arms by the degree of bending in the arm lines and the positions of the feet by the sole signs.

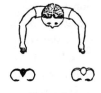

FIG. 416.

Fig. 416 shows the complete drawing of the sign, and the respective abbreviations for the symbols of the gentleman and the lady. The arm line of the gentleman has been drawn with the palm upward and that of the lady with the palm downward, for the reason that the gentleman "presents" his hands and the lady "gives" hers in these positions.

619. To further distinguish the sexes, the symbol of the gentleman has been filled in, while that of the lady is in outline. Also the figure described by the gentleman is represented by a continuous line and that described by the lady by a dotted one.

The symbol of the person is written at the starting point of the symbol of the figure, and the arrow head at its end, while the position signs are drawn at any point in the figure where distinctness demands them.

620. In order to be more readily understood, it is often well to simplify the script by representing only the part of the first dancer, as the figures of the other dancers are usually also indicated thereby.

621. Perhaps the best method of obtaining a correct picture of a figure is to actually

draw the course of the dancers upon the floor. This practical demonstration will convince the reader of the feasibility of the plan.

622. The representation of the various dancers by means of different colors would be very much easier to follow, but it would be difficult to show more than six different persons, and the cost of drawing and printing in more than one color is great, so small numerals by the side of the person signs, and along the direction lines, may be used to represent a number of dancers.

623. For the purpose of drawing figures for use upon the stage, a frame representing the floor plan of the stage must be shown which provides similar arrangements and conditions at all times. Fig. 417 shows such a frame.

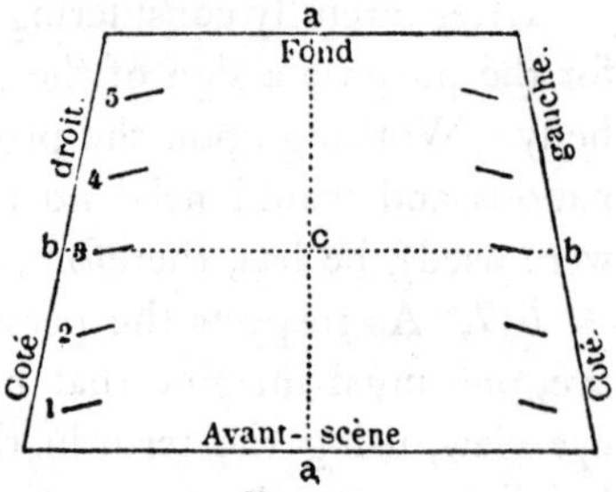

The line *a-a* runs from the front to the back of the stage, dividing it into halves, and is known as the perpendicular middle line. The term "right" signifies the right side of the dancer when facing the spectators.

The line *b-b* divides the stage into forward and backward halves, and is known as the horizontal middle line.

The point *c*, at which the middle lines cross one another, is known as "centre."

FIG. 417.

Five side scenes or "wings" are represented on each side; these are numbered from the front backward, and the ends of the third pair rest upon the horizontal middle line. A passage is left free behind these wings.

624. The term *descendre*, which means walking or dancing downward, signifies that the person approaches the front of the stage, and the term *monter* means the opposite. These expressions are literally correct, as applied to the stage, for the floor is slightly elevated at the rear, so as to render all parts of the stage perfectly visible to the spectators. No explanation is necessary as to dancing forward, backward or to the side, except that these directions radiate from the person of the dancer, without reference to his position upon the stage or his relation to the spectators.

625. A dancer may, therefore, move either upward or downward, by walking forward; or he may walk or dance in perpendicular, horizontal or irregular lines, forward, backward, diagonally or sidewise.

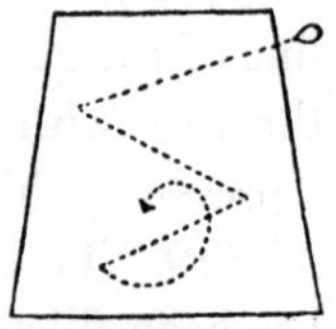

626. If the frame consists of a simple quadrilateral figure, it represents only that portion of the stage which is visible from the auditorium. Fig. 418 shows such a frame. The dotted zig-zag shows the opening figure of the first couplet of the Cachucha, a Spanish solo dance, which is fully explained later in this work [§ 921 *et seq.*].

FIG. 418.

627. Fig. 419 shows a group from the ballet *Amor*, by L. Manzotti, and plainly indicates that the entire group faces the spectators.

The representation of the figures of stage dances is very different from that of social dances, for the reason that spectators sit or stand around the hall in social dances, whereas they are all in the same relative position to the stage in theatrical work. Therefore, the invariable stage rule to turn the back to the spectators as seldom as possible cannot be applied in any degree to social dancing.

628. The French Quadrille has been selected as the first example of the application of the choregraphy of the figures, in social dancing, because that dance is universally known, and is, therefore, more easily demonstrated. In order to convey a proper idea of the figures and their choregraphy, it is necessary to give a description of the whole dance in detail.

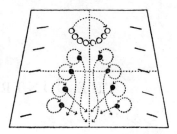

FIG. 419.

NOTE. — It may appear entirely superfluous to many readers to devote so many pages to the description of the ordinary *Contre Danse*, whereas other writers have found a single page quite sufficient to answer the purpose; but this description has not been written for those who merely desire to learn the various figures and their sequence. It has been completely and minutely given so that those who study the explanation carefully will be enabled to clearly and satisfactorily answer, both for themselves and others, any question that may arise regarding this beautiful dance.

# Chapter XIII

## THE CONTRA DANCE AND QUADRILLE

THE term *contre danse*, translated literally, means "opposite dance"; and the term *quadrille*, applied to dancing, means, technically, the assembling of four or more ladies and a like number of gentlemen, in the form of a square (*quarré*).

The Contra Dance and the Quadrille differ only in the positions of the dancers, for the same figures may be executed in either, in which case they retain the same names; although it is not customary to introduce so great a variety of figures in the Contra Dance, because only two couples form a set.

With respect to the names of the various simple and compound figures, this Grammar can recognize as authentic only the literal meaning of the term which is applied to each, for the reason that traditions and anecdotal references differ widely and not infrequently contradict one another [§ 413].

### THE THEORY OF THE POSITIONS IN THE QUADRILLE

630. There have been used two systems of numbering the couples in Quadrilles. They are as follows:

| SYSTEM A | SYSTEM B |
| --- | --- |
| 1 | 1 |
| 2      4 | 3      4 |
| 3 | 2 |

These systems have been advocated by twelve different masters in their respective works, and in the following table these authorities are divided under the respective systems they advocate:

| SYSTEM A | | SYSTEM B | |
| --- | --- | --- | --- |
| 1 Tschütter (Jahn), Dresden . . | 1835 | 1 Maedel, Erfurt . . . . . . | 1805 |
| 2 Dancing Teachers' Soc., Vienna | 1844 | 2 Dancing Teachers' Acad., Paris | 1860 |
| 3 Buchey, Greitz . . . . . | 1852 | 3 Balz, Ballet Inspector, Berlin . | 1861 |
| 4 Fricker, Dessau . . . . . | 1865 | 4 Scipio, Hamm . . . . . . | 1865 |
| 5 Cellarius, Paris . . . . . . | 1862 | 5 Göhle, Dresden . . . . . . | 1874 |
| 6 Martin, Philadelphia . . . . | 1864 | 6 B. Klemm, Leipzig . . . . | 1875 |

The fact that the advocates of the two systems balance so evenly is not due entirely to European authority, for it will be noticed that an American appears among the supporters of System A.

The Author had adhered consistently to System A for more than forty years, having learned it in childhood, but while preparing this work, he thoroughly contemplated each system, submitting each to every test, and, after mature deliberation, decided to adopt System B for the following reasons:

631. There are but two couples in a *Contre Danse;* the couples numbered 3 and 4 are, therefore, merely added to complete the Quadrille arrangement. In the execution of the Quadrille, the opposite couple always follow the first couple or the first lady, and that couple are, therefore, actually the second couple; while the couple at the right of the head couple follow in third place, and must therefore be considered the true third couple.

Again, suppose a teacher asks a new pupil which are the second couple — he will invariably signify that opposite the head couple, as that will appear to him to be the natural order.

System B has also been adopted by many of the more recent authorities, among them being Freising, Wallner and Guttman; the German Academy of the Art of Teaching Dancing also accepts that theory as correct.

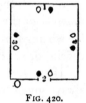

FIG. 420.

632. Let us suppose the floor plan of the hall to represent a map — at the top is North; at the bottom, South; at the right, East, and at the left, West. Let us say that the entrance is in the South side of the hall, and placing the four couples in the form of a square, the first couple stand in the North, the second in the South, the third in the West, and the fourth in the East [Fig. 420].

633. If the square be composed of eight couples, a letter is added to the number of the couple, and couple 1 a are opposite, and dance with couple 2 b (*vis-à-vis*) [Fig. 421].

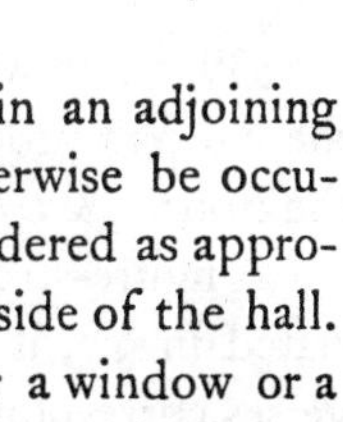

If three couples stand in each line, the letter *c* is added, and if there are four couples in each line, the letter *d*.

If two or more couples stand in each line, the couples marked *a* are the first in their respective lines.

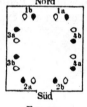

FIG. 421.

634. It is an almost universal practice to consider that the first couple in a Quadrille stand facing the orchestra, but there are frequent exceptions to this rule. Sometimes the couple facing the entrance to the hall are called the head couple. Very often the orchestra is placed in an adjoining room at the side, in order to save the space in the hall which would otherwise be occupied by the musicians, and in such cases the position opposite is not considered as appropriate for the head couple. The same is true where the entrance is at the side of the hall.

It is always necessary to provide a place for a piano which is not near a window or a heater, because heat and dampness injure that instrument; thus we have a certain limitation in placing an orchestra. If, however, there is only a violinist, as is often the case in teaching, a position may be given him which will be most convenient to the dancers, and if the dancing master himself plays the violin he may stand wherever his purpose is best served.

635. In case neither the orchestra nor the entrance can serve as a guide it is well to observe this general rule:

The first place or place of honour cannot be near the entrance, hence that place which is opposite the entrance should be considered the first. A throne is never placed at the entrance of a throne room.

636. **The First Person in a Quadrille.** It is usually conceded that the first place belongs to the lady, but some descriptions assign the initiative to the gentleman.

It is the Author's opinion that wherever the charms of the Muses are evoked for the beautifying of life, precedence should be given to the gentler sex, although man should always lead in points of strength and courage, being naturally adapted therefor. The first place is universally assigned to the bride at a wedding festival, and it is no more than proper to extend this same rule to all social functions.

637. In the Quadrille, the first lady begins the dance, and if at a private residence, the mistress of the house is always regarded as the first lady. If, however, she does not dance, for whatever reason, she delegates her position to an adult daughter, a younger sister, a cousin, or anyone else whom she may select.

If the function is given in honour of a prominent guest of either sex, the first rank is always given to that person and the guest of honour stands in the first place. At a birthday or engagement dance or other honorary affair, the person honoured is always assumed to be in the first place, wherever he or she may stand.

In case there is no lady present who has a peculiar right to the first place, that point is arbitrarily determined by the conductor in accordance with the conditions of the hall.

638. For the proper understanding of the diagrams which follow, it is necessary to specifically name each of the different parts, single and combined. We shall therefore first consider the explanations.


## Figure and Strophe, or Couplet


639. The word "figure," as has been already explained, signifies the lines upon which the dancers proceed. The term probably arose from the fact that it may be drawn upon the floor. A *traversé*, for instance, is a simple figure.

A figure-strophe is composed of the *enchainement* of such simple figures, and as has been stated in § 7, it may be likened to a stanza of poetry, composed of a number of lines or verses corresponding to the number of *enchainements* of eight measures which constitute it.

NOTE. — The word " couplet " has been adopted for this Grammar, after long and careful consideration, because it avoids the ambiguity which arises from the use of the word " figure."

French terms are accepted as technical names for movements, steps, figures, etc., in all countries where dancing is properly and scientifically taught; a step combination is therefore called *une phrase*, and a strophe, *un couplet*.

640. The Quadrille of the present day usually contains six couplets, which are called by the following names: *Pantalon, Été, Poule, Trénis, Pastourelle* and *Finale*.

The fourth couplet (*Trénis*) was inserted many years after the others, and even now it is not executed in all countries. It should perhaps be left out entirely, as it too closely resembles the *Pastourelle* which follows it.

Many dance managers add to the last couplet so many different logical and illogical combinations that one is often at a loss to decide which is most remarkable, the diligence of the orchestra, the good nature of the abused dancers, or the presumption of the so-called "manager" in undertaking to present something of which he is ignorant.

641. The number of figures and couplets varies from time to time. The Author saw at a very elaborate ball in Berlin in 1833 a French Quadrille of eleven couplets. In 1836 it was usual to dance seven couplets, in Norway, Sweden and Denmark.

It was customary, during the early part of the nineteenth century, for persons of fashion to study new couplets for the Quadrille each year, and every one of these was known by its specific name, and its peculiar combination of steps. Persons who had danced for years spent weeks in practice before taking part in the Quadrille.

642. The simple figures usually bear the names of the geometrical forms which they describe upon the floor, as, for instance, *chaîne, balancé, tour de main, traversé*. The couplets or strophes bear names that are seldom suggestive of any object or movement, the names being often derived from the title of a famous musical composition or of a song, or from the name of its inventor, or some celebrity.

The name of each couplet often appears at the beginning of the corresponding music, but these names are of no value, and are usually disregarded, because their derivation is uncertain.

643. The custom of speaking of simple figures as *tours*, and of entire strophes as "figures," has been common for more than a century, but this application of the words is technically incorrect.

The literal significance of the word *tour* is a circular movement, and the expression *un tour de roue* means a single rotation of a wheel. *Un tour de valse* means a single rotation of the Waltz, or sometimes, to waltz once around the hall.

*Balancé* and *traversé* may be called figures, but not *tours*, because, while they do contain movements which would describe certain lines upon the floor, they contain no turning, and the word *tour* implies that quality.

Certain rules relative to the execution of the various figures must be given, besides the exact description of each of the drawings which follow.

644. **Division of Time — Measure.** It is necessary, before applying music to the various movements, to "count" the different steps and figures, and in Quadrilles such counting is usually divided into periods running to eight.

In this division, however, the count relates to the number of music syllables or *tempi*, and not to the number of measures. A measure of Quadrille music contains two music syllables and two steps, but it is the number of music syllables that count in the figures and not the number of measures; in the same manner that a line of poetry is composed of a certain number of word syllables, irrespective of the number of words.

645. **Signal** (*Ritournelle*). To enable the participants to take their places in the set, either eight or sixteen measures of music are played before the actual execution of a Contra Dance or Quadrille. These introductory measures constitute the signal or *ritournelle*. The music of the Quadrille starts immediately after the various couples are placed and the " sets " completed.

646. *Prélude.* At the beginning, the dancers wait during eight measures of the music, which are played to indicate the *tempo*, after which the actual dancing commences. A similar period of eight measures is played at the beginning of each couplet or strophe. The most suitable *tempo* for the Quadrille, when the steps are properly executed in 2-4 or 6-8 time, is about M.M. 100; but for the walking steps now in use this may be increased to M.M. 116. In this connection it may be mentioned that the *tempo* in some countries runs as high as M.M. 144, which is nonsensical, as so great a speed precludes even a uniform and graceful walk.

## Original Steps

647. The steps formerly used in the various figures of Quadrilles and Contra Dances were as follows :

| FIGURE | STEP COMBINATION |
|---|---|
| *En avant* (forward). | *Pas chassé et deux pas élevés.* |
| *En arrière* (backward). | *Pas chassé et deux pas élevés.* |
| *À droite* (to right). | *Pas chassé et deux pas élevés.* |
| *À gauche* (to left). | *Pas chassé et deux pas élevés.* |
| *Traversé* (crossing). | *Trois pas chassés et deux pas élevés en tournant.* |
| *Balancé chassé* (balance). | *Un pas chassé et deux pas élevés à droit ou à gauche.* |
| *Tour de main* (turning by the hand). | *Trois pas chassés et deux pas élevés.* |

(See Exercises 84 and 85, and §§ 608 and 609.)

648. One *jeté* and one *assemblé* may be substituted for the *pas élevés*, if the dancer desires to still further improve the execution of the steps (Exercise 88, § 611).

It is a matter of profound regret that it is no longer fashionable to properly execute the steps,—that by so doing one renders himself ridiculous; but it is necessary, in teaching, to strictly observe the proper combinations. This applies especially to the teaching of children, and all competent and conscientious instructors follow the practice, for the æsthetic development of the pupils and of their movements which it affords [§ 611].

**649.** Four *pas de basques*, executed alternately to the right and left, are substituted for the *balancé* in North Germany; and, if well executed, they present a very pretty effect. In other places the *balancé-dégagé* (explained in § 608) is executed.

**650.** It is now an almost universal custom to walk through a Quadrille, but it is none the less desirable or advantageous to learn the proper steps, and the correct method of execution, for the training that is gained by their practice gives grace of movement and educates the sense of measure; while he who neglects to acquire these steps seldom, if ever, even walks according to measure in a Quadrille, or indeed walks properly, to say nothing of dancing.

**651.** It was for many years customary to exercise the utmost precision in the execution of the steps in a Quadrille, and not infrequently they were accompanied by artistic embellishments, so that the dance was far more beautiful than it now appears. Since that time, however, custom has changed, and fashion is a tyrant from whose decree it would be useless for the dancing master to appeal, so he has been obliged to follow it.

Even now, a person may endeavour to walk in measure without seriously offending the rules of social usage, although no attention is paid to the measure in many countries, and the figures are absolutely neglected, while certain persons exclaim, "*Ce n'est plus le bon ton de danser en mesure*" (It is no longer good form to dance in measure).

How is it possible to so far distort taste and reason as to find beauty and attractiveness in that which is positively unlovely, simply because it is fashionable? It would be as sensible to introduce inharmonious and discordant tones in musical compositions, for if taste can so far err in dancing, is it not possible that this may be the fate of music in the future? No conscientious teacher can find it possible to teach in such a manner, for such dancing is offensive to common sense, to artistic taste, and to beauty.

**652.** He who disregards the natural sense of measure, impairs it; and he who labours against the influence of the beautiful in art, in nature or in life, descends the ladder of human progress.

It is only fair to assume that a person who wilfully opposes the wishes of a conscientious manager at a ball, or who disregards the rules of social custom, would, if opportunity and occasion arose, violate the laws of the state. It should be firmly impressed upon the minds of the young that their dancing is sure to indicate their character, their education and their breeding.

**653.** In dancing, the lady always stands at the right of her partner. This is in conformity with the general rule which assigns that position to whomsoever one wishes to particularly honour, either in dancing, in walking, at table or in a carriage.

**654.** The Contra-Dance may be executed by as many couples as space will permit, and is always danced in two opposite lines.

**655.** In a Quadrille, however, at least four couples must participate to form the square, although six, eight, ten, twelve or even more couples may be used. Indeed, sets of twenty or thirty couples have been formed, but such a number is impracticable, and should be avoided, as it causes too great a distance between the *vis-à-vis* (opposite couples).

The music for a *traversé* (crossing) is composed of four measures, and provides for only eight walking steps; as the proper length of such a step is not more than that of one of the feet, a square of eight persons is best adapted to the music.

656. In case a person or a couple is lacking to fill a set, one or two persons may pass to the vacant place and dance, thus filling both positions. In such case, however, the gentleman should always inquire if the double exertion will be agreeable to his partner, before undertaking it.

It sometimes happens that a hall is so crowded that double squares are formed, consisting of, say, twenty-four couples. In such cases twelve couples dance through the first figure, and then rest, while the same is executed by the other twelve. This plan doubles the duration of the Quadrille, but it is usually tiresome to the dancers, and should therefore be avoided, whenever possible.

In cases where there are twice as many ladies as gentlemen, each gentleman may engage two partners, dancing first with one and then with the other, but unless this is done in all the sets it is improper to introduce the feature.

## Standing and Sitting during the Quadrille

657. While it is not only natural but desirable to sit during a Cotillion or a Mazurka, the practice should never be tolerated in a Quadrille.

The execution of an ordinary French Quadrille, it is true, affords sufficient time for sitting while two couples are executing the figures, and while it is, beyond question, more agreeable to be comfortably seated and to pass the time in conversation with an interesting lady, still the practice tends to cause the couple to neglect the dance and therefore to disturb the other dancers. The carrying of chairs is also inconvenient and unpleasant.

658. Before engaging a partner for the Quadrille, a gentleman should arrange for a *vis-à-vis*, that is, another gentleman who will dance opposite; if no *vis-à-vis* can be found, and he has engaged a lady, he is under the disagreeable necessity of excusing himself. He should at the time of finding a *vis-à-vis* arrange for a particular place in the hall, that they may not be compelled to hurriedly find a position when the signal is given.

## The French Contra Dance (*La Contredanse Française*)

### THE FIRST COUPLET OR STROPHE—PANTALON

**659.** It is said that the name of this couplet is taken from its original music, which was the air of a French song commencing with the word "*Pantalon*," although the Italians believe the strophe to be named for one of the characters of the old Italian comedies and pantomimes, in which certain mythical personages, such as Pantalon, Polischinello, Columbine, etc., always appeared.

**660.** In our language, a word like *Pantalon* would be entirely out of the question as a title for a strophe, and it sounds very strange to us, but it would not appear unusual to the French. We have incorporated into our language many French words—such as names of various articles for the use of ladies, especially toilet articles—which if translated literally would sound stranger still, but nobody thinks of avoiding them.

**661.** The First Figure in *Pantalon* is called Right and Left (*Chaine Anglaise Entière*).

Those figures in which the hands are alternately given in meeting are called *chaines*. Of these there are several different examples, such as *chaine anglaise, chaine des dames, chaine en trois, en quatre, en six, en huit*, which are named in accordance with the number of dancers, as well as the *grande chaine, chaine en ligne, chaine aux bras, tour de chaine*, and others. If the lines described by the dancers in these figures were drawn upon the floor they would look like chains, and were the dancers to halt at the precise moment in which all the hands are joined, an actual chain would be the result.

This particular *chaine* is called "*anglaise*," from the fact that it is said to be of English origin.

In the English language, although the name *Pantalon* is applied to the couplet, this figure is known as "right and left," while the *chaine des dames* is known as "ladies' chain," and the *demi-chaine anglaise* as "half right and left."

*Chaine anglaise entière* is so named because it leads to the opposite positions and back to place, thus describing a complete figure.

In this figure, although it is not at present customary in all countries, the hands should be given, as is indicated by the word *chaine* in its title. The practice is of advantage, for the reason that if one presents his right hand to his *vis-à-vis* in passing, and then joins left hands with his partner for the turn, it will be impossible to mistake the turning, which frequently occurs in such cases if the hands are not joined. In teaching, the instruction should at least begin with the joining of the hands, for the sake of demonstration.

The number of measures necessary for each figure will be found at the beginning of the following descriptions:

I., II. **Right and Left** (*Chaine Anglaise Entière*). Eight measures. The first couple exchange places in the set, by giving right hands to the *vis-à-vis* and then turning partners to position by the left hands. This consumes four music measures, and is called *demi-chaine anglaise* [Fig. 422]. The same movements executed upon the succeeding four measures restore the dancers to their original positions in the set, and form the *chaine anglaise entière* [Fig. 423]. In giving the hands, the arms should be moved gracefully in curved lines and in rounded form and one should look at the person to whom the hand is given [§§ 312–319].

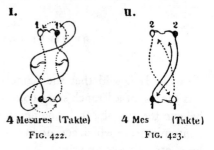

FIG. 422.                 FIG. 423.

662. III. Balance Partners (*Balancé*). Four measures. The term *se balancer* means to rock or swing, or to weigh, in which latter significance the English word "balance" is also used. The word is sometimes written in the imperative mood, *balancez*. While this is quite correct in "prompting," where the word is given as a command, it cannot be used as the name of a figure, for this use of the word renders it a noun instead of a verb and the noun is spelled *balancé*. This rule is also applicable to the terms *traversé*, *croisé* and other similar terms.

At the time of the composition of this figure, the dancers did actually rock from one foot to the other, in the same manner as in the *balancé sur place* and the *demi-balancé*, and later this movement was superseded by more elaborate steps, as fashion demanded, and it became customary to execute the *pas tendus* or zephyr steps. But now that the artistic steps have gone out of fashion, it is the almost universal custom to execute this figure by means of one chasing and two raising steps, first to the right and then to the left, although the movement is not, properly speaking, a real *balancé* [Fig. 424].

663. A Quadrille, if properly executed, may be said to represent a conversation, yet, in this dance, it is not at all uncommon to find even the most polite persons committing an entirely unnecessary, but none the less serious, breach of etiquette. It is a positive rule of politeness that one should face the person whom he addresses; this is so natural that one never thinks of disregarding it; still, in the *balancé* where the *chassés* are used, many, and we really believe most, dancers step directly forward instead of going to the right, and thus deliberately turn their backs to their partners, in supreme unconsciousness of the fault.

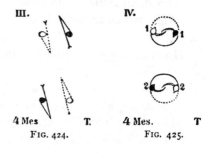

FIG. 424.                 FIG. 425.

The face should always be turned toward the person with whom one is to dance, so that conversation will be possible, if desired.

664. IV. Turning by the Hand (*Tour de Main*). In this figure the dancers join right, or both, hands with their partners and walk in a small circle around to place [Fig. 425].

It is at present the general practice to give both hands in this figure, but it is more correct to give the right only; first because the name of the figure only calls for the giving of one hand, and if both hands were intended, the plural form would be used and the name would be *tour des mains;* and second, because the figure extends through four measures of music, which provide for eight walking steps, each about the length of one of the feet.

If one hand is given, eight such steps will bring the dancers back to the exact place from which they started; but if both hands are given, eight such steps will carry them once and a half around the set. The same condition exists in the case of *chassé* steps.

665. V., VI. Complete Ladies' Chain (*Chaîne des Dames Entière*). Eight measures. The ladies advance, and give right hands, in the centre, pass by and give left hands to the opposite gentlemen, who also give left hands, and turn the ladies so as to face the centre, while the gentlemen regain those positions in the set which they have left at the commencement of the figure to meet the visiting ladies, for which purpose they advance diagonally to the right [Fig. 426].

This evolution requires four measures, and its repetition, upon the four measures succeeding, brings the ladies once more to their original places, and completes the figure [Fig. 427].

666. VII. Half Promenade (*Demi-Promenade*). This figure was at one time called *queue de chat* (cat's tail). In it, the couple join both hands, with the right crossed above the left, and proceed to the place opposite in the set [Fig. 428].

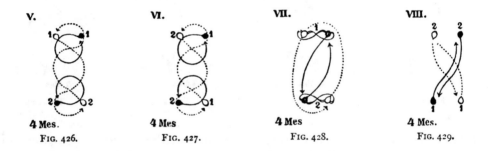

| V. | VI. | VII. | VIII. |
|---|---|---|---|
| 4 Mes. | 4 Mes | 4 Mes | 4 Mes. |
| FIG. 426. | FIG. 427. | FIG. 428. | FIG. 429. |

667. The word *demi* means "half," and signifies that the figure leads only to the opposite position, from which the couple regain their places by means of a *demi-chaine anglaise* [Fig. 429] which consumes the remaining four measures of the music and ends the strophe or couplet of a *Contre Danse*. If, however, the dance be a Quadrille, the entire couplet is repeated, and the first and second couples wait while the "second party" (third and fourth couples) execute the same figures.

## THE SECOND COUPLET OR STROPHE—L'ÉTÉ

668. The name *L'Été*, meaning "The Summer," which has been applied to this strophe, is also said to be derived from the opening words of a song, upon whose melody the figures were arranged. This couplet has been technically described for nearly two centuries by the following formula: *En avant deux et en arrière, chassé à droite et à gauche, traversé, chassé*

*à droite et à gauche, balancé et tour de main;* but there have existed differences of opinion as to the succession of the various figures, and notwithstanding the fact that the above succession has been the one most generally accepted, it is not exactly proper, for the combination would require twenty-eight measures of music; thereby contradicting the rules, as well as the sense of measure. This disparity is corrected by Gardel and Blasis, by omitting either the first *chassé à droite et à gauche* or the *balancé* (see p. 362, "Manuel de la Danse," by Blasis, revised by Gardel, published by Roret, Paris, 1830).

The probable cause of this misunderstanding is the improper placing of a comma and the word *et*. If, instead of writing *retraversé, balancé et tour de main,* we write *retraversé et balancé, tour de main,* it is clearly indicated that the *retraversé* and the *balancé* are connected, in which case only four measures of music are used, and the persons who remain upon their places during the *retraversé* of their partners execute a *balancé*, which is followed by a *tour de main* upon the succeeding four measures.

The most competent authorities show this couplet in this manner, and it is given in this order in the "Catechism of the Art of Dancing," by B. Klemm.

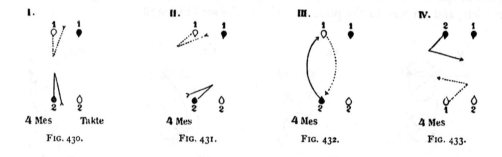

I.    FIG. 430.            II.    FIG. 431.            III.    FIG. 432.            IV.    FIG. 433.

**669.** In places where it is customary to execute the *balancé-chassé* (§ 609), the couplet is usually danced in the following order, which is recommended because of its natural sequence: Immediately following the prelude of eight measures, the first lady and the opposite gentleman (*vis-à-vis*) commence the figures (§ 637).

I.   Forward and Back Two (*En Avant Deux et en Arrière*). Four measures. One *chassé* and three *pas élevés* forward; same backward [Fig. 430].

II.   To Right and Left (*Chassé à Droite et à Gauche*). Four measures [Fig. 431].

NOTE. — One should never neglect to return to place after this figure, as the omission would disturb the succeeding figure. Many persons habitually go to the centre in the *chassé* left, but this is incorrect and only allowable where there is a great deal of space.

III.   Crossing (*Traversé*). Four measures. In this figure each walks to the left in a curved line to the place of the *vis-à-vis*, and turns to face the centre [Fig. 432].

IV.   To Right and Left to Centre (*Chassé à Droite et à Gauche au Milieu*). Four measures. Especial care must be taken in this figure to reach the centre by means of the *chassé* to the left, in order to regain one's position in proper time for the *balancé-chassé*, which follows instead of the *retraversé* [Fig. 433].

V. **Balance Partners** (*Balancé-Chassé*). Four measures. This makes it necessary for the partners to face one another and *balancé* to right and left [Fig. 434].

VI. **Turn by Hand to Original Positions in the Set** (*Tour de Main à votre Place*)[Fig. 435].

At the conclusion of the last of these figures, they are repeated by the second lady and the first gentleman, the third lady and the fourth gentleman, and the fourth lady and the third gentleman, in the order named.

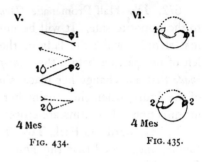

670. The custom of bowing in each *en avant deux* (forward two) is superfluous. The bows to partners and to centre at the beginning and the end of the .dance are sufficient for good taste. Repeated *révérences* during the figures are quite as unnecessary as they would be in a social call.

Of course these repeated salutations have their proper place in many Quadrilles, notably in the *Quadrille à la Cour*, where they form a part of the figures, and allowance is made for them both in time and in music. However, the most elegant and artistic salon dances, the Minuet and the Gavotte, contain but four bows, two at the beginning and two at the end, the first being to the spectators and the second to the partner, in each case.

## THE THIRD COUPLET OR STROPHE—LA POULE

671. It is said that the name of this strophe (The Hen) was taken from the original music, which, at the time of the *balancé*, resembled the cackling of a hen.

The figure is commenced by the first lady and second gentleman, as in the second strophe.

I. **Crossing** (*Traversé*). Four measures. This is executed by joining right hands and walking to the opposite places [Fig. 436].

II. **Crossing Back** (*Retraversé*). Four measures. In this the active couple join left hands upon the fifth music syllable, and pass by, giving

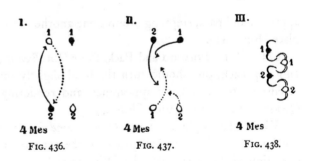

right hands to partners upon the seventh music syllable, thus forming an irregular line in which the dancers may conveniently face one another [Fig. 437].

III. **Balance in Line** (*Balancé en Ligne*). Four measures. In this figure, the ladies execute first one *chassé* and two *pas élevés* to the right, then the same steps to the left; while the gentlemen execute first one *chassé* and two *pas élevés* to the left, followed by the same steps to the right [Fig. 438].

This *balancé* is sometimes executed by one *chassé-tourné en avant à droite,* and the same movements back to place. This is very good, if properly executed.

Still others execute the original *balancé dégagé* or *pas de Basque sur la place.* One should always look at the person toward whom he directs his movement.

672. IV. Half Promenade (*Demi-Promenade*). Four measures. This figure leads only to the opposite side. It will be noticed that it is executed by one couple exactly as in the first strophe, while the lady of the other couple, who began the strophe, stands at the left of her partner before the *demi-promenade;* and, as it is not necessary to the *demi-prom- enade* that she change her place, she remains in this relative position, until the conclusion of the figure, when she regains her position at her partner's right, by means of a turn in his direction. The arms are crossed during the entire figure [Fig. 439].

V. Forward and Back, Two (*En Avant Deux et en Arrière*). Four measures. It is, of course, understood that this figure is executed by the same couple who commenced the figure [Fig. 440].

673. VI. To Right and Left (*Chassé à Droite et à Gauche*). Four measures. It was at one time customary to execute a *dos-à-dos* in place of this figure. In the *dos-à-dos* the dancers

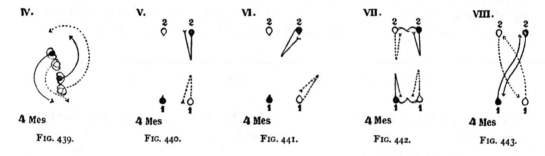

IV.            V.            VI.            VII.            VIII.

4 Mes          4 Mes          4 Mes          4 Mes          4 Mes

FIG. 439.      FIG. 440.      FIG. 441.      FIG. 442.      FIG. 443.

approach and pass, stepping around one another to the left, back to back, and returning to place [Fig. 441].

674. VII. Forward and Back, Four (*En Avant Quatre et en Arrière*). Four measures. In going back, one should turn the head slightly toward the partner, as if to speak; thus avoiding a too automatic appearance, and rendering more apparent the similarity of the Quadrille to a conversation [Fig. 442].

VIII. Half Right and Left (*Demi-Chaîne Anglaise*). Four measures. This figure brings the dancers to their original places in the set and restores the form of the square for the execution of the fourth strophe [Fig. 443].

### THE FOURTH COUPLET OR STROPHE—LA TRÉNIS

675. This strophe bears the name of Trénitz, a famous dancer who is said to have invented it about the year 1800. It is not to be found in works prior to that time, and is now omitted in most countries.

676. This strophe has undergone such changes that confusion often arises regarding it. It is executed in some places with *traversé-croisé*, in others with *croisé-traversé*, and in still others with the three hooks (*crochets à trois*). The Author has seen it danced with an additional *chaine des dames* in England, Norway and the East Indies; it is also danced with *chassé-croisé* and in other ways.

The best course is to drop the whole strophe, but it is necessary to represent and explain it here.

677. The original and correct sequence of the strophe, as composed by Trénitz, was as follows:

I. First Couple Forward and Back (*Première Couple en Avant et en Arrière*). Four measures [Fig. 444].

678. There exist essential differences between the words *couple*, *deux* and *paire*, but they are very easily explained and comprehended. Although a gentleman and lady who dance together as partners are regarded as a *couple*, a gentlemen and the opposite lady are not, but are designated by the term *deux*, which, as an unqualified numeral, does not imply any relationship between the persons to whom it is applied.

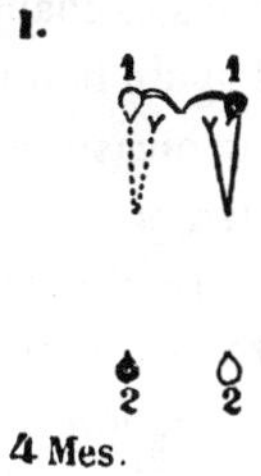

The word *couple* in French is particularly applied to two persons of opposite sex who are related either by marriage or by consent, and the word *paire* is applied to two objects of the same species; as, for instance, *une paire de bottes* (a pair of boots), but the expression *couple d'amis* and *paire d'amis* are both used, as are also the expressions *paire de chevaux* and *couple de chevaux*, etc. ("Dictionary" of Noël and Chapsal).

II. First Couple Forward; Lady Cross to Opposite; Gentleman Back to Place (*Première Couple en Avant, la Dame Traverse, et le Cavalier Retourne à sa Place*). Four measures. The first couple forward; the lady crosses to the left of her *vis-à-vis*, and remains there, while the gentleman returns alone to his place [Fig. 445].

III. Cross Over, Three (*Traversé-Croisé à Trois*). Four measures. In this figure the lone gentleman passes to the opposite side between the two ladies, who also cross to the side opposite them, each passing in a curved line to the outside, and crossing one another, turn to face their own partners who are now *vis-à-vis* [Fig. 446].

IV. Recross to Place, Three (*Retraversé Croisé Trois, Jusqu'à sa Place*). Four measures. In this the gentleman once more passes between the two ladies, and all proceed to their original positions [Fig. 447].

V., VI. Balance and Turn to Place (*Balancé et Tour de Main*). Four measures [Figs. 448, 449].

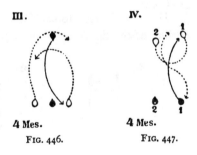

FIG. 444.          FIG. 445.

FIG. 446.          FIG. 447.

Following the execution of these figures, the entire strophe is repeated and danced by the second, third and fourth couples in their respective turns.

## VARIATIONS OF THE FOURTH COUPLET OR STROPHE

679. The third figure is sometimes varied by the execution of a *croisé-traversé* instead of *traversé-croisé*. In this, the ladies exchange places, before going across the set, and again before returning; pausing at the end of each four measures in the middle of the set and facing their own partners for the *balancé*. In these figures it should be noticed that the lady who begins the strophe crosses in front of the other, that is, inside the line of direction of the other lady, and recrosses behind or outside. This figure is more beautiful than the first because its execution is more rhythmic.

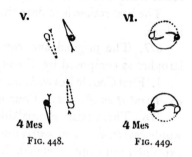

FIG. 448.                    FIG. 449.

680. In some countries still another style of dancing this strophe has been used for so long a time that dancing masters are obliged to teach it. It is executed as follows:

## THE THREE HOOKS OR THE SHELL (LES TROIS CROCHETS OU LA COQUILLE)

I. One Couple Forward and Back (*Un Couple en Avant et en Arrière*). Four measures [Fig. 450].

II. The Three Hooks (*Les Trois Crochets*). Four measures. In this, the name and the outline of the figure correspond very nicely. The lady walks in a circle around her part-

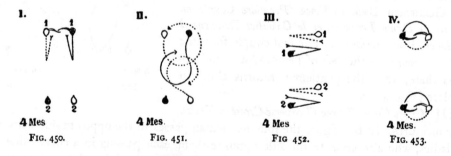

FIG. 450.          FIG. 451.          FIG 452.          FIG. 453.

ner, and returns to place, while the gentleman executes a *tour de main* with the opposite lady, in the centre of the set, presenting for the purpose his right hand, after which they remain in the centre, facing their partners (this circle is sometimes executed without joining hands) [Fig. 451].

III. Balance Partners (*Balancé-Chassé*). Four measures [Fig. 452].

IV. Turn by Hand to Original Positions in the Set (*Tour de Main à vos Places*). Four measures [Fig. 453].

While this figure is extremely graceful and beautiful, it is not technically correct, as it extends through only sixteen measures, whereas the music contains twenty-four. It may, however, be given, not as a part of *La Trénis*, but as an independent figure. Many persons refer to this figure as *La Coquille* (The Shell), but the name "The Three Hooks" is demonstrated by the drawings to be more fitting.

### THE FIFTH COUPLET OR STROPHE—LA PASTOURELLE

681. This strophe has been called *La Pastourelle* (The Shepherdess) from its original music, which was similar to the shepherd or pastoral songs.

I. First Couple Forward and Back (*Première Couple en Avant et en Arrière*). Four measures [Fig. 454].

This is the same as the first figure of *La Trénis*.

II. The Same Couple Advances and the Lady Crosses to the Left of her *Vis-à-Vis* while the Gentleman Returns, Alone, to His Place (*La Même Couple en Avant, la Dame Traverse et le Cavalier Retourne à sa Place*). Four measures [Fig. 455].

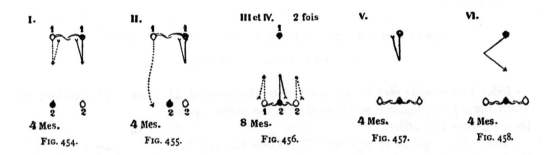

| I. | II. | III et IV.   2 fois | V. | VI. |
|---|---|---|---|---|
| 4 Mes. | 4 Mes. | 8 Mes. | 4 Mes. | 4 Mes. |
| FIG. 454. | FIG. 455. | FIG. 456. | FIG. 457. | FIG. 458. |

682. III., IV. Forward and Back, Three, Twice (*En Avant Trois et en Arrière deux fois*). Eight measures [Fig. 456].

This figure was sometimes called *chassé à la visite*, because the gentleman in advancing turned his head toward the lady at his right, and in retiring toward the one on his left, as though in pleasant conversation. This greatly relieves the figure of the stiff appearance which would be the result were the three to move forward and backward in too automatic a manner.

683. This figure may be varied by the use of different arm positions, and one may, if sufficiently skillful, turn the ladies under the uplifted arms, as in the *Allemande* or *Tyrolienne*. The variations, however, are left to the discretion of the dancers.

684. V., VI. Solo. Eight measures. The lone gentleman dances forward and back [Fig. 457] and to the right and left to the centre [Fig. 458].

Other than the ordinary Quadrille steps may, if desired, be danced; as, for instance, the so-called Cossack step; but unless the gentleman is capable of executing such steps beautifully, he should stick to the regular movements, rather than appear ridiculous by exhibiting his lack of skill.

This solo is sometimes omitted and the lone gentleman executes, instead, two *tours de main*, the first with his *vis-à-vis*, and the second with his partner.

Many dancers execute this solo as follows: " Forward and back, and right to centre," omitting the "left to centre," and thus filling only six measures of the music. This should be avoided, as it brings the figure to a close two measures ahead of its proper time.

VII. **Open Half-Circle to the Left** (*Demi-Ronde Ouverte à Gauche*). Four measures. This figure leads to the original places. It is called an open half-circle, because while the lone gentleman presents his right hand to his partner, he does not offer his left to his *vis-à-vis* [Fig. 459].

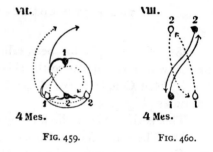

VII.                    VIII.

4 Mes.              4 Mes.

FIG. 459.          FIG. 460.

VIII. **Half Right and Left** (*Demi-Chaine Anglaise*). Four measures. This figure brings the dancers back again to their original positions [Fig. 460].

## VARIATION OF THE FIFTH COUPLET OR STROPHE
### THE GRACES (LES GRÂCES)

685. This strophe may be repeated under the name of The Graces (*Les Grâces*), in which the seventh figure is so changed that the ladies dance the solo, as in Fig. 461.

This name might be changed to " The Three Graces," for the Greek mythology represents such a group, composed of three of the daughters of Zeus or Jupiter. They were the dispensers of grace, beauty and refinement, and presided over festivals, entertainments, dancing, music, painting and sculpture. They were called Aglaia (splendour), Thalia (beauty) and Euphrosyne (gayety). Perhaps the title " *Pastourelle*, with solo for the lady," would be more correct.

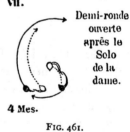

VII.

Demi-ronde
ouverte
après le
Solo
de la
dame.

4 Mes.

FIG. 461.

## THE LAST COUPLET OR STROPHE—LA FINALE

The name of this strophe is self-explanatory. Different combinations may be used to execute it.

686. The most simple combination of the *Quadrille à la Cour* is given in the " Dance Album" of A. Freising, and the most beautiful combination is to be found in the twelfth edition of the same book (page 42, No. 6).

**687.** The combination sometimes known as *La Rose à Quatre*, and which contains the changement of the ladies, is among the final strophes most commonly used. The name *La Rose* (The Rose) is derived from the figure itself, which, if drawn, presents a design resembling that flower. This resemblance is nearly lost in the *Contredanse*, where only two couples form a set, but with eight couples the similarity to the flower is more marked.

### THE ROSE (LA ROSE)

**688.** For two couples (*En deux couples*).
   I. Forward and Back, Four (*En Avant Quatre et en Arrière*). Four measures [Fig. 462].
  II. Exchange of Ladies (*Changement des Dames*). Four measures [Fig. 463].
 III. Forward and Back, Four (*En Avant Quatre et en Arrière*). Four measures [Fig. 464].
 IV. Return of the Ladies (*Reprise des Dames*). Four measures [Fig. 465].

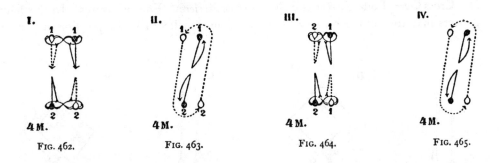

FIG. 462.     FIG. 463.     FIG. 464.     FIG. 465.

**689.** In the exchange of ladies, the gentlemen lead the visiting ladies, who approach them on the left, in a three-quarters circle to the left. In case the figure is danced by only two couples, the visiting lady is the gentleman's *vis-à-vis*, but if there are four couples (*Rose à huit*), then the gentleman turns the lady who stands at his left in the set; that is, the first gentleman and fourth lady, and so on.

**690.** As many couples as desire may participate in the Rose, but for each couple in excess of four, four measures of music must be added; and, as it is always necessary to maintain an even number of couples, the music will be increased by periods of eight measures, thus providing a proper ending for the figure.

Following the first strophe it is customary to execute *L'Été* (twenty-four measures) as the second, although the reason for so doing is not clear, and the combination probably has no logical explanation. The second strophe is followed by a repetition of the Rose, which is danced through by each couple.

**691.** Instead of exchanging ladies in this figure, the gentlemen sometimes "cheat" the approaching ladies, by wheeling quickly and turning their own partners, with whom they return to place. This figure may be permitted among friends, who will accept it as a pleasantry, but it should be avoided or at least very seldom used among strangers. It is necessary that this " cheating" be done twice, thus occupying sixteen measures of music in order that the figure shall not interfere with others who may, at the same time, be dancing the Rose or the Galop.

692. If one dances the Galop, he must hold his partner in Waltz position, and the gentleman should always commence with the left foot, while the lady commences with the right.

PAS DE GALOP

I. Forward and Back, Four (*En Avant Quatre et en Arrière*). Three Simple Chasing Steps and One Whip Syllable to the Centre (*Trois chassés simples et un fouetté au milieu*). Four measures. Both execute three simple chasing steps and one whip syllable forward, and the same movements backward [Fig. 466].

(See §§ 478 to 482, and Exercises 59 and 60.)

II. Cross Over, Four (*Traversée à Quatre et en Arrière*). Four measures. In this figure the dancers may turn either once or twice to the right or left in Waltz position (if it can be

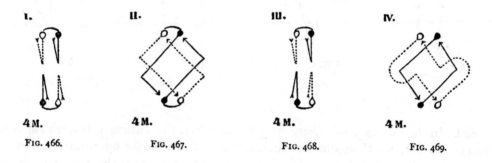

<table>
<tr><td>I.</td><td>II.</td><td>III.</td><td>IV.</td></tr>
<tr><td>4 M.</td><td>4 M.</td><td>4 M.</td><td>4 M.</td></tr>
<tr><td>FIG. 466.</td><td>FIG. 467.</td><td>FIG. 468.</td><td>FIG. 469.</td></tr>
</table>

properly done and the execution does not interfere with the other dancers), provided that the *tempo* is maintained. In an ordinary *traversée à deux* the dancers, upon meeting, pass to the left, allowing the *vis-à-vis* to cross upon their right; but in the Galop, the Waltz position renders it necessary to pass by upon the right of the approaching couple [Fig. 467].

III. Forward and Back, Four (*En Avant Quatre et en Arrière*). Four measures [Fig. 468].

IV. Recross, Four (*Retraversé à Quatre*). Waltz position. Four measures [Fig. 469]. This figure is followed by another repetition of *L'Été*, upon twenty-four measures, and this is unchanged whether the Rose or the Galop is danced, for its figures always follow one another in the same sequence.

If, however, in dancing the Galop, the couples rotate to the right, the figure is as represented in No. II. [Fig. 467], but if " the reverse" (*à l'envers ou à rebours*) is danced, the figure is as shown in No. IV. [Fig. 469].

## LADIES' WINDLASS (MOULINET DES DAMES)

**693.** The following beautiful combination, which is very popular in North Germany, is executed by four couples only, and may be substituted for the preceding as a final strophe.

I. **Cross with Chasing Steps, Eight** (*Chassé Croisé à Huit*). Four measures. All *chassent* to the side, ladies to the left, gentlemen to the right and behind the ladies; upon meeting, all execute a *demi-balancé* which consists of a *pas dégagé*, either to right and left or to left and right.

II. **Recross, Eight** (*Recroisé à Huit*). Four measures. The same figure in counter-motion.

III. **Ladies' Windlass** (*Moulinet des Dames*). Four measures. Four ladies join right hands to form a cross and retain same while they walk once around the set to place.

IV. **Balance in Windlass and Turn to Place** (*Demi-Balancé en Moulinet et Demi-Tour de Main*). Four measures. The gentlemen, who have so far remained inactive in their places, now receive the left hands of their partners in their own right hands, and all execute a *demi-balancé*, after which the ladies return to place by means of a half-turn, which leaves the gentlemen in the centre and prepared for the succeeding figure.

V. **Grand Promenade** (*Grande Promenade*). Eight measures. In this figure, each gentleman gives his left hand to his partner, to form the crossed position for the promenade, and all proceed once around the set. This figure is executed four times, and is followed upon the succeeding twenty-four measures by the entire strophe *L'Été*.

Upon the fifth repetition of this figure, the gentlemen offer their right arms to their partners and conduct them to seats.

This strophe may be still further extended by the execution of one or more of the figures which follow.

**694.** As the execution of these various figures and combinations depends largely upon the number of dancers, their ability, the size of the hall, and the time allowed for dancing such figures, no positive rules as to their use can be set down. The matter must therefore be left to the discretion of the director, who may select the figures and combinations which are most suitable. A dancing-master may, it is true, drill his pupils for the execution of a certain *Finale*, but even he may be forced by circumstances to alter the figures or to substitute others where a large number participate in the dance, as the most thoroughly drilled figures may sometimes fail; while, in other instances, figures that are entirely *impromptu* are very successful.

## LARGE CIRCLES (GRANDES RONDES)

I., II. **Grand Circle to Left and Right** (*Grande Ronde à Gauche et à Droite*). Eight measures. In this figure all join hands and form a closed circle, making an eighth turn to the left, placing the right foot forward in 3d position, and take either six walking or three chasing steps in a circle. Upon the seventh and eighth music syllables, all turn to the right and repeat the movement in the opposite direction to place [Fig. 470].

III. Ladies to Centre and Return (*Les Dames au Milieu et de Retour*). Four measures. The four ladies execute *chassé-tourné* to right to the centre, and repeat the same to place [Fig. 471].

IV. Gentlemen to Centre and Balance (*Les Cavaliers au Milieu et Demi-Balancé sur Place*). Four measures. The four gentlemen execute a *chassé-tourné* to the right to the centre,

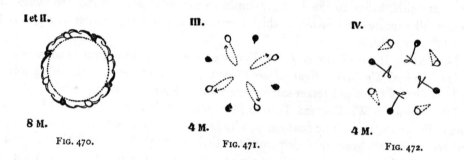

I et II.

8 M.

FIG. 470.

III.

4 M.

FIG. 471.

IV.

4 M.

FIG. 472.

where they then execute a *demi-balancé* while the ladies do likewise. This *demi-balancé* consists of a *dégagé* upon the right while the left is drawn into posterior 3d position and the same movement is executed on the other foot, and requires two measures or four syllables of music [Fig. 472].

V., VI. Balance Partners and Turn to Place (*Balancé avec vos Dames et Tour de Main*). Eight measures. These figures are executed with ordinary walking steps, and need no explanations, as the cuts speak for themselves [Figs. 473, 474].

V.

4 M.

FIG. 473.

VI.

4 M.

FIG. 474.

VII.

FIG. 475.

695. VII. Grand Right and Left, Half Round (*Demi-Chaîne à Huit*). Four measures. In this all turn to partners and present the right hand upon the first step, and the left hand to the next lady, and so on [Fig. 475].

During this figure the gentlemen pass in front of their ladies and continue in a serpentine line half around the circle, where they meet their own partners, who have simultaneously taken the same steps in the opposite direction.

Although this figure is very simple, frequent mistakes arise from improper placing or position. It should be noted that the gentlemen start *toward the inside*, while the ladies start *toward the outside* of the circle.

696. Eight measures have been prescribed for the *demi-chaine à huit*, but if the prompter calls merely "*grande chaine!*" it is always understood to mean *grande chaine entière*, or grand right and left all the way around; in which figure the dancers do not stop upon meeting their partners, but continue the movement to places, thus requiring sixteen measures of music.

697. VIII. **Promenade to Seats** (*Promenade Finale*). Eight measures. This figure is designed especially for the escorting of the ladies to their seats, for which purpose the gentlemen offer their right arms, and all retire from the floor with ordinary walking steps.

698. This is the most commonly used final strophe, but even this is frequently prolonged.

699. It is not at present customary to "prompt" for Quadrilles in well-regulated parties.

700. It is natural to suppose that only well-drilled and competent dancers would attempt to lead in the execution of the figures, but this is not the case. Persons who know so little regarding the figures as to be ignorant even of their names, to say nothing of their combinations, frequently attempt to direct Quadrilles, prompting one thing and leading another, until, when the confusion has become complete, they call "*cherchez vos dames!*" when all the dancers struggle to find their partners and to untangle the snarl into which they have been led.

For the information of dance managers, certain final figures, which may be combined according to personal taste, are given herewith:

701. **Grand Right and Left Half Round; Turn, and Repeat to Place** (*Chaine et Chaîne de Retour*). Sixteen measures. In this figure the chain is executed in the same manner as in the *demi-chaine à huit* until the partners meet, when they join right hands and, after a *demi-tour de main*, return in the direction from whence they came to place. The gentlemen start inside and return outside the ladies.

This figure has been composed for four couples and allows four measures for the first *demi-chaine*, two measures for the *demi-tour de main*, two measures to pause, facing the direction from whence they came, four measures for *demi-chaine de retour*, and four measures for final *tour de main*. If more than four couples participate, the pause must be lengthened accordingly, *i.e.*, two measures for each additional couple.

**Balance and Turn to Place** (*Balancé et Tour de Main*). Eight measures. This figure affords time for those who are tardy about arriving at their places to right themselves for the succeeding figure.

702. **The Diagonal Lines** (*Les Lignes Obliques*). For four couples. In this the arms are crossed as in the Promenade (§ 666), and the first and second couples turn respectively to the third and fourth, thus forming two lines of four, diagonally across the set.

I. **Forward and Back, Eight** (*En Avant Huit et en Arrière*). Four measures.

II. **Exchange of Ladies** (*Changement des Dames*). Four measures. In this the first and third ladies cross to the next gentlemen at the right, who present their left hands and execute a *demi-tour de main* to place.

Forward and Back, Eight (*En Avant Huit et en Arrière*). Four measures.

Repeat to next gentleman.

These figures are then repeated, the second and fourth couples turning respectively to the third and first, and so on, until the ladies are once more restored to their original positions in the set.

This is a very beautiful figure, if the lines are kept straight, but it loses by the widening if eight couples participate.

703. The term *en avant huit* is used in all cases in which eight or more people participate in the figure. Such expressions as *en avant seize* (sixteen) are not used, because the figures are all planned for eight persons.

### THE OPPOSITE CIRCLES (LES RONDES OPPOSÉES)

704. Not less than eight couples should be used in these figures, because a smaller number makes too small an outer circle.

I. Ladies to the Centre (*Les Dames au Milieu*). Four measures. All the ladies execute a *chassé-tourné* toward the centre, turning to the right and facing partners, and then exe-

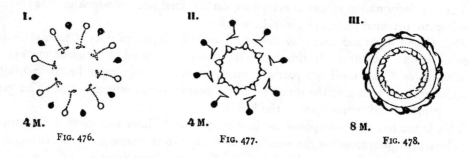

I.                     II.                     III.

4 M.                  4 M.                    8 M.

FIG. 476.              FIG. 477.               FIG. 478.

cute a *balancé sur place*, at the same time joining hands and forming a closed circle in the centre, with their backs turned to the middle of the set [Fig. 476].

705. If such a closed circle is entirely composed of ladies or of gentlemen, the right hand is *presented* palm upward and the left is *given* palm downward, and in the following manner: upon the first step of the *balancé* which goes to the right, the right hand is *presented*, and upon the first step to the left, the left hand is *given*, thus closing the circle.

II. Gentlemen Forward (*Les Cavaliers Approchent*). Four measures. The gentlemen take two short steps toward the centre, where they execute a *demi-balancé sur place*, during which they join hands to form a circle facing the ladies [Fig. 477].

III. **Opposite Circles to the Left** (*Rondes Opposées à Gauche*). Eight measures. The ladies turn in a circle to their left, and the gentlemen in another circle to their left, thus forming two opposite circles as they are facing one another and producing a very attractive appearance [Fig. 478].

706. Every figure is rendered easier by the execution of exact steps and the maintenance of even *tempo*.

This figure, which contains sixteen steps, presents a better appearance if danced upon eight measures than upon four.

IV. **Opposite Circles to the Right** (*Rondes Opposées à Droite*). Eight measures [Fig. 479].

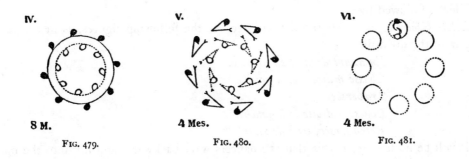

FIG. 479.          FIG. 480.          FIG. 481.

V., VI. **Balance and Turn to Place** (*Balancé et Tour de Main*). Eight measures [Figs. 480, 481].

After these figures, the complete strophe is repeated, as follows:

I. **The Gentlemen to the Centre and Giving of the Hands** (*Les Cavaliers au Milieu et Donnez les Mains*). Four measures.

II. **The Ladies Approach** (*Les Dames Approchent*). Four measures.

III. **Opposite Circles to the Left and Right** (*Rondes Opposées à Gauche et à Droite*). Sixteen measures.

IV. **Balance and Turn to Place** (*Balancé et Tour de Main*). Eight measures.

## THE WREATH (LA GUIRLANDE)

707. This strophe may be danced by as many couples as space permits.

I. **The Ladies Advance to Form a Circle** (*Les Dames en Avant pour Former une Ronde*). Four measures. The ladies advance, either with four small walking steps or with one *chassé* and two *pas élevés*. They do not turn, but during a *demi-balancé* give the hands and form a closed circle.

II. **The Gentlemen Advance to Form the Wreath** (*Les Cavaliers en Avant pour Former la Guirlande*). Four measures. The gentlemen advance to the ladies, cross their arms in front and over the ladies' arms and join hands, thus forming another closed circle intertwining that of the ladies, and completing the wreath.

III. **Wreath, Circle to Left** (*Guirlande, Ronde à Gauche*). Four or eight measures. Retaining the form of the wreath all walk to the left, half around the set.

IV. **Open the Wreath** (*Ouvrez la Guirlande*). Four or eight measures. The first couple release their left hands and fall back simultaneously with those at the other end of the line to form a straight column, thus utilizing the remainder of the music.

V. **Ladies Pass Through** (*Traversée de Dames*). Four measures. In this figure, the gentlemen raise their hands so that the ladies may pass under and to the opposite side, forming what is known as an " English column," the ladies being upon one side and the gentlemen upon the other.

This is followed by :

*L'Eté Générale,* in which the dancers execute the following figures, as in the second strophe of the quadrille :

> *En avant deux et en arrière.*
> *Chassé à droite et à gauche.*
> *Traversée.*
> *Chassé à droite et à gauche.*
> *Retraversée, tour de main.*

It will be noticed from this that the dancers walk backward, and not into the middle during the second *chassé à gauche,* and that that figure is followed by a real *traversée,* immediately after which a *tour de main* is made with the now opposite partner, while the whole concludes with a march by couples, from which may proceed either a Finale Promenade, a Polonaise, a Grandfather Dance or any other movements that may be desired.

708. In case too many couples participate to permit the formation of a single wreath, two or more may be formed and the figures may be executed alike in each wreath. At the command " Open ! " both wreaths fall back and form two lines *vis-à-vis.*

In these cases the strophe *L'Été* is executed first by all the ladies, then by all the gentlemen, and upon the second *chassé à gauche* they dance to the centre, and execute a *balancé* with partners instead of *retraversée.* The figure ends with a *tour de main.*

709. Various other and similar combinations may be added to the *Finale,* but the conductor should always bear in mind that too long a *Finale* is not only tiresome to the dancers, but wearies the spectators and overtaxes the musicians.

# The Polonaise

(M. M. 88 = ♪)

710. Properly speaking, the Polonaise is not really a dance, but rather a Promenade or Procession. Its particular office is to afford opportunity for the lady in whose honour the ball may be given to greet the guests, and to invite them to participate in the entertainment.

For this purpose, the lady so honoured makes a tour of the hall accompanied by her partner, saluting each couple in turn. The gentleman naturally joins in the *révérences*. Each couple, after having been greeted, fall into line behind the first couple who continue their way around the room until all have taken places in the procession.

The usual step for the Polonaise is the alternation of the feet in the 4th, 3d, and 4th positions as in the Polka, but in different rhythm (3-4 measure). The step usually commences with the right foot.

711. This being neither a difficult nor a tiresome movement, even the oldest and the youngest of the gentlemen present should be sufficiently polite to invite some lady to participate in the pleasure of it, especially at private or house parties. It would be well for the young gentlemen of to-day to follow the example of the old Polish and French gentlemen, who are, in this respect, perfect models of politeness.

712. It was at one time customary to exchange ladies at different points in the Polonaise, but the practice is now obsolete.

713. If no one lady has a particularly prominent part, as in the case of public parties, where an admission fee is charged, the manager or director should ask one of the older ladies to commence the Polonaise.

714. This beautiful beginning to a social function should never be omitted, because of its sentiment, and the dignity that it casts upon what follows it.

715. The Polonaise is sometimes executed at the conclusion of a ball, but when this is done, the *révérences* are made at the end instead of the beginning of the dance, and are expressive of a farewell.

The different figures and changes of the Polonaise are of little moment, and are left to the judgment of the leading couple, who should, in selecting them, bear in mind at all times, (1) the amount of space necessary for their execution, (2) the number of participants, and (3) their ability.

716. Many exquisite figures for the Polonaise have been published in the various works upon dancing, both old and new, with and without drawings. It would be impossible to describe them all, but the following are recommended for their beauty and simplicity.

717. In placing pupils for the Polonaise, they present a better appearance if the tallest are at the right and the shortest at the left, in regular gradation. Indeed, such a formation

facilitates the work of a teacher. The Polonaise or March commences with the smallest pair, who wheel to the left and are followed by each successive couple in order.

I. Grand Promenade (*Grande Promenade*). This figure has already been described (§ 693). It should be continued once or twice around the hall until all the couples have joined.

II. Column of Twos (*Colonne à Deux*). In this, all other couples fall in line behind the leading couple and march up the centre of the hall, where the column is divided, and the gentlemen proceed to the left and the ladies to the right, around the room, meeting again at the starting point, and passing once more in *colonne à deux* to the head of the hall (§§ 632, 635).

III. Casting off Twos. In this, the first couple go to the left, the second to the right, and so on, passing again to the starting point, where they form the

IV. Column of Fours (*Colonne à Quatre*). In this the procession passes to the head of the hall for the execution of the next figure.

V. Casting off Fours. In this figure the platoons wheel alternately to left and right, and pass around to form the

VI. Column of Eights (*Colonne à Huit*). This formation is retained until the head of the hall is reached, where it divides in the centre, and wheels in platoons of four to left and right. Proceeding simultaneously to the foot of the hall, the two columns combine, the couples of the right column falling in between those of the left, and thus forming again the

VII. Column of Fours. The procession passes once more to the head, where the dividing process is repeated and after forming a Column of Twos, the line once more casts off to left and right, in preparation for the

VIII. Passage of the First Half Column (*Passage de la Première Demi-Colonne*). Upon meeting, that portion of the dancers which is led by the first couple passes, arm in arm, between the partners of the couples whom they meet, who separate for the purpose, but immediately rejoin their arms when the last couple has passed through. From here all proceed to the head of the hall, for the

IX. Passage of the Second Half Column (*Passage de la Seconde Demi-Colonne*), in which the first half-column separates and allows the second to pass through.

X. Passage of the Ladies Through the Middle (*Les Dames Passent au Milieu*). In this the couples separate and the ladies pass between the partners of the advancing columns.

XI. Passage of the Gentlemen Through the Middle (*Les Cavaliers Passent au Milieu*). On meeting this time, the gentlemen pass between the partners of the opposite columns.

XII. Column of Twos. After this meeting, the half columns consolidate and form the original single Column of Twos, which proceeds to the head of the hall, and divides for

XIII. The Half Moon (*La Demi-Lune*). Upon separating, the ladies join hands and face the centre of the hall, passing to the right; and the gentlemen join hands and move to the left, facing the wall. Both lines proceed in this manner to the meeting-place, where the gentlemen pass in front of the ladies and face them.

As soon as the two lines have entirely passed one another, they turn, and the gentlemen face the centre, while the ladies face the wall, and continue thus to the opposite ends of the hall, where the ladies pass again to the inside, and all proceed to the starting point to begin the next figure.

718. XIV. **The Snake** (*Le Serpent*). This figure may be executed in single file or by couples. The single file is better adapted to classes in which the sexes are not mixed, and the formation by couples is preferable where both ladies and gentlemen participate. At the conclusion of this figure, a large closed circle is formed for the

719. XV. **Grand Circle** (*Grande Ronde*). The Polonaise may, at the beginning of a ball, lead into a Waltz or a Polka, but if at the end, it should be concluded by a *révérence*, which may be done in two ways.

720. The first and more dignified manner is as follows: The first couple, still retaining the hands, turn to the second and address, then pass to the third and address them, and so on to the last couple, beside whom they take their places, and are followed in turn by each of the other couples, until the last have passed the first, when the Polonaise is ended.

721. The second manner of ending is less elaborate, and is preferred among acquaintances. It is as follows: Having formed a large circle, the ring is broken, and falls back in four lines to the ends and sides of the hall; the head and foot lines advance, address and retire to their places, and the side lines repeat the figure, after which each gentleman offers his arm to his partner and leads her to her seat.

722. If the hall or the company is too large, some of the foregoing figures may be omitted, or others may be substituted or added if desired; or more intricate figures may be introduced, where there is a sufficient number of couples upon whose ability in dancing dependence may be placed. This, however, must be left to the conductor, who is usually in a position to judge as to the abilities of his guests.

# Chapter XIV

## THE MINUET

THE music of the Minuet of the Queen, which is presented here together with its text [Fig. 452], has been taken from a manuscript copy which is said to have come down to us from Gardel. The text above the lines refers to the movements which are executed during the first rendering of the music, and that which appears below the lines refers to the movements during the repetition.

724. Herr A. Freising, dancing teacher of the Royal University of Berlin, is in possession of an authentic and exact description of this classical dance.

725. It has, therefore, been possible, with the aid of these works, for the author of this grammar to choregraphically represent the Minuet of the Queen in its original form ; as well as a collection of other important dances, which will be published later as a separate work.*

### Minuet of the Court (*Le Menuet de la Cour*)

726. Although much significant information regarding the Court Minuet may be found in the " Lexicon of Dances," of Rudolph Voss, and the " History of the Art of Dancing," by Albert Czerwinski, a more complete description is given by Bernhard Klemm in his " Catechism."

The Minuet is a grave and dignified dance for two persons, containing steps peculiar to itself; it is executed upon the lines of the letter " Z."

Its name (*Menuet*) is derived from the French word *menu*, which comes in turn from the Latin word *minutus*, meaning " small " or " dainty." From this fact we may infer that the steps should be small and daintily executed.

727. The music is in 3-4 time, the *tempo* slow (M.M. 56 = ♩.) and the music should be executed in a majestic manner (*maestoso*), with the accent falling upon the first music syllable, while the third is rendered prominent by the accompaniment, if not by the melody.

The music for the Minuet consists of two parts of eight measures each, and a so-called

---

* It is to be regretted that Herr Zorn never published the collection to which he refers. — ED.

"trio" which is of like duration (sixteen measures), and each of these parts is repeated. Inasmuch as the entire melody is played through twice, and there is also a Prelude and a Postlude of eight measures each, the entire dance, as hereafter described, extends through one hundred and forty-four measures of music.

728. The Minuet was first introduced at the court of France. This particular Minuet (*Menuet de la Cour*) is ascribed to Pecour, who was perhaps the most celebrated dancer of

Musique du Menuet de la Reine.

FIG. 482.

his period (1674–1729), while the *Menuet de la Reine*, which is accounted the most beautiful as well as the most perfect and the most difficult ever written, is the work of Gardel, and was composed for the celebration of the marriage of Marie Antoinette to Louis XVI., from which circumstance its name is derived. It was generally executed in conjunction with the Gavotte of Vestris, and its music was probably composed by Rameau.

729. Minuets have been written by many of the most celebrated composers, but the *Menuet de la Cour* is generally danced to the "Boat Song" from "Don Giovanni," by

Mozart. This melody contains two parts of eight measures each, and is played twice through for each couplet.

730. The Minuet has been frequently termed the "queen of dances," and justly so, for no other dance contains such elegance of manner nor is so exquisitely graceful. It spread to many countries, was practiced in every European court, and it is executed, even now, in many places where one would hardly expect to find so beautiful a dance.

NOTE. — The Author was greatly surprised to see the peasants of a small and out-of-the-way Norwegian village executing the Minuet. He had gone to the place to study the national dance, and had no idea that so beautiful a conception was known to them.

731. Although it no longer appears upon the list of social dances, and is perhaps ridiculed by persons of little taste, and by those who are too ignorant to appreciate its beauty and its value, the Minuet is considered by all competent dancers and teachers of dancing as a most valuable assistance in æsthetic training. It frequently reappears, even now, at social functions, among those persons who still retain some vestiges of taste and some appreciation of the beautiful.

732. An illustration showing a Minuet which was danced in the new hall of the "Diana Bath," in Vienna, may be found upon page 220 of the German periodical, "Ueber Land und Meer," for 1861 (No. 14).

733. A Minuet Quadrille, composed by A. Freising, dancing teacher at the Royal University in Berlin, has been adapted by the members of the German Academy and incorporated in their course of instruction, for the purpose of aiding to revive the Minuet.

734. A new minuet, with choreographic script and musical supplement, appeared in the "Frauenzeitung," of Berlin (Vol. XIII., No. 1), January 1st, 1886. It is called the "Minuet of Louis XV.," and was written by M. de Soria, ballet master of the Grand Opera at Paris. The music is by E. Etesse.

735. There also appeared, during the latter part of 1886, another new Minuet, which was published by Franz Pechel, in Graz. It was presented and explained by means of three choregraphic drawings, with text, and was the work of Edward Eichler, graduated academic dancing master in Graz. The music was original and was composed by Franz Rafael.

Thus we may see that, even now, efforts are made to do honour to this beautiful dance.

## Steps of the Minuet (*Pas de Menuet*)

736. There are, in the Minuet, four different combinations of steps that belong exclusively to it. They are as follows:

Minuet step to the right (*Pas de menuet à droite*).
Minuet step to the left (*Pas de menuet à gauche*).
Minuet step forward (*Pas de menuet en avant*).
Minuet balance (*Balancé de menuet*).

**737.** Although the music of the Minuet is in 3-4 time, it is customary to so phrase it as to make four step movements coincide with six syllables of music. In teaching, however, it is preferable to divide the movements into six syllables of music, as this method is more easily understood by pupils, and by its use the simple movements are more easily accommodated to the music.

**738.** Exercise 102 shows the choregraphic representation of the different Minuet steps :

Minuet Step to the Right (*Pas de menuet à droite*) [Fig. 483].

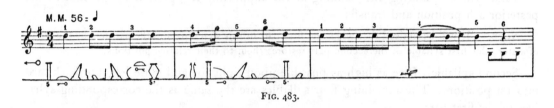

FIG. 483.

Execution. — Preparation: 5th Position of Right.

First syllable. The right foot glides upon the toe into 2d position.

Second syllable. Raise the left heel and transfer the weight, thus bringing the left into 2d position.

Third syllable. Bend the supporting knee and glide the left foot, with slightly bended left leg, into the posterior 5th position.

Fourth syllable. Stretch both legs and transfer the weight, thus bringing the right foot into anterior 5th position.

Fifth syllable. Glide the right foot lightly to 2d position and transfer.

Sixth syllable. Glide the left foot lightly into posterior 5th position and transfer, thus bringing the right once more into anterior 5th position, and ready to begin the succeeding movement.

In the Minuet, two of these *pas droits* are always used in succession.

**739.** Minuet Step to the Left (*Pas de menuet à gauche*) [Fig. 484].

FIG. 484.

Execution. — First Part. Preparation: 5th Position of Right.

First syllable. Bend the supporting knee and raise the heel, at the same time gliding the right foot forward into 4th position, where it receives the weight.

Second syllable. Rise upon the right toe and glide the left foot lightly into 1st position.

Third syllable. Glide the left foot to 2d position, at the same time lowering the right heel, and bending the right knee.

Fourth syllable. Transfer.

Fifth syllable. Bend the left knee slightly, glide the right foot into posterior 5th position and transfer.

Sixth syllable. Glide the left foot lightly to 2d position, at the same time stretching the left leg, and transfer.

Second Part.

First syllable. During the bending of the supporting leg, glide the right foot to the posterior 4th position and transfer.

NOTE. — It will be noticed that while the first part of this step separates the partners by the width of a step, this first syllable of the second part restores them to their relative positions.

Second syllable. Rise as high as possible upon right toe and glide left foot backward into 1st position. The remaining four syllables are the same as the corresponding syllables of the first part.

740. Minuet Step Forward (*Pas de Menuet en avant*) [Fig. 485].

FIG. 485.

Execution. — First Part. Preparation: 2d position of right.

First syllable. The right foot glides lightly through the 1st into the anterior 4th position and receives the weight.

Second syllable. Raise the right heel and glide left foot through the posterior 3d and into the 2d flowing position.

Third syllable. Lower the right heel, at the same time putting down the left foot in posterior 3d position.

Fourth syllable. Glide left foot to 1st position and transfer.

Fifth syllable. Advance right foot to anterior 4th position and transfer.

Sixth syllable. Glide left foot to 1st position and transfer.

Second Part. The second part is begun by the right foot which starts from 1st position, and the first four syllables are exactly similar to those of the first part.

Fifth syllable. Place the right foot in front of the left in an over-stepped 5th position, rise upon the toes and execute a half-turn to the left.

Sixth syllable. Lower into anterior 5th position of left and transfer, thus allowing the right foot to begin the succeeding step.

This half-turn accomplishes the change of direction necessary to the execution of the figure of the Minuet.

741. Minuet Balance (*Balancé de Menuet*) [Fig. 486].

Execution. (*a*) Preparation : 2d point position of right.

First syllable. Glide right foot into anterior 4th, marking the 1st position in transit, and transfer.

Second syllable. Glide left to posterior 3d position.

Third syllable. Carry same (left) into 2d flowing position.

Fourth syllable. Put down left and glide same through the 1st to posterior 4th position and transfer.

Fifth syllable. Glide right to anterior 3d, and

Sixth syllable, thence into 2d flowing position.

742. Didelot, Bournonville, and certain other celebrated dancers have executed the *Balancé de Menuet* in the manner which follows [Fig. 486*b*]:

(*b*) First syllable. Same as in *a*.

Second syllable. Mark with the toe of the left foot the posterior and anterior 3d positions in passing, and

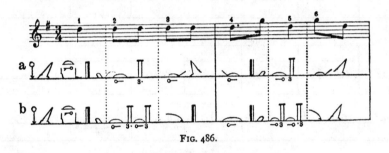

FIG. 486.

Third syllable, proceed into anterior 4th point position.

Fourth syllable. Glide left a whole step backward to posterior 4th position and transfer.

Fifth syllable. Mark lightly with the right foot the anterior and posterior 3d positions, and

Sixth syllable, proceed into 2d flowing position.

743. The Minuet may be executed by either one or more couples. If it is danced by more than a single couple they form a column, one behind another, about forty inches apart, with the shortest couple in front. The head of the column should face the place of honour, and the line usually runs lengthwise of the hall [Fig. 487]. If space permits, more than one column may be formed.

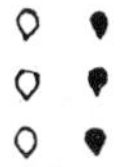

FIG. 487.

The description which follows is for a single couple. In case there are others, all the couples execute the same steps and figures, and exact uniformity of movement is one of the most important elements of the dance.

744. The division of the couplets refers to the music, and the numerals at the right of the line show the number of measures required for the execution of the figures.

745. Exercise 103. Minuet of the Court (*Menuet de la Cour*) [Fig. 488].

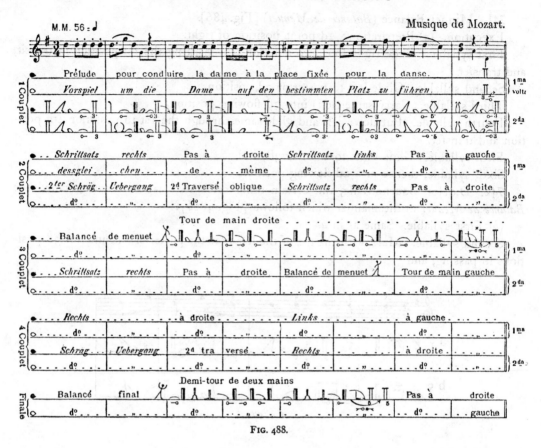

FIG. 488.

| SYLL. | FIRST COUPLET | MEAS. |
|---|---|---|

**Prelude.**    8

During the first eight measures of the music, each gentleman conducts his lady to the position in the column which has been assigned to them, and, releasing her hand, stands at her left side.

| | THE LADY'S PART | THE GENTLEMAN'S PART |
|---|---|---|
| 1 | The lady extends her right foot to 2d position. | The gentleman extends his right foot to 2d position. |
| 2 | Transfers, and executes a quarter-turn to the right. | Transfers and executes a quarter-turn to the left. |
| 3 | Draws the left foot into posterior 3d position. | Draws the left foot into anterior 3d position. |

At the conclusion of these movements the hands are joined.    I

Arrangement original par Pécour.                    Chorégraphie de F. A. Zorn.

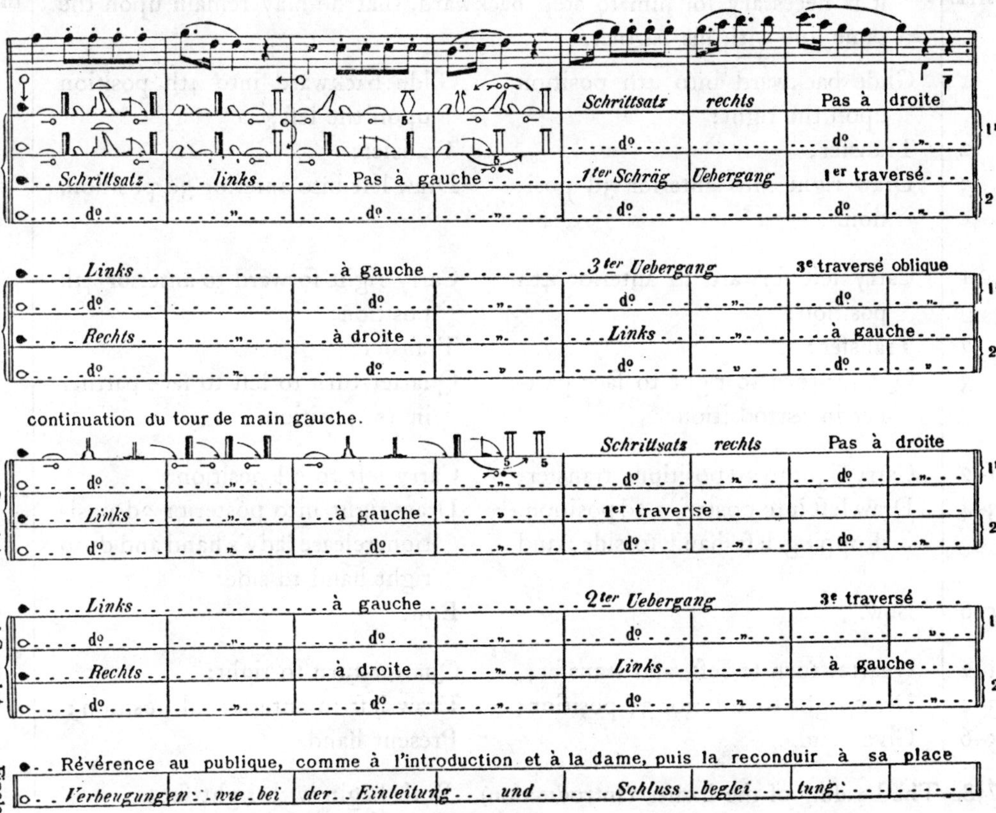

**1 Couplet**

Schrittsatz    rechts   |  Pas à  |  droite

......do.....    do.....

Schrittsatz ... links ..... Pas à gauche ..... 1ter Schräg | Uebergang | 1er traversé ....

...do...    do ..... do ..... do .....

**2 Couplet**

.... Links ........... à gauche ........ 3ter Uebergang   3e traversé oblique

.... do .......... do ....... do ....... do .....

.... Rechts ......... à droite ..... Links ..... à gauche ....

.... do ......... do ....... do ...... do .....

continuation du tour de main gauche.

**3 Couplet**

Schrittsatz   rechts   Pas à droite

....do.... do ..... do .....

.... Links ...... à gauche ..... 1er traversé .....

...do... ....do..... do ..... do .....

**4 Couplet**

.... Links ........... à gauche ........ 2ter Uebergang   3e traversé ...

.... do .......... do ....... do ....... do .....

.... Rechts ......... à droite ..... Links ..... à gauche ....

.... do ......... do ....... do ...... do .....

**Finale**

.. Révérence au publique, comme à l'introduction et à la dame, puis la reconduir à sa place

.. Verbeugungen : wie bei der Einleitung ... und ..... Schluss begleitung.

FIG. 488.

## 746. Bow.

| SYLL. | | | MEAS. |
|---|---|---|---|
| I | The lady inclines the body and bends the knees, at the same time slightly raising the right heel; | The gentleman inclines the body without bending the knees; | |
| 2 | Glides right foot to posterior 4th position; transfers; sinks and rises again | Glides left foot backward to posterior 4th position; transfers | |
| 3 | And draws the advanced foot backward to anterior 3d position. | And draws the advanced foot backward to anterior 3d position, at the same time rising to an erect position. | I |

747. The ordinary bow of the gentleman is executed in 1st position and upon the place, but in order to coincide with the figure of the Minuet,

| SYLL. | | | MEAS. |
|---|---|---|---|
| | it is necessary for him to step backward, that he may remain upon the same line with his partner. | | |
| 1 | Glide backward into 4th position upon the right; | Glide backward into 4th position upon the left; | |
| 2 | Transfer; | Transfer; | |
| 3 | Draw right into anterior 3d position. | Draw left into anterior 3d position. | 1 |
| 1 | Carry left forward to anterior 4th position; | Carry right forward to anterior 4th position; | |
| 2 | Transfer; | Transfer; | |
| 3 | Quarter-turn to right to face partner in 1st position. | Quarter-turn to left to face partner in 1st position. | 1 |
| 1–2 | Carry right to 2d position; transfer; | Carry left to 2d position; | |
| 3–4 | Draw left into posterior 3d position, dropping left hand to side; and | Draw right into posterior 3d position, release lady's hand and drop right hand to side; | |
| 5–6 | Bow. | Bow. | 2 |
| 1–2 | Quarter-turn to left, and transfer; | Quarter-turn to right; | |
| 3–4 | Draw right to anterior 3d position; | Draw left to anterior 3d position; | |
| 5–6 | Give hand. | Present hand. | 2 |

**748. The Leading of the Ladies (Introduction).** Both begin with right foot.

| | | MEAS. |
|---|---|---|
| *Pas de Menuet en avant.* | *Pas de Menuet en avant.* | 2 |
| *Pas de Menuet en avant.* | *Pas de Menuet à droite.* | 2 |

II.

This brings the dancers into the position shown in Fig. 489, when the hands, which have until now been joined, are released.

FIG. 489.

| | | MEAS. |
|---|---|---|
| *Pas de Menuet à droite.* | *Pas de Menuet à droite.* | 2 |
| *Pas de Menuet à droite.* | *Pas de Menuet à droite.* | 2 |
| *Pas de Menuet à gauche.* | *Pas de Menuet à gauche.* | 2 |
| *Pas de Menuet à gauche.* | *Pas de Menuet à gauche.* | 2 |

III.

These movements bring the dancers back to place, as shown in Fig. 490, and ready to commence the execution of the principal figure.

FIG. 490.

SECOND COUPLET (THE PRINCIPAL FIGURE)

**749.** The principal figure consists of the following combinations: *traversée oblique, pas de Menuet à droite double*, and *pas de Menuet à gauche double.*    12

Fig. 491 shows the drawing of the principal figure.

**IV.**

FIG. 491.

NOTE. — The first couplet of thirty-two measures ends with the *traversée oblique*, and the second couplet commences with the *pas de Menuet à gauche double*, and calls for the repetition of the entire melody.

750. The principal figure is usually repeated twice in both the first and second halves of the Minuet.

First repetition of principal figure.                                            12

Second repetition of principal figure.                                           12

In case it becomes necessary, or desirable, to abbreviate the Minuet, these repetitions may be omitted; thereby reducing the dance to only ninety-six measures, without seriously affecting it. But unless both repetitions of the principal figure are omitted in each half of the dance, there will result a very disturbing condition, as the music will contain one hundred and twenty measures.

It is customary for the first dancer to inform his followers if the principal figure is to be executed only once, and the usual signal is a light clapping of the hands, immediately preceding the last *pas de Menuet à gauche*. By this signal all the other participants understand that the *balancé* shall be executed.


### THIRD COUPLET


Minuet balance (*Balancé de Menuet*).                                            2

751. During the conclusion of the *balancé* the right arm should be raised in readiness to give the hand for the *tour de main droite*, which consists of two *pas de menuet en avant*, one *pas de menuet de côté* (*droit ou gauche*).

**V.**                                                                           6

FIG. 492.

Fig. 492 represents the *tour de main droite*.

At the conclusion of the first *pas en avant*, the couple should be in such a position that the lady faces the spectators; at the conclusion of the second, they should have passed entirely around one another. In the *pas de côté*, the hands are released and the partners separate, passing to their original positions, the lady by means of *pas de menuet à gauche*, and the gentleman by *pas de menuet à droite*.

Following this is the *pas à droite double*, during which the right arm is lowered gently,    4

           *Balancé de Menuet*, and raise left arm,                                 2

           *Tour de main gauche*,                                                    6

**VI.**

Fig. 493 shows the figure of the *tour de main gauche:*

FIG. 493.

           *Pas de Menuet à droite double*,                                          4

           *Pas de Menuet à gauche double*.                                          4

### FOURTH COUPLET

MEAS.

After this the principal figure is again executed three times, the first *traversée* thereof filling the last four measures of the third couplet, and the remainder the entire thirty-two measures of the fourth couplet; at the conclusion of which the dancers are in the positions shown in Fig. 494.

VII.

FIG. 494.

36

### FIFTH COUPLET — CODA (CONCLUSION)

752. *Balancé de Menuet,* with raising of both hands, preparatory to execution of *demi-tour des deux mains* and two *pas de menuet en avant,* which bring the dancers into the relative positions shown in Fig. 495, from which they again come to their original places; the lady by means of a *pas de menuet à gauche* and the gentleman by *pas de menuet à droite.*

VIII.

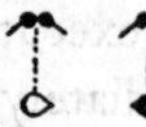

FIG. 495.

8

753. The dance is finished by two bows similar to those at the beginning, but instead of retreating upon the seventh and eighth measures, the gentleman conducts the lady to her seat.

8

# Chapter XV

## THE GAVOTTE

THE oldest description of the Gavotte now extant, or at least the oldest intelligible description, is to be found in the " Orchesographie" of Thoinot Arbeau, published in 1588. But the music there given is so entirely out of date, that it would be impossible to adapt it to dancing purposes to-day without changing it completely, and making alterations which would destroy the originality of the dance, and therefore render reproduction of no value.

**755.** The music of the Gavotte which reached the highest mark of favour, and which was said to be the work of Louis XIII, King of France (born in 1601), must have been composed at a much later date than is supposed, or altered to correspond with the more recent rules of musical composition.

**756.** The Gavotte which has lived to receive the title of *la danse classique* in our day was written by Gaetano Vestris. Its steps are so well chosen and so admirably combined that one could hardly conceive a more beautiful effect; and as the dance may be executed with either simple or artistic steps, it is little wonder that so worthy a production has received so fitting an honorary title.

**757.** The first part of the *Menuet de la Reine*, by Gardel (§ 728), is generally danced at the commencement and conclusion of this Gavotte, before which the strain of eight measures is played twice through. During the first rendering, the gentleman conducts his lady to the appointed position; and during the repetition the usual introductory bows are executed. At the conclusion a similar strain is played, first for the final bows, and then for the leading of the ladies to seats.

### COUPLET AND FIGURE

**758.** It should always be borne in mind that the term "couplet" means a "strophe," which contains the entire melody of the music, and that the word "figure" refers only to the lines described by the dancers upon the floor. A single figure requires only from eight to twelve measures of music.

**759.** Exercise 104. La Gavotte de G. Vestris [Fig. 496].

## La Gavotte de G. Vestris.

Chorégraphie de F. A. Zorn.

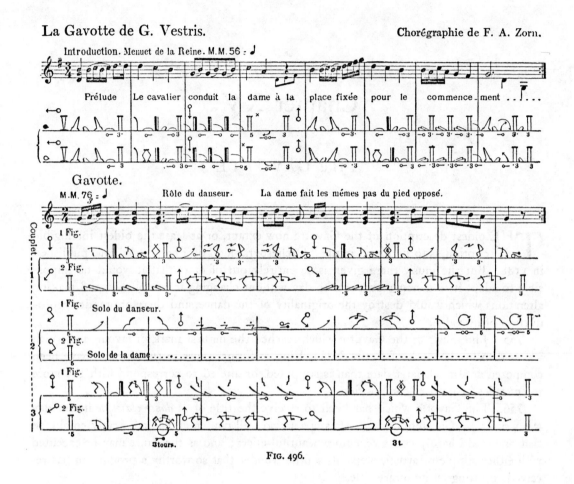

FIG. 496.

| SYLL. | | | MEAS. |
|---|---|---|---|
| | **Introduction. "La Menuet de la Reine."** | | |
| | **Prelude.** | | 8 |
| | The gentleman leads his partner to the place from which the Gavotte is to start, and both stand in 1st position. | | I |
| | THE LADY'S PART | THE GENTLEMAN'S PART | |
| 1 | Carry right foot to 2d position; | Carry right foot to 2d position; | |
| 2 | Transfer; | Transfer; | |
| 3 | Draw left into anterior 3d position preparatory to the curtesy. | Draw left into posterior 3d position preparatory to the bow. | I |

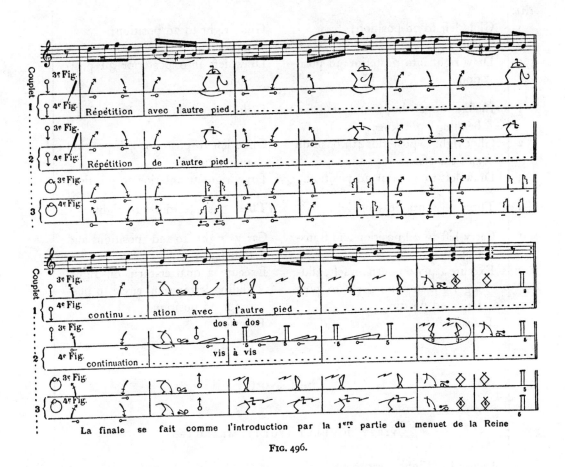

FIG. 496.

| SYLL. | | | MEAS. |
|---|---|---|---|
| 1 | Incline upper body and transfer; | Incline upper body and transfer, simultaneously bending right knee; | |
| 2 | Glide left to posterior 4th position and transfer; | Glide right to posterior 4th position and transfer; | |
| 3 | Draw right to anterior 3d position. | Draw left to anterior 3d position. | 1 |
| 1–3 | Three walking steps forward, beginning with left foot. | Three walking steps forward, beginning with right foot. | 1 |
| 1 | Carry right to anterior 5th position; | Carry left to anterior 5th position; | |
| 2 | Execute a quarter-turn to left on both feet; | Execute a quarter-turn to right on both feet; | |
| 3 | Sink to anterior 3d position of left. | Sink to anterior 3d position of right. | 1 |

| SYLL. | | | MEAS. |
|---|---|---|---|
| 1 | Glide left to 2d position; | Glide right to 2d position; | |
| 2 | Transfer; | Transfer; | |
| 3 | Draw right into posterior 3d position. | Draw left into posterior 3d position. | 1 |
| 1 | Incline upper body and transfer, bending right knee; | Incline upper body and transfer; | |
| 2 | Glide right to posterior 4th position and transfer; | Glide left to posterior 4th position and transfer; | |
| 3 | Draw left to anterior 3d position. | Draw right to anterior 3d position. | 1 |
| 1–3 | Three glissades dessous, left. | Three glissades dessous, right. | 1 |
| 1 | Carry left to 2d position and transfer; | Carry right to 2d position and transfer; | |
| 2 | Execute a quarter-turn on left, gliding right in semi-circle to posterior 3d position; | Execute a quarter-turn on right, gliding left in semi-circle to posterior 3d position; | |
| 3 | Transfer.* | Transfer.* | 1 |

## The Gavotte†

### FIRST COUPLET (FORTY MEASURES)

**Figure 1.** (Eight measures.)

| | | MEAS. |
|---|---|---|
| 1–3 | Preparation: Anterior 3d position of right. | 1 |
| 1 | Forward.    One *temps levé* into 4th position. | |
| 2 | One *assemblé dessus* with left. | |
| 3 | One *changement de jambes sauté* into 3d position. | 1 |
| 1–6 | Backward.   Three *jetés dessous* and one *assemblé dessus*. | 2 |

NOTE. — The first *jeté* is always toward the supporting foot.

Forward :   One *temps levé* into 4th position.
           One *assemblé dessus* with left.
           One *entrechat quatre*.          2

---

\* This transfer brings both dancers into proper position for the execution of the Gavotte.

† The description which follows is of the gentleman's part. The lady executes the same steps and figures, but in counter-motion.

| | MEAS. |
|---|---|
| Backward: Two *jetés dessous* and one *assemblé dessus*, thus bringing left into anterior 3d position. | 2 |

Note. — The rhythm of the music of the fourth and eighth measures renders this variation necessary.

### Figure II. (Eight measures.)

| | |
|---|---|
| Cross to right, behind lady. | |
| Three *glissades croisées* (*dessous, dessus-dessous*). | 2 |
| Backward: Four *pas ailes de pigeon*. | 2 |
| Recross to left behind lady. | |
| Three *glissades croisées*. | 2 |
| Backward: Three *pas ailes de pigeon*. | 2 |

### Figure III. (Twelve measures).

| | |
|---|---|
| Upon the place: Half-turn to right, facing lady, with right in anterior 3d position. | |
| One *pas ballotté, dessus et dessous*. | |
| One *pas de zéphire* into intermediate (2-4) position with *demi-rond de jambe gauche en dehors* and 1-4 turn to left. | 2 |
| Repetition of preceding two measures, commencing with left foot. | 2 |
| Repetition of same two measures, commencing with right foot. | 2 |
| Beginning with left foot, one *ballotté dessus et dessous*, and one *assemblé dessous* into posterior 3d position of left. | 2 |
| Upon the place: Four *jetés dessous*. | 2 |
| Upon the place: One *assemblé dessous*, one *entrechat-quatre* and one *changement de jambe* to anterior 3d position of left. | 2 |

### Figure IV.

| | |
|---|---|
| Repetition of third figure with other foot (*Répétition avec l'autre pied.*) | 12 |

### SECOND COUPLET (FORTY MEASURES)

### Figure I. Gentleman's Solo (*Solo de Danseur*). (Eight measures). [Exercise 100, § 613].

| | |
|---|---|
| Cross to left and right. Two *pas de basque*. | 2 |
| Backward. Two *pas bourrées*, and one *assemblé dessous*. | 2 |
| Cross to right and left. Two *pas de basque brisés*. | 2 |
| Backward. Two *pirouettes basques* to right. | 2 |

### Figure II. Lady's Solo (*Solo de la Dame*). Eight measures.

| | |
|---|---|
| The same steps as the gentleman's solo, but in the counter-motion. | 8 |

**Figure III.** (Twelve measures.)

| | | |
|---|---|---:|
| Forward. | Gentleman beginning with right, lady with left. | |
| | One *pas ballotté* and one *pas de zéphire*. | 2 |
| | One *pas ballotté* and one *pas de zéphire*. | 2 |
| | One *pas ballotté* and one *pas de zéphire*. | 2 |
| | One *pas ballotté* and one *assemblé dessous* with left foot, during which the gentleman executes a quarter-turn to left, thus coming *dos-à-dos* to partner. | 2 |
| Backward. | Four *glissades croisées* to left. | 2 |
| Three-quarter-turn. | Two *jetés dessous* and one *assemblé dessus*, by which the gentleman comes into anterior 5th position of left. | 2 |

**Figure IV.** (Twelve measures.)

| | |
|---|---:|
| Repetition of Third Figure, beginning with other (gentleman's left, lady's right) foot, by which the dancers are brought *vis-à-vis* in the eighth measure. | 12 |

### THIRD COUPLET (FORTY MEASURES)

**Figure I.** (Eight measures.)

| | | |
|---|---|---:|
| Forward. | One *tempo levé sauté* into 4th position. | |
| | One *contretemps dessus* with left into 3d position. | |
| | One *changement de jambe*. | 2 |
| Backward. | Four alternate *temps de cuisse*, right, left, right, left. | 2 |
| Forward : | One *temps levé sauté* into 4th position. | |
| | One *contretemps dessus* with left into 3d position. | |
| | One *entrechat quatre ou huit*. | 2 |
| Backward: | Three alternate *temps de cuisse*, right, left, right. | 2 |

**Figure II.** (Eight measures.)

| | | |
|---|---|---:|
| Cross to right behind lady : | One *chassé*. | |
| | One *pirouette battue* of two or more turns (depending upon ability of dancer), by which the left foot comes into anterior 5th position. | 2 |
| Backward : | Four *pas ailes de pigeon*. | 2 |
| Cross to left before lady. | One *chassé*. | |
| | One *pirouette battue* of two or more turns ending in anterior 5th position of right. | 2 |
| Backward. | Three *pas ailes de pigeon*. | 2 |

**Figure III.** (Twelve measures.)

Slightly forward. One *ronde croisée entière*, the gentleman to right inside and the lady to left outside the circle.

One *pas ballotté*.

Two *temps fouettés dessus*.                                    2

Repeat preceding two measures.                                    2

Repeat preceding two measures.                                    2

Upon the place. One *ballotté* and one *assemblé dessous* with left foot.

Backward. Four *jetés*, one *assemblé* and two *changements de jambes*, ending in anterior 5th position of left.                                    4

**Figure IV.** (Twelve measures.)

Slightly forward. *Ronde séparée;* gentleman to left with left foot, and lady to right with right foot, with same steps as in *ronde croisée*, but in counter-motion.                                    6

Upon the place. One *ballotté* and one *assemblé dessous* with right.                                    2

Backward. Four *ailes de pigeon*.

One *assemblé dessous* with right foot, and

Two *entrechats quatre ou huit*, ending in anterior 5th position of right.                                    4

**761. Postlude.** Following the third couplet, the first part of the *Menuet de la Reine* is again executed, with the final *révérences*, the first to the spectators and the second to the partner; upon the seventh measure of which the gentleman offers the lady his right arm and courteously leads her to her seat.                                    8

# Chapter XVI

## SOCIAL ROUND DANCES

### The Galop and the Galopade

THE usual significance of the word "galop" is the most rapid pace of a horse, and the word "galopade" refers to a similar movement in dancing. "Galopade" is, therefore, a more correct *terme de danse* than "galop." The dance which is now known as the Galop was formerly called the Galopade, which name signifies a dance movement to the side by means of simple chasing steps. The word Galop refers technically to a waltz-like turning by means of alternate chasing steps (*chassés alternatifs*).

763. This dance, being one of the simplest of the round dances, and having been already introduced in the closing figures of the Quadrilles, will undoubtedly appeal to the teacher as the most natural transition to the round dances.

The Galop is written in 2-4 measure, and the accent is equally placed upon both *tempi*. The steps are either simple or alternate chasing steps. (See §§ 476 and 477.)

Simple chasing steps to the side should be practiced until the student is competent to execute them smoothly, either in repetition or alternately, after which a *temps fouetté* may be added to the exercise. (See §§ 476 and 488.)

By combining a whip-step (*fouetté*) with three simple chasing steps upon two measures of music, the phrase may be immediately repeated in the opposite direction; if, however, the *enchaînement* is to extend through four measures, seven chasing steps and a whip-step should be used.

Exercise 105. Galop of the Amazons (*Galop d'Amazones*). [Fig. 497.]

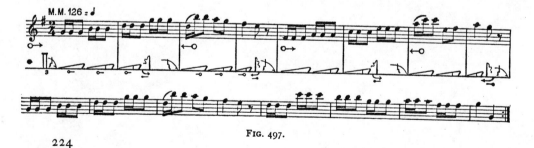

FIG. 497.

**764.** The following figure is not only of great value in practicing the above combinations, but it affords the pupil an agreeable diversion: —

## THE STAR OF FOUR COUPLES (L'ÉTOILE À QUATRE COUPLES)

As the Waltz position is assumed in this figure, it will be necessary to make a digression and explain it.

**765.** The carriage of the arms in the Waltz position has as its foundation the 3d arm position, as shown in Fig. 498. The dancers stand facing one another, and near enough for the gentleman to pass his right arm behind the lady, in order to hold and guide her.

The lady places her right hand, palm downward, in the gentleman's left, and her left hand upon the gentleman's right arm. Care should be taken that the feet do not touch. The position is illustrated by Figs. 499 and 500.

FIG. 498.

FIG. 499.

FIG. 500.

**766.** The gentleman must never place his arm so far around the lady's waist as to bring her left shoulder in line with his right, nor should he allow himself to raise his left elbow, thus drawing her hand close to him; neither should he contract the habit of supporting his left hand upon his hip, as that position is a constant menace to other dancers. The hand stretched horizontally to the side is not only awkward and uncomfortable, but takes too much room; the idea that such an attitude is "smart" is absurd.

The lady must never allow her weight to rest upon the right arm of her partner, for such a position not only interferes with freedom of movement, but is offensive to good taste. This lack of reserve is more common in our day than ever before.

**767.** The most correct Waltz position is a perfectly natural carriage of the body with both arms in 3d position. This is clearly shown in Fig. 498, above.

**768.** Had not our judgment and taste been perverted by that most unreasonable tyrant we call fashion, there is little doubt that we should unhesitatingly pronounce the Waltz position to be indecent, for even now it would be considered a flagrant insult should a gentleman place his arm around the waist of the lady with whom he is sitting. Why then, should such a liberty be excused, merely because the music of the dance is in the air? It would never be tolerated beyond the duration of the music. Where is the logic of it?

769.  But to return to the figure of the star (*l'étoile*). The four couples stand in the Waltz position, in the respective corners of a square, as shown in Fig. 501.

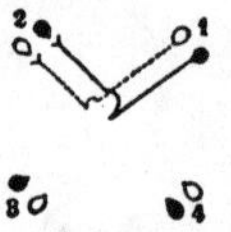

FIG. 501.

NOTE. — It is always understood that the gentleman commences with the left, and the lady with the right foot, in the waltz position.

| | MEAS. |
|---|---|
| All execute three *chassés simples* and one *fouetté* with quarter-turn to right. | 2 |
| All execute the same steps to next corner at right. In this the gentleman begins naturally with the right and the lady with the left foot. | 2 |
| It will be found that by turning the head slightly in the direction of the steps, the turning will be more easily made, and the entire figure will present a more pleasing appearance. | |
| Repetition of preceding four measures to next corner to the right. | 4 |
| Repetition of preceding eight measures, which restores dancers to original places in the square. | 8 |

770.  The above figure, if executed by four couples, is known as *l'étoile simple* or *étoile à quatre couples*. If executed by eight couples, it is known as *la double étoile* (the double star), in which case the dancers form an octagon, as shown in Fig. 502. Couples 1, 3, 5 and 7 are known as the first party, and couples 2, 4, 6 and 8 as the second party.

FIG. 502.

| | |
|---|---|
| First party.  Forward to centre and thence to next corner at the right. | 4 |
| Second party.  Forward to centre and thence to next side at the right. | 4 |
| First party.  Repetition of first four measures. | 4 |
| Second party.  Repetition of second four measures. | 4 |
| Repetition of same movements to original places. | 16 |

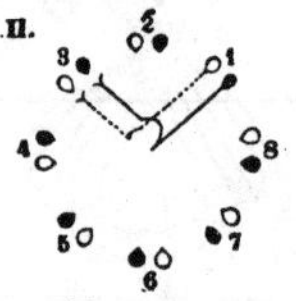

Either star may be executed as a Cotillion figure with Galop steps, or by substituting therefor the steps of the Mazurka-Polka.

The application of the Galop step to the last figure of the Quadrille is plainly demonstrated by this figure (§ 692).

## The Galop-Waltz

771.  Literally, the word "waltz" means to turn forward from the place, or to advance by turning; and in waltzing one either moves from his place by turning or causes his partner to move from place. Thus we may say that every round dance is a Waltz, the particular kind of Waltz being designated by prefixing another word.

If, for instance, the music is that of a Galop and the dancer executes Galop steps, the addition of the turnings makes the dance a Galop-Waltz; in the same manner, Polka steps produce a Polka-Waltz, Mazurka steps a Mazurka-Waltz, and so on.

772. The steps of the Galop-Waltz are neither more nor less than the alternate simple chasing steps (*chassés alternatifs*) in which the rear foot is drawn into posterior 3d position after each *chassé* to the side, thus forming the necessary preparation for the succeeding *chassé*, which completes the turn.

A half-turn must be made upon each *chassé*, and for this purpose the gentleman turns to the left backward, and the lady to the right forward upon the first; and the gentleman to the right forward and the lady to the left backward upon the second *chassé*.

773. The Line of Direction. By means of the turns above described, the dancing couple proceed, almost involuntarily, along the line of a large circle, around the hall.

To illustrate: let us imagine such a circle drawn upon the floor, as the line upon which we are to waltz. If one faces the centre, the direction line to the right is at his right, and that to the left is at his left side.

### THE FIGURE OF THE WALTZ-DANCES

774. As a rule, round dances proceed along the line to the right, and the ordinary Waltz turns to the right upon the line of direction are shown in Fig. 503.

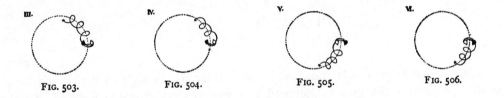

III.    IV.    V.    VI.

FIG. 503.  FIG. 504.  FIG. 505.  FIG. 506.

The reverse of this movement to the right is represented in Fig. 504.

Figs. 505 and 506 show the Waltz turns in ordinary and in reversed form, going to the left along the line of direction.

## The Reverse of the Galop (*Le Galop à L'envers*)

775. For the sake of variety, skilful dancers frequently turn in the opposite direction upon the direction line. This variation is what is known as "reversing" or "waltzing to the left" (*à l'envers ou à rebours*). The movement calls for considerable dexterity, for while the ordinary Waltz turn along the direction line to the right contains somewhat less

than a whole turn, depending upon the size of the grand circle, the reverse turn calls for something more than a whole turn.

776. The line of direction remains unchanged in the "reverse" and the dancers continue in the same general direction, because other couples who may be following have no way of learning that those in front contemplate changing, and for some couples to start around the hall in the other direction would render collisions almost unavoidable.

777. It is the general custom to commence the Galop with several simple chasing steps to the side, without turning. Particular attention must be paid to the music, else the dancer will fall into false cadence, in which case his steps will not coincide either with those of the couples who are dancing correctly, or with the rhythm of the music.

## The Pursuit (*La Poursuite*)

778. The Galop is varied by dancing directly forward without turning, in which movement the dancers move along the line of direction without revolving. This figure is called *La Poursuite* by the French, and in it the gentleman should always dance backwards, allowing the lady to follow him dancing forwards, particularly if her dress reaches the floor. Indeed, this rule is generally conceded to be invariable, notwithstanding the fact that the figure could be executed in reversed order.

## The Waltz (*La Valse*)

779. As has been already stated, any round dance may be called a Waltz, and the particular species of Waltz may be indicated by prefixing a denominative word. If, however, no such word is prefixed, and the dance is spoken of simply as a "Waltz," one always understands that the sociable national dance of Germany is meant.

780. Originally, only the three-step Waltz was danced, and that slowly, sometimes very slowly($56 = \downarrow$). This gave good dancers so smooth and easy an appearance that it was often said that they "could dance upon a plate."

781. Since that time, however, the beautiful three-step Waltz has disappeared in all but a few of the German states, and even there it is danced in more rapid tempo, the dancers sometimes demanding as nonsensical a tempo as 88 to 100.

782. The proper tempo of a dance depends upon its nature, as has been explained in § 407. If the music is too slow, the dancer is unable to prolong the rhythm to coincide with it, and if the next step is begun before its time the effect is extremely annoying. If the music is too rapid, it is difficult for the dancer to follow it without becoming "winded," and to dance in that condition is neither agreeable nor artistic.

**783.** As the result of many experiments with the metronome, the Author has come to the conclusion that the most rapid tempo in which the waltz can be properly executed is seventy-two measures per minute.

**784.** Johann Strauss, senior, the Waltz king, played Waltzes at about 72, and Lanner rendered them at about 76. In Germany, the tempo runs from 69 to 72; in Paris, as high as 76; in tranquil England, from 66 to 69; and in Russia many young persons waltz at a tempo so rapid that few musicians can follow it.

## The Two-Syllable Waltz (*La Valse à Deux Temps*)

**785.** This Waltz should be called the *Chassé*-Waltz, or chasing step Waltz, and it is rather a six than a three step Waltz. The real *Valse à deux temps* is described in § 834, under the name of the Hop Waltz or Two-Step.

**786.** The so-called Vienna Waltz or *Valse à deux temps* has, during the last fifty years, come into vogue and nearly displaced the beautiful three-step Waltz. This so-called Vienna Waltz is, in reality, only the Galop danced in Waltz time, for the Viennese delight in rapid dancing and make everything a Galop, compelling even fashion to follow them by their bewitching merriment.

**787.** It is the rhythm, and not the step combination, which constitutes the difference between the Galop-Waltz and the *Valse à deux temps*.

For the Galop-Waltz the music is written in 2-4 measure and rendered with practically the same accent on each syllable; the dancer therefore requires an equal length of time for each step-syllable.

For the *Valse à deux temps*, the music, which is in 3-4 measure, is played with a strongly accented first syllable, and the dancer in accenting his first step-syllable to correspond with the music, almost involuntarily prolongs it to fill the second quarter-note of the measure. His sense of measure will almost invariably lead him to this prolongation if the music is properly phrased for the *Valse à deux temps*.

Exercise 106 [Fig. 507].

FIG. 507.

**788.** Although Waltz music is always written in 3-4 measure there is as wide a difference between the various compositions as between the different interpretations of them. For the *Chassé* Waltz or *Valse à deux temps*, the syncopated rhythm, such as one may find in the "Parisian Waltz" by Johann Strauss, is best adapted [Fig. 508].

FIG. 508.

789. For the slow three-step Waltz, the music of the Ländlers is best, viz., M. M. 54–60 = ♩.[Fig. 509].

FIG. 509.

790. The Fairy Waltz of J. Labitzki contains a most exquisite rhythm, if played at about 72 [Fig. 510].

FIG. 510.

791. Still, notwithstanding all that has been said regarding the various compositions, more depends upon the rendering of the music than upon the music itself, and a really efficient musician can interpret any Waltz composition so that it will fit the requirements of either style of the dance [Figs. 511 and 512].

For Two-Step Waltz

FIG. 511.

For Three-Step Waltz

FIG. 512.

792. All that has been said regarding the Waltz position, direction, figure and changes, in connection with the Galop, is equally applicable to the Waltz.

## The Three or Six-Step Waltz (*La Valse à Trois ou à Six Temps*)

**793.** There is little more to be said of this beautiful dance beyond what has been already explained. An entire rotation or step-sentence contains two measures or six syllables, and for that reason we may style it the six-step Waltz, which title is literally proper.

**794.** Exercise 107. Three-or Six-Step Waltz (*Valse à trois ou à six temps*) [Fig. 513a].

FIG. 513.

The key indicates that the regular waltz turn to the right is to be made along the line of direction to the right, and the symbol of the gentleman means that the choregraphy shows the step combination for the gentleman only. The lady begins the same combination upon the first syllable of the second measure, the gentleman having by that time completed a half-turn.

Preparation: Anterior 3d position of right.

**First Syllable.** Carry the right foot forward slightly toward the right into 4th position, and transfer.

**Second syllable.** Glide left foot forward into the crossed 4th position, executing at the same time a half-turn upon the right, and transfer.

**Third syllable.** Draw the right backward into anterior 3d position, transfer and carry left to posterior 4th balancing position (*coupé dessus*) as a preparation for the commencement of the next measure.

**Fourth syllable.** Put down the left in posterior 4th position and transfer.

**Fifth syllable.** Glide right backward into crossed posterior 4th position, at the same time executing a half-turn upon the left, and transfer.

**Sixth syllable.** Draw the left foot forward into posterior 3d position and transfer, immediately carrying the right into anterior 4th balancing position (*coupé dessous*), ready to repeat the sentence and completing the Waltz turn.

**795.** It is therefore plainly to be seen that to execute a complete Waltz turn the dancer requires two measures of music, upon which he makes either more or less than a complete rotation, in accordance with the requirements of maintaining the line of direction as explained in § 775.

**796.** It is customary for the gentleman to commence upon the first note of the first measure and the lady upon the first note of the second measure.

The acquirement of the Waltz step is far from difficult, but in order to waltz smoothly and gracefully one must practice long and diligently.

**797.** There is no other round dance so conducive to dizziness as the Three-Step Waltz. One should therefore immediately stop upon the first appearance of this sensation, and either turn three times in the opposite direction, thus dispelling it, or wait a short period until it has passed. In this way one may rapidly accustom himself to the movement, but unless the dizziness is avoided at once it is likely to result in headache or some other disagreeable feeling.

**798.** In the Three-Step Waltz, as in the Galop, one may dance directly forward or backward, or turn to the left, but these variations require considerable practice and ability.

These variations were first acccepted in Germany under the Bohemian name *Redowak*, (see § 811), about 1830.

## The Reverse Waltz (*La Valse à l'Envers*)

**799.** The execution of this movement is explained by Bernhard Klemm in his "Catechism" in a masterly manner:—

"The gentleman executes alone, and as a preparation, the first three steps of the ordinary Waltz (to the right), after which he immediately commences the succeeding six steps with the left foot, turning to the left, while the lady begins the same six steps with her right foot and turns in the same direction as the gentleman."

**800.** Exercise 108 shows the choregraphy of the "Reverse." In dancing it the gentleman commences with the first half of the sentence, and the lady with its second half [§794, Fig. 513*b*].

## The Polka (*La Polka*)

**801.** Rarely, if indeed ever, has a dance received so much honor, or so much attention, as was paid to the Polka in 1844, when the whole world wrote and talked about it, and apparently thought little of anything else.

Every newspaper contained essays singing the praises of the dance, and persons dressed their hair *à la polka*, with *pomade à la polka*, ate cakes *à la polka*, wore gowns *à la polka*, and so forth; and almost numberless musical compositions for the dance were published. Every music store put out "original Polkas," every picture store displayed "Polka" pictures, and so many "true" and conflicting stories were told about the origin of the dance, that Professor Schlosser might have spent months had he reviewed them all.

At that time the author travelled from Odessa to Vienna and Paris, for no other reason than to visit the most celebrated teachers of the Polka. And what did he find? Only the dance which, as a child, he had learned from his father under the name of the "Scotch Waltz,"·and which he had shown to his pupils in Dresden in 1835, in Christiania in 1836, and in Paris in 1837. It was not, however, until 1844 that this dance became known in Paris to those persons who understood how to advertise it.

802. The Tour or the Parisian Polka, once so popular, has long since disappeared, and the Polka-Quadrille, composed in 1845 in Paris, never achieved a fashionable position.

803. The music of the Polka is in 2-4, or more properly 4-8 measure, of which the first eighth-note is strongly and the third lightly accented. The step-sentence, however, may be said to commence upon this third eighth-note.

804. The Amazons Polka, by Emil Titl, was among the first of the so-called original Polkas, and The Tour (*La Tour*) or Parisian Polka, as well as the Polka-Quadrille were arranged upon that composition.

The composer gave this music the title of "The Bohemian Amazons," and the degree of the metronome was so slow (88) that the steps could be executed with the utmost precision. In social dances, however, few young people are satisfied with such a tempo, and it was accordingly accelerated. The most rapid tempo in which the steps can be accurately executed is 108.

Exercise 109. Original Polka (*Polka Originale*) [Fig. 514].

FIG. 514.

805. As indicated by the key the steps are executed along the lines of the regular Waltz figure upon the direction line to the right, and the symbol shows that the script is the gentleman's part. He commences with the left foot.

806. Execution. Preparation: Anterior 3d position of left, with light raising on the right and lifting of the left in the part-measure.

First syllable. Put down left foot, and transfer.

Second syllable. Carry right to posterior 3d position, and transfer.

Third syllable. Glide left forward and sidewise, upon the sole, and transfer (this must be done whether one is dancing directly forward or is turning).

Fourth syllable. Draw right into posterior low 3d balancing position, ready for the commencement of the succeeding step.

The movement is *staccato*.

807. The "pursuit" and the "reverse" are easier of execution in the Polka than in the Galop or the Waltz, because of the hopping, and are therefore more often danced.

**808.** The Polka has been known by various names, such as the Hop-Polka, the *Polka Tremblante*, and the Parisian Polka, but they are all identical in execution.

In certain of the Rhine countries there is danced, under the name of the " Bavarian Polka," a combination which in Russia, England, France and in various other countries is called the " Scotch Polka," and which in Bavaria is known as the " Rheinländer."

**809.** In Vienna and certain other portions of Austria, a so-called " Rush Polka " is danced, in which there is no hopping, and which is played in more rapid tempo than the ordinary Polka. Indeed, this tempo is often so rapid as to change the dance to a Galop. Many authorities claim that there should be no hopping in the Polka. Let us consider — who is right?

**810.** There is but one way in which to bring about uniform opinions among the various authorities upon the art of dancing, as to the different terms and expressions relating to it, and that is, by maintaining a society or a committee of thoroughly educated masters to whom questions may be referred for consideration, and whose findings shall be final. Until such a board of authority is established, we need not hope for anything but a Babel in the language of the dance.

A plan of this character has already been undertaken by the German Academy of the Art of Teaching Dancing, in Berlin, which includes members from other countries; and it is to be hoped that all friends and connoisseurs of the art will coöperate with this movement, in order that a Universal Academy of the Art of Dancing may be effected.

## Redowa (*Rejdovak*)

**811.** In the Bohemian language the word *rejdovat* signifies to push by turning to and fro, in the same manner that one would grasp the shafts of a wagon and push it backward, at the same time turning the shafts to guide it to a given place; and the noun of the word is spelt *rejdovak*.

This term may therefore be applied to the " pursuit " in the round dances; as, for instance, the Three-Step Waltz, in which one dancer is pushed backward along the line of direction.

**812.** The number of turns in the same direction is a matter of little or no consequence; but a change of figure every four measures as follows is recommended:

Four measures, Waltz turn to right.
    "     "    Gentleman going backward.
    "     "    Waltz turn to left.
    "     "    Lady going backward.

**813.** This combination of figures was adopted in Southern Germany about 1830, under the name of " Redowak," and the original music was as follows:

Exercise 110. *Redowa Originale* [Fig. 515].

FIG. 515.

## Redowaczka (*Redowatschka*)

814. The same variations were afterward applied to the Galopade, with a corresponding change to 2-4 measure, and the dance was called the " Redowaczka."

Exercise 111. *Redowaczka Originale* [Fig. 516].

FIG. 516.

815. At the time of the general acceptance of the Polka, similar variations were applied to that dance, and it was called the Redowa-Polka, which name has clung to it to this day.

NOTE. — The French write and pronounce the word " Redowa," following their usual practice of suppressing the final consonant.

816. Many beautiful and worthy compositions having been published under the title of " Redowa," by Karl Faust and others, in which a peculiar rhythm, similar to that of the Mazurka, was employed, it was thought worth while to invent a new step-sentence to correspond to them, and it is this that we now call the Redowa; and by an unimportant change in this sentence, or rather, by its repetition, the dance called the Mazurka-Polka was produced. (See § 823.)

817. Exercise 112. Modern Redowa-Step (*Pas de Redowa Moderne*) [Fig. 517].

FIG. 517.

Execution —Preparation for gentleman : Anterior 3d position of left.

First syllable. After a light hop upon the right foot in the part-measure, the gentleman glides the left foot into the 2d position (*temps levé glissé*), and transfers.

Second syllable. The right foot now follows into anterier 3d position, while the left is slightly raised and pushed sidewise from its position (*coupé latéral*).

Third syllable. The left foot, which hangs in the 2d balancing position, is now put down and receives the weight, while the right is carried immediately into the posterior 3d balancing position.

These three syllables fill one measure of music and contain a half-turn, and the same combination is repeated in the second measure with the other foot, to complete the rotation; the *enchainement* therefore extends through a period of two measures.

818. In this dance the reverse and pursuit are greatly facilitated by the lifting movement which it contains, and which consists principally of the throwing step (*jeté*). Such variations are therefore more common in the Redowa than in most of the round dances; indeed it is these variations which are responsible for its name.

819. The Redowa is frequently executed under the name of " Tyrolienne," and there are many compositions for it which have been made up solely of genuine Tyrolese airs. The disagreement which arises from such a condition is readily understood when one pauses to consider that few dancers or composers are competent to discriminate between the Bohemian and the Tyrolese music which determines the proper title of the dance. Indeed, such questions could only be suitably decided by a board of experts.

820. Again, the Redowa is, in certain other countries, known as the " Hunters' Schottische " or the " Hunters' Polka." These names, like those of many other dances and steps, are difficult to account for. The name " Hunters' Schottische " appears to have been first given to the dance in Berlin, and as the story is at least plausible, we will recite it.

About the time that the dance was introduced there was garrisoned in Berlin a military body known as the "Neuchatel Hunters," composed largely of good-looking young men whose handsome uniforms were greatly admired by the young ladies. It is said that one of the " Hunters " executed the steps of the dance is so exquisite a manner that his comrades endeavored to imitate him, and that the ladies therefore gave the dance the name of the " Hunter " Schottische or Polka, which title eventually spread to other places.

821. It sometimes happens that the same combination of steps is invented at two different places, and therefore receives correspondingly different names. Such a contingency is quite possible in the case of such combinations as the Polka step and in others which coincide so completely with the musical rhythm. This will, perhaps, account for the disparity of names in this case. Would it not be possible that such a coincidence might extend to a third or even a fourth location?

822. Young persons are seldom at a loss to find a name for that which pleases them, regardless of its absolute correctness, and this is only further evidence of the need of a universal academy of the art of dancing.

## Mazurka-Polka or Polka-Mazur

823. This dance is usually referred to as the " Mazurka-Polka," although most of the musical compositions for it are marked " Polka-Mazur." Which is the correct title?

824. Although the position, the figure, the line of direction, and at least a part of the step combination coincide with the Polka, the music is in 3-4 measure, and the rhythm so exactly similar to that of the Mazurka that one has only to quicken the tempo to be able to dance the Mazurka by it.

Now, if in the other round dances the music designates the character of the dance, as, for example, in the Galop-Waltz, which is danced to Galop music, and in the Mazurka-Waltz, which is danced to Mazurka music, why should not the same rule apply to this dance, which, being executed to Mazurka music, should be called the Mazurka-Polka?

825. It may be that the transposition has been made for the sake of easier pronunciation.

826. The invention of the dance is attributed to the Russian Princess, Marie Nicola-ewna; but, although the Princess was reputed to be an excellent dancer, and the Russian Court is a great patron of the art, still the author cannot affirm of his own knowledge that such was its origin. He will state, however, that the dance came to Odessa from St. Petersburg long before it was practiced in other countries.

The original music is said to have been that which is given herewith:

Exercise 113. Mazurka-Polka [Fig. 518].

FIG. 518.

Execution (The Gentleman's Part). Preparation: Anterior 3d position of left.

First syllable. *Temps levé glissé* and transfer.

Second syllable. *Coupé dessous latéral* (§ 493).

Third syllable. *Fouetté dessous* (§ 487).

Fourth syllable. *Glissé.*

Fifth syllable. *Coupé dessous latéral.*

Sixth syllable. *Jeté dessous* upon the left, followed by immediate lifting of right foot into posterior 3d balancing position.

This combination extends through two measures of music, and as a consequence the entire *enchaînement*, which contains a complete rotation, requires a period of four measures.

**827.** For the sake of variety, one may execute the first two measures *à rebours* and the remainder backward.

**828.** The *enchaînement* may also be combined with the Galopade. In this case the first two measures may be danced *à rebours* with a half-turn, and the remaining two measures filled in by the Galopade, which consists of five *chassés simples* and one *fouetté*.

This combination, applied to the star figures, presents a beautiful appearance (see Exercise 105 and § 770).

**829.** It would, however, be an improper combination to execute the first three syllables twice, and the last three only once, because the repetition of such an *enchaînement* would constitute a period of only six measures, and would throw the dancers into false cadence; but this would be remedied by executing the first three syllables three times and the last three once, as that combination would constitute an *enchaînement* of eight measures, thus ending in correct cadence.

## The Tyrolienne (*La Tyrolienne*)

**830.** The melodies of the Tyrolese dances are Alpine songs called *Yodlers* and *Ländlers*, to the accompaniment of which the boys and girls dance at weddings and festivals. In these dances the youth leads his partner gently by the hand, turns her beneath his arm, revolves most skilfully, and sinks upon one knee, while she dances around him ; he perhaps finishes by lifting her high in the air, all of which is done to the music of a charming Three-Step Waltz.

**831.** The author saw, at Dresden, in 1835, a dance called the Tyrolese or Balance Waltz, the music of which was a genuine Tyrolese air. Following is its choregraphy :

Exercise 114. *Tyrolienne Originale* [Fig. 519].

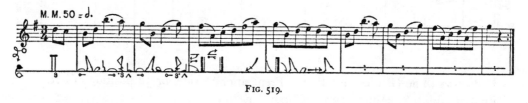

FIG. 519.

Preparation : Waltz position. Gentleman in anterior 3d position of left; lady, anterior 3d position of right.

### FIRST PART (SIXTEEN MEASURES)

**First Measure.**
The gentleman executes a *demi-balancé* to left, with inclination and turning to partner, while the lady executes a *demi-balancé* to right with corresponding inclination, but no turning.

First syllable. The gentleman glides left into 2d position and transfers.

Second syllable. Raises upon left foot and glides right into posterior 3d balancing position.

Third syllable. Lowers left heel (*une chute*). (See § 374.)

Second Measure. Repetition in opposite direction.

The lady executes the same steps in countermotion.

Third and Fourth Measures. Execute a complete rotation of the three-step Waltz, in which the gentleman leads backward with the second half, and the lady follows forward with the first half of the Waltz step.

This *enchainement* requires four measures of music, and is executed four times, necessitating the repetition of the period of eight measures of music.

### SECOND PART (SIXTEEN MEASURES)

The Three-Step Waltz.

### THIRD PART (SIXTEEN MEASURES)

Repetition of the first part.

### FOURTH PART (SIXTEEN MEASURES)

*Balancé* as in first part, but merely join hands. Two measures.

Turn, disengage hands and execute Waltz turn, the gentleman to the left and the lady to the right, again joining hands. Two measures.

Repeat figure three times. Twelve measures.

### FIFTH PART (SIXTEEN MEASURES)

Waltz.

Other Tyrolese figures may be added at will, and any number of couples may join in the dance. Indeed, certain couples may retire and make way for others to take their places, provided the regularity of the lines and the coincidence of the figures is maintained.

832. *Tyrolienne de l'Académie.* A *Tyrolienne* composed by Herr A. Freising has been unanimously adopted by the members of the German Academy and incorporated in their course of instruction. It is composed of various genuine figures of the Tyrolese national dances and is so arranged that it is suitable for use at the finest balls. The music, which corresponds both in motive and in rhythm to the peculiarities of the Tyrolese airs, is by Edouard Herold of Berlin.

833. A complete choreographic exposition of this very elegant dance will be given in another collection.

Its figures are briefly outlined in Freising's " Dance-Album " of 1885, page 52.

NOTE. — Herr Zorn never published the " Collection " referred to. — ED.

## Hop Waltz (*La Valse Sautillée*)

834. At the beginning of the nineteenth century there was danced, to very lively music, a Waltz in 2-4 measure known as the "Hop Waltz." The step consisted of one *jeté* and one *fouetté*, as shown in the following exercise:

Exercise 115. Hop Waltz (*La Valse sautillée*) [Fig. 520].

FIG. 520.

The key signifies the ordinary Waltz turns toward the right, and the symbols represent the role of the gentleman.

Preparation: Waltz position; gentleman, posterior 3d position of left; lady, posterior 3d position of right.

During the part-measure, the gentleman lifts the left foot into 2d balancing position.

First syllable. *Jeté* into 2d position, with immediate lifting of right into posterior 3d balancing position.

Second syllable. Hop upon left and extend left into 2d balancing position, as preparation for the succeeding *jeté*.

During these two syllables a half-turn is executed, and the rotation is completed in the second measure by the repetition of the same combination with the other foot.

The hop (*sauté*) may, as shown in the script of the third and fourth measures, be substituted by a *fouetté*, which will embellish the movement.

## Balance Waltz (*Valse Balancée*)

835. The same steps are also applied to the regular 3-4 Waltz, in which case there is no *jeté* in the first syllable, and the transfer of weight is accomplished without hopping. This movement is known as the two-step Waltz, and the same movement is also called the Balance Waltz (*La Valse Balancée*), under which name it is explained in Klemm's "Catechism."

While the name "Two-Step" or "Two-Step Waltz" is in itself literally correct, inasmuch as only two transfers of weight are made during a complete Waltz turn, it might be well to call it the "*Dégagée* Waltz," to distinguish it from the *Balancée* Waltz of the *Tyrolienne*.

Exercise 116. Balance Waltz (*Lá Valse Balancée*) [Fig. 521].

FIG. 521.

Execution. — Preparation : First position. During the part-measure, the gentleman carries the left foot into 2d position, at the same time hopping upon the right.

First syllable. Put down left in 2d position and transfer.

Second syllable. Hop on left foot, simultaneously executing a *rond de jambe en dehors* with the right.

Third syllable. Put down right in 2d position, and transfer.

Fourth syllable. Hop on right and carry left into 2d balancing position as preparation for the next step.

These four syllables contain a complete Waltz turn and require two measures of music. It is unnecessary to state that the lady executes the same movements as the gentleman, but in counter-motion, thus maintaining the coincidence of their respective parts.

Persons of sufficient skill may make this a very beautiful dance, by doubling the *rond de jambe* and "beating" the *temps levé* in the part-measure; but unless one is especially proficient such attempts will be extremely unlovely.

## The 5-4 Waltz (*Valse en Cinq Temps*)

**836.** A Waltz in 5-4 measure, which was said to have originated in Paris, was at one time brought out, but its rhythm was so greatly at variance with the ordinary sense of measure that it was very short-lived and the endeavor to make it fashionable resulted in utter failure.

**837.** Nearly the same fate overtook the *Sicilienne* and the *Impériale*, which were published, with notes and descriptions, in 1854. They were too complicated to attain popularity.

## The Varsovianna (*La Varsouvienne*)

**838.** This was another round dance of the same period, but it was more favorably received than the three preceding, and thus lived longer and spread farther. It is occasionally danced even at the present time.

**839.** The original music and choregraphic description are given herewith.

Exercise 117.  The Varsovianna (*La Varsouvienne*) [Fig. 522].

FIG. 522.

The key indicates that the dance is to proceed by means of the regular Waltz turns, along the line of direction to the right, and the auxiliary keys, which are under the part measures, indicate the particular direction in which the movements should go at that point, and which must be maintained until changed by another auxiliary key.

It is true that the direction may be ascertained by referring to the signs of the positions and movements, but the use of auxiliary keys often serves to expedite matters by increasing the clearness of the script.

**840.** Preparation: Gentleman's part. Posterior 3d position of left with inclined direction of sole.  During the part-measure the gentleman carries the left foot to the side.

### FIRST PART (EIGHT MEASURES)

First syllable.  Put down left in 2d position and transfer.

Second syllable.  *Coupé dessous latéral* with right, thus forcing the left into 2d balancing position.

Third syllable.  *Jeté* upon left, with immediate carrying of right into posterior 3d balancing position, with simultaneous half-turn to the left backward.

Fourth and fifth syllables.  Put down right foot in 2d position and hold same for the duration of a half-note.

Sixth syllable. Carry right backward into the posterior 3d and thence to 2d balancing position.

This step-sentence requires two measures of music, and its repetition by the other foot in the succeeding two measures constitutes an *enchainement* of four measures, and completes the rotation. It will be noted, however, that the gentleman must, in order to complete the Waltz turn upon the second *jeté*, execute a half-turn to the right forward.

The same *enchainement* is repeated upon the next four measures.

### SECOND PART (EIGHT MEASURES)

841. In this the rhythm of the music necessitates a different combination of movements, as follows:

Part measure. The left foot is raised into posterior 3d balancing position and then stretched into 2d balancing position.

First syllable. Put down left in 2d position and transfer.

Second syllable. *Coupé dessous latéral* with right.

Third syllable. *Fouetté dessous* (§ 487).

Fourth, fifth and sixth syllables. Repetition of first, second and third.

Seventh syllable. Put down left in 2d position and transfer.

Eighth syllable. *Coupé latéral.*

Ninth syllable. *Jeté* upon left, carry right into posterior 3d and thence to 2d balancing position with simultaneous half-turn to the left backward.

Tenth and eleventh syllables. Put down right foot in 2d position, and hold same for duration of a half-note.

Twelfth syllable. Carry left backward into posterior 3d, and thence to 2d position.

This sentence is repeated upon the succeeding four measures with the other foot; the whole *enchainement* therefore extends through a period of eight measures.

842. In the original music, which was composed by Johann Strauss, still other rhythmic variations occur, but it will be easy for dancing teachers and other persons who have followed these examples closely to discover or to invent suitable combinations for these variations.

843. If, however, the measure is changed from 3-4 time, it will be necessary to adapt the movements to the requirements of the case.


## Krakoviak (*Cracovienne*)


844. That this dance originated in Cracow may be inferred from its very name; but although it is not, as sometimes stated, the actual national dance of the Cracovians, but merely a social dance intended for the drawing-room, its music and its movement are alike true to the national characteristics of that people.

Of the many compositions that have been published for this dance, the most popular is that which follows:

Exercise 118. Krakoviak (*Cracovienne*) [Fig. 523].

Fig. 523.

Preparation: Both stand in anterior 3d sole position of right.

Position: The gentleman holds the lady as in Walz position, but allows his left arm to hang naturally at the side, or supports it by placing the back of the closed hand upon his hip.

Note: Some prefer to carry the left arm behind the back or to raise it to 4th position.

The lady rests her left hand lightly upon the right shoulder of her partner, and either holds her dress gracefully with the right hand, or supports her hand open upon her hip. The Polish ladies assume this attitude with an inimitable grace, quite in keeping with their extraordinary talent as dancers.

FIRST HALF

Both begin with the right foot and execute three *pas ordinaires* and one *frappé* forward, along the line of direction, in the same manner as in the Mazurka (§§ 880 to 883), but in 2-4 measure; finishing in the part measure by a simultaneous raising upon the left foot and lifting of the right into an anterior balancing position.

First Measure.

First syllable. Put down right foot, which glides forward into 4-5 position, and transfer, immediately lifting left foot into posterior 4th balancing position with slightly bended knee, and inclined or perpendicular direction of the sole.

Second syllable. Hop on right foot and carry left forward in a circle to anterior 4th balancing position, at the same time "raising" upon the right foot, in preparation for the succeeding step.

Second Measure. Repetition with left foot.

Third Measure. Repetition with right foot.

Fourth Measure.

The lady executes a fourth *pas ordinaire*, and then crosses over by means of a *tour boiteux*, which consists of four *pas boiteux*, while the gentleman executes the following enchainment:

First syllable. Put down left in 2d parallel position, at the same time turning the right foot upon the ball into corresponding position.

Second syllable. Strike the heels together, thus coming into a half-outward 1st position, and immediately carry the left into posterior 5th ball position, in readiness for the *pas de ciseaux en tournant*.

Many dancers execute, in place of the beating of heels, three audible steps in 3d sole position (*pas frappés*), of which the first and third are more strongly accented than the second. This figure is quite in harmony with the spirit of the dance, but in large parties, where excitement is almost unavoidable, may so degenerate as to become nothing more than a rude tramping.

These four measures constitute the first half of the *enchaînement*.

SECOND HALF

845. The Second Half consists of the *tour boiteux*, in which, as has been already stated, the lady goes around her partner by means of four *pas boiteux*, while he executes three *pas de ciseaux en tournant*, carries the left foot into parallel 2d position, and strikes the heels together, or else executes three *pas frappés*; thus finishing the *enchaînement* of eight measures in such time that the part-measure may be used as preparation for a repetition.

Unless the *enchaînement* is begun with the commencement of the *clausula*, the dancers will fall into false cadence, and the entire movement will appear ridiculous.

## Mazurka-Waltz (*Valse de Mazourka*)

846. The title of this dance is self-explanatory, for it is a Waltz movement executed in either 3-4 or 6-8 Mazurka time in periods of eight or sixteen measures. The dance has become widely spread, but is particularly popular in Poland.

Execution. Preparation: Gentlemen left and lady right foot in anterior 3d position.

The gentleman holds the left hand of the lady in his right and leads her through the first half of the *enchaînement*, but assumes the regular Waltz position for the second half. The dance may be very beautifully varied by carrying the disengaged arms in different graceful ways.

Exercise 119. Mazurka-Waltz (*Valse-Mazourka*) [Fig. 524].

FIG. 524.

FIRST HALF

*a. Promenade:* Both execute, upon the first four measures, four *pas ordinaires*, the gentleman commencing with the left foot and the lady with the right.

SECOND HALF

During the succeeding four measures, which constitute the second half of the *clausula*, the dancers assume the Waltz position, and execute the same steps with Waltz turns along the line of direction.

This *enchainement*, therefore, requires eight measures, and particular care should be taken in it to observe the proper cadence.

847. Any of the Mazurka steps other than the *pas boiteux* (which cannot be alternated) may be used in this *enchainement*.

848. The Poles usually dance the Mazurka-Waltz, or, as they pronounce it, the *Valse-Mâzur*, as a *promenade* of eight measures, combined and alternating with eight measures of turning, as in the Waltz.

For the sake of brevity, only four measures of the figures have been written in Exercises 119 *a* and 119 *b*.

849. Execution of Exercise 119 *b* [Fig. 524].

Preparation: 1st position. During the part-measure the gentleman carries the left foot into the low balancing 2d position, turning the toe slightly forward.

First Measure. *Pas battu parallèle.* (This is explained in § 885, and written choregraphically in Exercise 119*b*).

Second Measure. *Pas ordinaire* to left, turning in that direction on the left foot upon the third syllable.

Third and Fourth Measures. Repetition of the 1st and 2d with other foot.

850. Exercise 119 *c* [Fig. 524]. (This exercise is described in Klemm's " Catechism " as the *Valse Russe* or " Russian Waltz."

Execution: The preparation and the first measure of this are exactly similar to the corresponding portion of Exercise 119 *b*, and finish in the balancing 2d position of the left. The second measure is executed by the gentleman as follows:

First syllable. *Jeté* to left and transfer.

Second syllable. Carry the left backward into the crossed 4-5 ball position, and execute a half-turn to the left backward, finishing in anterior 3d position of left.

Third syllable. Finish by *coupé dessous* with left.

The same step-sentence is repeated in counter-motion with the other foot upon the succeeding two measures.

The lady, as in all other round dances, executes the same steps as the gentleman, but in the opposite direction, thus maintaining the coincidence of movement along the line of direction.

## Galop-Polka or Glide-Polka (*L'Esmeralda*)

**851.** This combination of steps, which consists of two simple Galopade steps to the side and one clearly accented Polka-step, is perfectly described by the name "Galop-Polka," and is so absolutely in harmony with the rhythm of a properly arranged musical composition that its execution becomes almost involuntary. The "Apropos Polka," by Karl Faust (Op. 68), is a good instance of this.

Many dancing-masters, among whom was the Author, had, previous to the appearance of this dance, discovered the step-sequence and given it the name of the Galop-Polka, little thinking that the euphonious Spanish name *Esmeralda*, which was derived from a similar combination occurring in the chorus of a ballet of that name, had elsewhere been applied to it.

**852.** The music is in 2-4 measure, and in the absence of a specially arranged composition, any Polka music may be used, provided the rhythm given above the lines of the following example is applied. The dance is executed in Waltz position, and the part of the lady is the exact counterpart of that written below for the execution of the gentleman.

**853.** Exercise 120. Galop-Polka or Glide-Polka (*L'Esmeralda*) [Fig. 525].

FIG. 525.

Preparation: Anterior 3d position of left. In the part measure glide to the left, at the same time raising upon the right and transferring to left upon the first beat of the measure. This is immediately followed by two *chassés simples*, one *coupé*, and one *jeté* to the left, during which one executes a half Waltz turn along the line of direction, as indicated by the key. For variety, the same movements may be executed *à rebours*.

NOTE.—The different abbreviations which occur in the choregraphy have been explained in §§ 462, 479 and 493.

## Schottische, Rheinländer, Bavarian Polka

**854.** In the year 1850 there appeared, in all parts of Europe, the "Schottische," a round dance which had, as early as 1844, been executed in Bavaria under the name "Rheinländer," and in the Rhenish countries it was known as the "Bavarian Polka." These names have in some places been retained until this time. The music, which is in 2-4 measure, is rendered very slowly, with the effect of 4-4 time.

855. This dance was known in France, England, Russia, Italy, Greece and various other countries as the "Scottish," and it would be difficult to explain, if indeed, it could be satisfactorily determined, how the title "Schottische," which is the German form of the word, ever came to be so definitely applied to the dance as to warrant its adoption, untranslated, into the languages of all the countries referred to.

The Polka (§ 801) was known as the "Schottische Waltz" about 1840.

856. The music given in the following exercise, which was composed in Paris by A. Decombre, corresponds exactly with the rhythm of the dance and attained great popularity.

Exercise 121. Schottische [Fig. 526].

FIG. 526.

Execution: Gentleman's part.

Preparation: Waltz position: anterior 3d position of left.

Direction: To the right, by means of regular Waltz turns.

**First Measure.** First syllable. Glide left to 2d position and transfer.

Second syllable. Draw right into posterior 3d and transfer.

Third syllable. Glide left into 2d position and transfer.

Fourth syllable. Draw right into posterior balancing 3d position.

**Second Measure.** The same movements are executed during the second measure with the other foot, and the first and third syllables of each measure are accented, thus giving a rocking movement to the combination. There is no turning during this rocking (*balancé*) movement.

**Third Measure.** First syllable. One *jeté* to left.

Second syllable. Hop upon left and raise right into posterior balancing 3d position.

Third and fourth syllables. Repetition of first and second with other foot.

**Fourth Measure.** Repetition of third measure.

857. A whole turn is executed in each of these (the third and fourth) measures, and the entire *enchaînement*, therefore, extends through a period of four measures. For the purpose of teaching, the step-sentence may be divided, and the first two measures may be termed *balancée* or rocking, while the last two are called *sauteuse* or hopping. The first step-

sentence is composed of two *chassés-glissés alternatifs*, and the second of four *jetés-relevés en tournant*, otherwise known as *Pas de Rigaudon* [§ 474]. It is a common fault among dancers to neglect the exact execution of this latter portion of the *enchainement* and thus produce a peculiarly crude effect. The foot must not be allowed to remain in the balancing 2d position with horizontal sole at the end of the sentence, but must be carried backward from that place into posterior balancing 3d position, thus finishing in a closed position.

858. The whole combination, however, has a more graceful appearance if executed as shown in Exercise 121 *b*, in which the *balancé* is expressed by means of the abbreviated symbols of the *chassés alternatifs* [§ 479], under the second of which is the sign of accent. This accentuation of the final movement of the second *pas chassé* may be regarded as a sufficient preparation for the succeeding movement (*sauteuse*). The third measure contains the complete script, and commences with the putting down of the left foot (upon the first syllable), which immediately glides into 2d position, where it receives the weight. The light spring in the preceding part-measure serves as preparation.

Upon the second syllable there occurs a hop upon the left foot, during which the right is raised and carried by means of a *rond de jambe en l'air*, through the posterior 4th and again into 2d position balancing, from which (upon the third syllable) it is put down, glides to 2d ball position, and receives the weight.

The fourth syllable is marked by a hop upon the right foot, with simultaneous lifting of the left in preparation for the repetition of the combination during the fourth measure.

859. The slow tempo in which this dance is executed so clearly accentuates the four syllables of each measure that such a division of the movement is as natural as if the music were in 4-4 time, like that of the *Impériale*.

860. If, as sometimes happens, the guests desire a Rheinländer or a Schottische, and the musicians have no music for either of these dances, any Polka played in half-time will answer the purpose.

861. Many dancers find it more convenient to vary this movement by substituting regular Galop steps for the *jetés en tournant*, but this alteration, while it may, perhaps, simplify the execution, detracts from the beauty of the dance.

Another variation which became extremely popular in Greece and Italy, was for a certain period in use. In it the dancers, instead of assuming the Waltz position, stood *vis-à-vis* with their partners and balanced, after which they separately executed a *tour sur place* upon one foot, the lady turning to the right, and the gentleman to the left.

862. In Germany and France this balancing is usually executed parallel to the line of direction, but in England it is the custom to execute the movement diagonally, with the gentleman's face and the lady's back to the line of direction.

## Hungarian Waltz (*Valse Hongroise*)

**863.** As its name implies, this dance is of Hungarian origin. It was first executed in Odessa by two sisters who, upon their return from Hungary, danced it as a variation of the Rheinländer or the Schottische, to the music of which dances it may be fitted. The dance created a favorable impression upon all who saw it, pupils endeavoured to learn it, and it spread rapidly, meeting everywhere a ready welcome.

**864.** Exercise 122. Hungarian Waltz (*Valse Hongroise*) [Fig. 527].

FIG. 527.

The dance is executed in regular Waltz position.

Preparation. Lady: Anterior 5th sole position of right. Gentleman: Anterior 5th sole position of left.

The entire *enchaînement* contains four measures of four syllables each. During the first half of the step-sentence the lady's part is the exact counterpart of the gentleman's, which is made up of two *ballonnés* to the left, one *assemblé* and one *tortillé bipède*.

The Gentleman's Part. During the part-measure, hop strongly upon the right foot, and carry left into balancing 2d position.

### FIRST HALF

First syllable. Put down left in 2d position and transfer.

Second syllable. Bend left knee and carry right foot into posterior balancing 3d position with perpendicular sole and point turned strongly outward, and transfer.

Third and fourth syllables. Same as first and second.

Fifth syllable. *Assemblé.* In this the left foot is carried backward into anterior 5th sole position during a hop upon the right.

Sixth syllable. *Temps tourné en dedans.* In this the heels are raised and turned entirely outward. This and the succeeding syllable constitute what is known as a *tortillé bipède contraire* [§ 530].

Seventh syllable. Bring the heels forcibly together in 1st position with feet turned half-outward.

Eighth syllable. Carry left backward into 5th position.

SECOND HALF

The second half of the *enchaînement* contains two *pas de sissonne* with backward turning, one *assemblé*, and one *tortillé*, which are executed as follows : —

First syllable. Bend both knees with weight upon right foot.

Second syllable. Stretch forcibly, hopping upon right and lifting left foot into high balancing 2d position.

Third and fourth syllables. Repetition of first and second syllables.

Fifth syllable. *Assemblé*, ending in posterior 5th position of left.

Sixth and seventh syllables. *Tortillé bipède contraire*, ending in 1st position.

Eighth syllable. Final pause, or in case of repetition of *enchaînement*, preparatory hop upon right foot and carrying of left into balancing 2d position.

During these two measures, the gentleman executes a complete turn backward upon the right foot.

865. It being supposed that pupils have learned the simple step-syllables, one may use the term *ballonné* to prompt the first half of the *enchaînement* and the term *sissonne* or *tour de ciseaux* to prompt the second half for the purpose of teaching [§ 468].

866. **The Lady's Part.** During the first half of the *enchaînement* the steps of the lady correspond with those of the gentleman, but are of course executed in counter-motion. In the second half, however, she executes a *tour boiteux*, for which the abbreviated sign of the *pas ballonnés* is used [§ 529].

## Execution of the Figure

**Part-Measure.** *Temps levé.* This is executed as follows : during a hop upon the left foot carry the right, by means of a *demi-rond de jambe en l'air*, from the posterior into the anterior balancing 4th position.

First syllable. Put down right foot in 2d position and transfer.

Second syllable. Carry left foot forward into narrowed 4th position and transfer.

Third and fourth syllables. Repetition of first and second.

Fifth syllable. Carry right foot forward into 5th position.

Sixth and seventh syllables. *Tortillé bipède contraire.*

Eighth syllable. Preparation for succeeding step. These movements carry the dancers along the line of direction in a circle, the same as in the other round dances.

867. The gentleman may, if he wishes, vary the movement, by himself executing the *tour boiteux*. This variation will be very agreeable if the right leg has become tired, as is frequently the case. The dance may also be varied by executing the figure *à rebours*. In order to give the steps the genuine Hungarian characteristics, one may knock the heels together alternately upon the fifth, sixth and seventh syllables, as shown in the seventh and eigth measures of Exercise 37 [§ 249]. In order to do this the *assemblé* which occurs upon the fifth syllable is omitted.

868. The dance may be executed to any Rheinländer or *Impériale* music, in case no Hungarian composition is available, provided a proper tempo is observed.

869. The following beautiful and genuinely Hungarian combination may be executed by sufficiently skilled dancers:

Direction: To the right sidewise along the line of direction. The gentleman executes two *ballonnés* and one *frappé* to the left with the left foot, and two *battements élevés* with the right heel, by which a whole turn to the left is made. The lady executes the same step-sentence in counter-motion.

This figure is followed by a *tour boiteux* to the right in which both place the left arm around the waist of the partner, and raise the right arm into 4th position.

This figure may be varied by so strongly swinging as to execute a turn and a half, which brings the dancers into a position which enables them to repeat the *enchaînement* along the line of direction with the other foot. In this case the *tour boiteux* is executed to the left, and the left arms are raised.

## The Mazurka (*La Mazourka*)

870. This dance, which is sometimes called *Masur* or *Masurek* by the people of Poland, derives its name from the tribe called Masures, who dwell in what was once the Duchy of Masovia. In English, the word "Mazurka" would be translated "Masovian woman."

871. In all parts of Poland this dance is preferred above all others, and it is also practiced in many other parts of Europe. It found its way into the aristocratic circles of Paris, where it was for a time extremely popular, but it never had such vogue as did the Polka, the Waltz and similar round dances.

872. The reason is evident, for the Mazurka required much time, patience and artistic ability not called for in learning the other dances. As a result, many dancers never learned the Mazurka, and in localities where that dance was not in special favor, there was frequently so strong an opposition to it as to prevent its execution.

The existence of this feeling of opposition is largely attributable to the fact that the mazurists, not satisfied with a half-hour (which any experienced manager will agree is enough) for the execution of the dance, aroused the antagonism of the non-mazurists, by demanding a full hour. There is little wonder that those who were unable to participate became impatient.

873. The Mazurka is, beyond question, the most beautiful social dance of our time, and the author knows by his experience of more than fifty years that everyone who has properly acquired the dance prefers it to all others. This is true of the dancers of all nations.

874. Perhaps the principal attraction in this singular dance lies in the fact that the dancer is at liberty to vary his steps at will, provided he observes the proper measure, and does not interfere with others. The succession of the figures is not fixed, as it is in Quadrilles, and one may therefore give his fancy free rein, for there is such a variety of figures that some change is always possible. Besides, the first dancer, or the manager, may improvise whatever figures he desires.

There is in this dance a certain inspiration not to be found in any other. Nearly every good Mazurka dancer feels an indescribable sensation entering his very soul and driving away all fatigue, immediately the first strains of a properly composed and correctly rendered Mazurka fall upon his ear.

875. It would be difficult, indeed, to accurately describe the characteristics of this dance; in fact, to fully appreciate its beauties one must have seen it executed again and again by accomplished dancers. The Mazurka is a combination of exalted pride and martial boldness, knightly gallantry and the most graceful devotedness.

While it is commonly admitted that the Poles, as a nation, are skilful dancers, it cannot be affirmed that all Poles are good Mazurists, nor is it beyond the possibility of other nations even to excel them in that particular dance.

876. The national character of the Mazurka is apparent among all classes of Polish dancers. The peasant, who accentuates the measure with his heavy ironshod shoes, lacks neither agility nor grace; but his dance is fit only for the yard or the village inn.

The aristocrat executes the same steps, but in a manner so elegant as to be perfectly in keeping with the brilliant company, the glistening parquet, and the magnificent decorations of his gorgeous ballroom.

The middle classes execute the Mazurka in a manner distinct from either, combining the elements of both the peasant and the aristocratic performance. In aristocratic circles one finds the *pas courant* and the *pas de Basque;* in the middle class *pas ordinaire* is the favorite step.

877. It seems to be the opinion of many people that a great deal of noise and the most extravagant movements of all parts of the body add to the beauty and national character of the Mazurka, but this is not true. The dance may be perfectly executed without any such accompaniments. It may, of course, like anything else, be overdone, but if so, it ceases to be beautiful.

878. The music of the Mazurka is in either 3-4 or 3-8 measure, of which the second syllable is accented, as shown by a point or an accent placed above it; but the regular accentuation of the first syllable is also observed.

In teaching the steps, a tempo of about M. M. 144 is the most practicable, but in the actual execution of the steps, the swing of the dance leads the participants, almost involuntarily, into a much quicker tempo; it should, however, never be allowed to exceed M. M. 176, and it is always affected by the composition to which it is danced.

879. Owing to the fact that competent mazurists frequently execute figures which are original and peculiar to themselves, it is impossible to determine the actual number of Mazurka steps, but we may take as fundamental those which are choregraphically described in the following exercise:

### TECHNICAL STEPS OF THE MAZURKA

880. Exercise 123. Mazurka Steps (*Pas de Mazourka*) [Fig. 528].

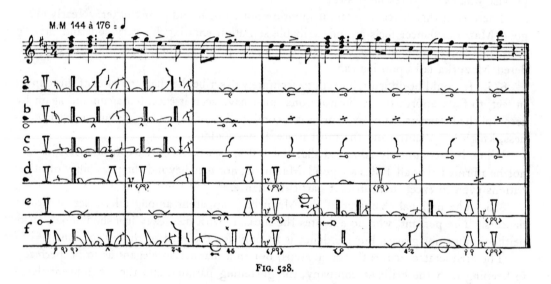

FIG. 528.

*a. Pas Glissé* or *Pas Ordinaire* or *Pas de Flore,* etc. (Usual step of the gentleman).

This step is the one most commonly used by gentlemen, both in the promenade and in the figures. It is described in several works upon the art of dancing under the name *pas glissé,* but many Polish dancing masters call it *pas de flore* and by other names.

The Author has carefully examined the various names and he has finally concluded that the name *pas ordinaire* is most appropriate, for the reason that other and different steps and movements may be understood by the term *glissé,* while the term *flore,* being inexpressive of any quality or attribute of the step, appears to be merely an arbitrary expression, which is, at best, unsatisfactory.

Preparation: 1st position.

Part-measure: Hop lightly upon the left foot, at the same time lifting the right.

First syllable. Put down right foot, which glides forward into 4th position.

Second syllable. Transfer, and carry left foot backward into low balancing 4th position.

Third syllable. Hop on right, and carry left foot forward as preparation for the succeeding step.

This step is executed alternately, and in it the legs should be well stretched, the points of the feet turned strongly outward and down, and the lifting should not be too high. A certain swing of the body and crossing of the legs render this step particularly attractive.

In the example, the first two measures have been written in complete choregraphic form, but the remainder contains only the abbreviated signs.

The backward step is executed in the same manner, but in counter-motion.

The ladies do not, in the simple Mazurka as commonly danced, execute this step, but in certain figures of the Mazurka Quadrille, which attained high favor, it becomes particularly beautiful if executed by them in their peculiarly graceful way.

881. **Limping Step** (*Pas Boiteux*) [Exercise 123 *b*]. For both lady and gentleman.

Preparation: 1st position.

Part-measure: Hop on left and extend right forward.

First syllable. Put down right gently in anterior 4th position.

Second syllable. *Dégagé* and carry left forward a whole step.

Third syllable. Put down left foot audibly in anterior 4th position, and *dégagé*.

Fourth syllable. Hop, falling audibly upon left, and carry right into preparation for next step.

The width of this step varies according to the requirements of the figure and the space.

In the example, the movement is written with complete choregraphy in the first and second measures, but only the abbreviation is given in the remaining measures. This step is always executed with the same foot, for to alternate would cause it to cease to be a *pas boiteux*. It is used principally in the closing figures, or in the turn upon the place, *tour sur place*, and that figure is therefore frequently termed *tour boiteux*. The figure generally extends through four measures of music, and is known in Poland as the *holupiec* or *holupza*, although these names are seldom heard except in the Polish countries.

Many ladies carry the foot forward in a large circle upon the second syllable, with the leg turned strongly outward, and perpendicular direction of the sole. This creates a very pretty effect. *Pas boiteux* is very often executed in connection with other steps, or combined with the *changements de pieds*, to restore a lost cadence. It may also be executed backward.

882. **Basque Step** or **Running Step** (*Pas de Basque* or *Pas Courant*) [Exercise 123 *c*]. For ladies.

This step, which is executed in a free and rapid manner, resembles the running step and is sometimes known as *Pas Courant*. It has been referred to by that name in § 449.

The step has also, and for a similar reason, been known as *Pas de Basque* [§ 521 *et seq.*]. There is, however, an important difference between the dancing step of the people who dwell around the Bay of Biscay and the so-called *Pas Courant* of the Mazurka. The Spanish Basque dance is in either 3-8 or 3-4 measure, and in executing this step they cross the legs strongly and put the feet down in 5th position; while the French Basques execute the same step in 2-4 time, as in the Gavotte. In the Mazurka, the so-called *Pas de*

*Basque* is always made without crossing the legs, and no such measure as 2-4 is ever employed.

This step is sometimes referred to as the *Pas de Pas* or *Pas de Bas*, but these names are the result of mispronunciation of the word " Basque."

In view of the facts above mentioned, it seems to the Author that the step would better be called the *Pas Courant* or Running Step, and he therefore makes that recommendation.

Preparation: 1st position.

Part-measure: Carry right foot into anterior low balancing 4th position.

First syllable. Throw weight lightly upon right foot (*jeté*).

Second syllable. Glide left forward a whole step and transfer.

Third syllable. *Coupé.* This is executed by bringing the right foot so forcibly into 1st position as to cut the left from its place; the weight is immediately transferred, and the now free left foot carried forward, as in the preceding part-measure, in preparation for the succeeding step. The abbreviated sign of the *coupé* has been already explained in § 526.

*Pas courant*, although principally used by ladies, is sometimes executed by gentlemen as well; but they accentuate the third syllable to a more marked degree than do the ladies; this audible accentuation, while quite proper in the dance, should never descend to the level of a rude tramping.

*Pas courant* should be practiced both forward and backward, for it occurs very frequently in the various combinations and figures, and even in the promenade.

If one fancies the crossed position, the *coupé* should be made into 3d, instead of 1st position.

**883. Collecting Step** (*Assemblée*) [Exercise 123 *d*].

This movement consists in striking the heels together in 1st position, with the feet turned half outward. It can be used only in connection with other movements. Its simplest and most common application is in connection with a preceding *pas boiteux*.

Upon the third syllable of the *pas boiteux*, the free foot, instead of passing into 4th position, is carried only into 2d parallel, and the supporting foot is simultaneously turned to a corresponding angle. The heels are brought forcibly together upon the first syllable of the next measure as shown in Fig. 521.

The first half of the *clausula* contains the complete choregraphy; the fifth and sixth measures, the abbreviated script; and the seventh and eighth measures, the regular musical symbol of repetition.

**884. Step-Sentences** (*Phrases*) [Exercise 123 *e*].

One may, by combining these various steps, form what is known as *phrases* or step-sentences; for example, in the first half of Exercise 123 *e*, which contains two *pas ordinaires*, one *boiteux*, and one *assemblé*, constituting a *phrase* which extends through four measures.

After this has been thoroughly practised, add a *tour boiteux*, which consists of three *pas boiteux* and one *assemblé*, and also requires four measures. This constitutes the second half of Exercise 123 *e*.

**885. The Striking Steps to the Side** (*Les Pas Battus Latérales*). This step is also known as Polish step (*Pas Polonais*) or Striking of the Heels (*Coup de Talon*).

Any genuine Mazurka step should be done after the manner of the Poles, and might, therefore, be called a *pas polonais*, and the *coup de talon* appears in so different a manner in other steps, that that title is not sufficiently significant. The word *coup* refers only to the actual movement by which the striking is effected.

The word *battre*, in dancing, signifies the striking of one foot with the other, and as one foot is, in this movement, struck against the other sidewise, the name " Sidewise Striking Step" or *pas battu latéral* appears to be the proper expression.

In striking the heels together one is liable to come in contact with the ankle, if the feet are turned outward; and as such an accident is extremely painful, the feet should be held nearly parallel for the execution of this step. For this reason it might be called *pas battu parallèle* or "Parallel Striking Step." The word lateral signifies the direction of the beating. For the sake of abbreviation, we may refer to the step as *pas battu*.

886. Execution. — Part measure. Raise the left foot into 2d balancing position, turning the point slightly forward.

First syllable. Strike the left heel audibly against the right, during a hop on the right foot.

Second syllable. Carry left foot sidewise to 2d position, turning the leg outward, and transfer.

Third syllable. Glide right foot into 1st position and immediately lift the left into 2d as preparation for the succeeding step.

Here also the syllable is audible, and although this attribute is agreeable to the dancers, and quite in harmony with the character of the Mazurka (especially if the dancer wears spurs) one should, nevertheless, keep within the limit of good taste.

This step should be practised with equal diligence both to the right and to the left, as it is applied in both directions; although in the promenade it is most commonly executed to the left, as by this means the gentleman turns entirely toward his partner.

887. Two or more *pas battus* may be executed in succession. If two of them be performed, the first falls upon the third syllable of the preceding measure, and the second upon and clearly marking the cadence of the music.

Three successive *pas battus* require a full measure of music, and are always followed by a *pas ordinaire*, and four *pas battus*. When executed consecutively, they extend through one and one-third measures, the fourth falling upon the cadence of the second measure. This combination is always followed by the extension of the free foot into 2d position, after which the other is immediately drawn to it.

888. *Pas Battu et Pas Ordinaire.* The nature of this combination of steps is self-evident. It extends through two measures of music, and consists of one beating step and one *pas ordinaire* in regular *enchaînement*. If the first step is executed to the left, the second continues that direction; and the last syllable of the *pas ordinaire* serves as preparation for the repetition of the combination, which commences with the beating to the right, thus alternating the movement. This sentence is sometimes used in the *Promenade*, wherein a turn to the left brings one directly facing the partner, and one to the right brings the partners *dos-à-dos*. One should, however, avoid this as far as possible; it is

only allowable under any circumstances to turn the back to the partner at the moment of striking.

This combination occurs very frequently in the set figures.

889. *Pas Battu, Ordinaire, Boiteux et Assemblée.* This combination forms a very simple and agreeable *enchaînement* of four measures, the first of which contains the *pas battu* ; the second *pas ordinaire* ; the third, *pas boiteux* ; and the fourth, *assemblée.*

If the *pas battu* is executed to the left, the *pas ordinaire* follows the same direction, and the *pas boiteux* must be made with the right. Both feet participate in the *assemblée.*

The movement to the right is in counter-motion.

By executing a complete rurn in the *pas boiteux*, with corresponding movements of the head, body and arms, one may improvise very graceful and attractive figures ; indeed, the Mazurka-Quadrille, which has been highly favoured is made up of just such combinations.

890. Exercise 123 *f* contains the choregraphic script of this enchainment, which may be described as follows : —

Preparation : 1st position.

During the part-measure, the left foot is carried into the 2d low balancing position and the points of the feet are turned parallel.

**First Measure.**

First syllable. Hop lightly upon the right and bring the left heel audibly against the right sidewise.

Second syllable. Turn left foot forward and carry same to 2d position, where it is put down audibly and receives the weight, and immediately raise right into 2d position.

Third syllable. Put down right foot audibly in 1st position, again carrying left into balancing position, in readiness to commence the repetition.

These three syllables constitute the so-called sidewise striking step (*pas battu latéral*).

**Second Measure.**

First syllable. Put down left foot and glide same lightly into 2d position.

Second syllable. Transfer upon left foot, simultaneously carrying the right backward into the slightly bended half-high 2-4 position.

Third syllable. Hop on left foot, maintaining same attitude.

**Third Measure.**

First syllable. Hop lightly upon left foot, and carry right through the half-high 2d into half-high anterior 4th position, thus beginning a whole turn, which is finished upon the Second syllable.

Third syllable. Put down right foot in anterior 4-5 position, and turn upon the tip of the left into 2d position, parallel.

**Fourth Measure.**

Upon the first syllable of this measure, the heels are brought forcibly together sidewise and into 1st position, which is held during the remaining two syllables.

The entire *enchainement* of four measures is repeated in the opposite direction upon the remaining half of the *clausula.* The key in the fifth measure indicates that the movement shall be to the right, and the script is written in the abbreviated form.

## Pounding Step (*Pas Frappé*)

**891.** This phrase, which extends through two measures, is very often combined with other steps, as, for instance, two *pas ordinaires*. It is executed in the place of the combined *pas boiteux* and *assemblée*.

If this phrase is begun with the right foot, it will finish in posterior 4th balancing position at the conclusion of the second *pas ordinaire*.

Execution of the *pas frappé*:

First syllable. *Jeté* into 1st solo position and put down right foot audibly, at the same time bending the left leg and carrying the left foot backward into balancing position.

Second syllable. Put down left foot audibly in 1st position.

Third syllable. Turn both heels outward.

Fourth syllable. Strike heels together.

Fifth syllable. Rest in 1st position.

Sixth syllable. Preparation for succeeding *pas frappé*.

**892.** Although it is entirely opposed to all the rules of art to support the weight between the two feet, in amplified 2d position, some dancers, in turning the heels outward (third syllable) glide into this attitude, and if this is done in a sufficiently skilful manner it is not without grace. Dancers of exceptional ability may often assume attitudes and execute movements which, if attempted by others, would appear wholly ridiculous, and which in reality may be directly opposed to every law of dancing. These deviations must be permitted to those whose skill is so consummate as to render them beautiful. No other dance so freely lends itself to these deviations as does the Mazurka. This may be attributed to the individual freedom which it bestows upon the dancers.

## Pushed Cutting Step (*Pas Coupé Poussé*)

**893.** This combination possesses a certain similarity to the *pas boiteux*.

Preparation: 3d position.

During the part-measure hop upon the left foot and carry the right into anterior 4th balancing position.

First syllable. Put down right in anterior 4th position.

Second syllable. Transfer.

Third syllable. Bring left forward into posterior 3d position, knocking (audibly) against the supporting right, transfer, and carry right immediately into anterior 4th balancing position in preparation for the succeeding step.

This phrase may be repeated consecutively, but can only be alternated by combining it with other steps.

## Chasing Step (*Pas Chassé*)

894. The ordinary alternating chasing step is frequently substituted for the *pas courant* (§ 882) in the Mazurka, and if the lady can impart to the movement more than its ordinary grace, the change is delightful. However, unless she fully understands this movement and performs it with exquisite ease, she would better stick to the running step; for, although the movement may be executed in a most beautiful manner, it is still a French step, and therefore entirely foreign to the character of the Mazurka.

## Sidewise Chasing Step (*Chassé Latéral* or *Chassé de Côté*)

895. This combination, although of French origin, is more or less Polish in character, It consists of *chassés simples* to the side, and may be used in the promenade, in which the gentlemen always execute it to the left and the ladies to the right (§ 476).

The movement is commenced by gliding the left foot into 2d position and transferring, thus bringing the right into preparatory 2d position with the weight upon the left, which is assumed to be in 1st position.

The phrase begins upon the 3d syllable of the measure, upon which the right foot strikes against the heel of the left, which immediately glides to the side.

This is repeated upon the first syllable of the next measure, and upon the second syllable the weight is transferred, thus restoring the preparatory position for the phrase.

In executing this movement, the feet are held nearly parallel, and the two beatings should follow one another in such rapid succession that the rest upon the second syllable and the cut in the rhythm are thrown into bold relief.

There can be no other or more definite rule for the number of repetitions of the various Mazurka steps than that they must clearly mark a cadence of either two, four or eight measures.

## Scissor Step (*Pas de Ciseaux*)

896. This combination has been already explained in connection with the Cracovienne (§ 844) and the Hungarian Waltz (§ 863). The change of name from its general form, *sissonne*, to *ciseaux* is accounted for in § 468.

Section 470 contains a description of the movement as executed in the Mazurka, in which it is supplemented by subsequent raising (*Pas de ciseaux relevé*). The choregraphic description of this movement may be found in Exercise 62 (§ 470).

This step is sometimes executed by the gentlemen in dancing the Mazurka, in place of the *pas boiteux*, and is generally applied to the *tour sur place*, going backward upon the right foot.

897. It has already been stated that the variety of Mazurka figures is great, and it may be added that in attempting to exactly describe them all, one might fill a large volume and yet find it incomplete. Still, those who have practiced and acquired the steps and combinations which have been mentioned above, will not only readily comprehend almost every other step, but will be competent to improvise original combinations — indeed the new enchainments will come to them involuntarily in the animation of the dance.

## Mazurka Figures

In order to properly describe the different Mazurka figures, the author has found it necessary to first evolve a system by which the various positions and combinations may be exactly denominated; for even the oral teacher sometimes feels the inaccuracy of recognized names, notwithstanding the fact that he has the great advantage of being able to demonstrate his meanings and to actually place his pupils in the requisite positions.

In the case of written instruction, however, one often meets with the necessity of describing movements, etc., difficult to put into words, which, although they would never really hinder an oral instructor, must be thoroughly and precisely explained and distinguished from other similar points, and the writer is compelled to enter into more or less lengthy deductions as to the propriety of this or that expression before completing his description.

Aside from all this there is little chance that a teacher of experience will be particularly embarrassed by the criticisms or questions of his pupils; whereas, he who writes a book of instructions may be positive that any real errors he may chance to make will be very severely criticised.

Indeed, the fear of such criticism has so affected the author of this book that he has pondered for whole days over a single simple expression, searching every available authority before he dared to declare an accepted term incorrect, or to suggest the use of a term not hitherto utilized by other choregraphs.

The various kinds of positions and formations have been more deeply studied by military instructors than by masters of dancing, and the author has therefore adapted their system of denomination to the positions and the movements of the dance, because of their greater distinctness.

## Instructions Regarding Cotillion and Mazurka Figures

**898.** Several pupils placed side by side in one line form what is known as a " Rank," and those who stand at the right and left of the middle of this line constitute, respectively, the right and the left wings. If several such ranks stand one behind another, the front line is called the first rank, the next the second rank, and so on.

**899.** If the pupils stand in a line one behind another, they constitute what is known as a " File." Therefore, if persons forming a rank execute a quarter-turn, either to right or left, they immediately become a file. If several ranks of equal length be placed one behind another, they constitute as many files as there are persons in each line, and the first file is composed of those who stand at the extreme right, those at the extreme left forming the last file.

900. If several ranks stand one behind the other the whole body is known as a " Column," and if the number of ranks exceeds that of the files, the column is longer than it is wide and is called a " Long Column." If the number of files exceeds that of the ranks, it is called a " Broad Column." In action, broad columns are generally used, and in marching, long columns. A long column becomes broad by means of a quarter-turn and *vice versa*. Two ranks of eight files form, therefore, a broad column.

901. If two ranks stand one behind the other, and the first rank executes a half-turn, there is formed an *allée vis-à-vis*. If, however, the first rank remains quiet and the rear one makes a half-turn, there is formed an *allée dos-à-dos*. If such an alley is composed of all ladies or all gentlemen it is called respectively " a ladies' " or " a gentlemen's alley."

902. If the front rank consists of gentlemen and the rear rank of ladies, a half-turn by the gentlemen produces an *allée vis-à-vis*, commonly known as an " English Column," because in early English dances the dancers stood in this form. If the ranks are transposed and the ladies execute a half-turn, the result is what is known as a " Reversed English Column."

903. If the front rank consists of gentlemen, and the rear of ladies, and each rank executes a quarter-turn to the right, the result is a regular dancing formation known as *colonne à deux*, in which the lady is, as the rule demands, at the right of her gentleman. A similar quarter-turn to the left produces what may be called a reversed *colonne à deux*, in which the lady stands at the left of her partner.

904. The position for the *Contredanse* has been described in §§ 653 and 654. The regular position for *Contredanse* may be formed by dividing a *colonne à quatre* into halves, each of which constitutes a mixed rank which is turned *vis-à-vis*.

905. If a column is divided lengthwise, it is called " split " (*colonne crevée*) and if divided crosswise, it is " cut " (*colonne coupée*); if the two divisions face one another, they form a *colonne coupée vis-à-vis*, and if back to one another, *colonne coupée dos-à-dos*.

## Space

906. For the purpose of ascertaining beforehand how many persons may sit in a circle of a given size, deductions based upon practical experiments have demonstrated that each couple so seated require a space occupying four feet of the length or width of the hall ; and although this unit is large enough to appear well-nigh ridiculous, it is in reality correct.

Around a hall thirty-six by twenty-four feet, there may therefore be seated thirty couples, nine at each side and six at each end. More than that number would be crowded.

Twenty couples may be seated around a hall 24 x 16 which contains   384 sq. ft.

Thirty  couples may be seated around a hall 36 x 24 which contains   864 sq. ft.

Forty  couples may be seated around a hall 48 x 24 which contains  1536 sq. ft.

Fifty  couples may be seated around a hall 60 x 40 which contains 2400 sq. ft.

From this one may readily see that a small hall will seat more persons in proportion to its size than a large one, and that this proportion of seating accommodation around a hall is still further varied by the shape of the hall. For example, if the hall is longer than it is wide it will accommodate more persons than a perfectly square one would. This is shown by the following table:

A hall 50 x 50 contains 2500 sq. ft. and will seat 50 couples.

A hall 60 x 40 contains 2400 sq. ft. and will seat 50 couples.

A hall 70 x 30 contains 2100 sq. ft. and will seat 50 couples.

A hall 75 x 25 contains 1875 sq. ft. and will seat 50 couples.

If the persons are seated in two circles in a hall 70 x 30, each circle will be 35 x 30 and will seat thirty-two couples, and the entire hall sixty-four couples.

If in a hall 75 x 25 the persons are seated in three circles each 25 x 25, each circle will contain twenty-five and the whole hall seventy-five couples.

In case more couples participate than the space mentioned permits, the ladies take seats in front of the gentlemen, thus nearly doubling the seating capacity.

The rules above given regarding the positions, terms, and calculations of space apply both to the Mazurka and the Cotillion.


## Large and Small Circles


907. For the Mazurka, the entire company is seated in a single large circle, each lady at the right of her partner. It was formerly the custom in many Polish cities, to divide the company into several small circles; but although under certain conditions this is advisable, fashions have changed in this respect since that time.

908. Each formation has its good and its bad points which depend largely upon circumstances. If the hall is very large, and particularly if it is much longer than it is wide, and the number participating in the Mazurka is large, the division of the company into smaller circles is advisable. In this case, those persons who desire to dance in the same circle should sit together. The experienced dancers usually endeavor to congregate in one circle, in order that they may execute the more beautiful and difficult figures without being disturbed by those less efficient than themselves.

Likewise, the less skilful dancers form a circle of their own, and if the manager is sufficiently thoughtful to provide them with a competent leader, they may execute figures so simple that even the least experienced guests may participate in them with pleasure. This division of the dancers provides for every one, and even those who are acquainted with only a very few figures may dance oftener in a small circle than in a single large one. More persons may participate in two circles than in one.

If, however, the single circle is not too large, the manager can conduct it more easily, and more pleasure may be given to each dancer, as there will result a greater number of well executed figures in a given time.

909. In a large circle, a single *tour* of the *promenade* becomes monotonous and consumes a great deal of time; besides, one manager is unable to properly conduct more than a certain number of couples. The varying abilities of the dancers present another disadvantage. Expert dancers desire to execute new and difficult figures, but these are ruined by inexperienced persons who necessitate corrections, which are always unpleasant and annoying.

On the other hand, the less skilful demand the easy figures, of which the others have long since tired, and so it is often impossible to execute harmoniously more than a very few figures.

910. Notwithstanding all this, the company should not be divided unless circumstances demand it, for a single circle is of particular advantage in private parties, when the company is not too large. A single circle contains more of the element of unity, leaves the space freer for the *promenade*, imposes fewer limitations upon the selection of figures and affords the spectators a better opportunity to distinctly observe the various figures.

But the prime essential, whether there is a single large circle or various smaller ones, is an efficient leader, a man who is a thoroughly experienced dancer. It is a matter of regret that the part is so often assumed by persons who are ignorant of even the names of the figures, to say nothing of their combination and sequence.

## Introduction

911. The Mazurka is generally commenced with a *grand tour* (grand right and left), followed by a *tour boiteux* upon the place, after which the dancers take their seats.

If the company is very large in proportion to the space, a few steps forward to the centre and back will answer the purpose of the *tours*.

With less than eight couples, five measures to the left and five to the right are recommended; but for more than eight couples eight measures should be allowed for every tour.

A *promenade* may be substituted for the *tours* as an introduction, in which case the first couple lead around to the right, returning to their original position, and there execute a *tour sur place*, after which they are again seated. The next couple at the right follow as soon as the first couple have passed, and the figure continues in the same manner until all have returned to their seats.

912. The Promenade is the most important thing in the whole Mazurka, as it displays the grace and ability of each dancer.

Having arrived at their respective places, each couple executes a *tour sur place* and address. If, after the *promenade*, new partners are to be selected, the turn should be made in order that each dancer may have a better opportunity of seeing the entire company, and thus be better able to locate the desired person. After the figure, however, the gentlemen must lead his partner to her own seat, where, after a *tour sur place* and a bow, he leaves her, and retires to his original position in the circle.

**913.** **The Selection of Figures** should always depend upon the circumstances of number and space, for there are figures which may be begun by one, two, three, four, five or even a larger number of couples.

In case there are not more than seven couples, as frequently happens at private dances, the manager should choose figures which do not call for more than three couples; if there are from eight to fifteen, he should never commence with less than two couples and he may introduce certain figures which begin with three or four; if there are from sixteen to thirty-one couples, one should begin with from four to six, and so on.

In addition to this, the manager should always keep in mind the skill of his dancers, which he usually knows. He should place the good dancers together, and with his own partner commence a line for the less skilful. In this manner he may easily lead the dancers by demonstrating the various figures, and those who fail to follow figures thus demonstrated will be conspicuous.

**914.** Where all are experienced dancers and acquainted with one another, it is often agreed that each group shall dance a different figure, and the practice renders the Mazurka more attractive to both dancers and spectators.

A group of twenty competent dancers may execute ten or fifteen different figures in the space of half an hour without allowing the interest to flag for a single moment. A manager who is unacquainted with the company should always begin with simple figures which will be readily understood.

**915.** These rules all apply to the Cotillion as well as to the Mazurka, and many figures may be applied to either dance.

**916.** The number of Mazurka and Cotillion figures is so great that it would be impossible to extend the Grammar so as to include them all, and for that reason the choregraphy and even the description of them will not be undertaken.

# Chapter XVII

## CONCLUDING REMARKS

THE purpose of this Grammar is to establish a universal method of teaching dancing and the invention and demonstration of a satisfactory system of dance script, by means of which the movements of any and all dances may be definitely and intelligibly shown.

918. In addition to this work, the author has devoted many years to the preparation of a collection of the social dances of the present and of other days, and the different national and stage dances, but it will be a long time yet before the work will be in shape to put upon the market. *

919. On account of this necessary delay, and in order to give an idea of the manner of representing the movements of the upper body, the author has added to this Grammar the following choregraphic description of the beautiful Spanish solo-dance called " *La Cachucha.*"

This description is given principally to demonstrate the fact that the choregraphy set forth in this work is capable of expressing, in a satisfactory way, all the movements of the various members of the body — the legs, arms, head, rump, etc, which form so important an element in the proper rendition of a dance, and the *Cachucha* has been selected as a model because all the members are particularly active and expressive therein.

Should not such a demonstration prove, at least, the possibilities of the system suggested in this book?

920. Regarding this description, it may be well to state that it is presupposed that the reader has carefully studied the Grammar, and that if he has not committed the expressions and symbols to memory, he is at least sufficiently acquainted with the index to easily find anything he may desire to have explained.

## The Cachucha (*La Cachucha*)

921. The *Cachucha* is a Spanish solo-dance, better adapted for execution by a lady than by a gentleman, which is danced to the melody of an Andalusian national song containing two parts of eight measures each, to which, for the sake of variety, there has been

---

* This refers to the collection before mentioned, which was never published. — ED.

added a third part of similar duration, and the whole is completed by an introduction and a coda.

The celebrated Fanny Elssler, by her wonderful execution, won for this dance a popularity in keeping with its merits.

The word *cachucha*, in Spanish, is a term of endearment, which is applied to particularly attractive or graceful persons or things, and is also used as the name of a certain kind of cap.

922. The music and complete choregraphic description of the Cachucha, which is executed in 3-8 measure, is placed at the top of the succeeding pages.

The clicking of the castanets, which forms so essential a part of the Spanish dances, is generally neglected by all save Spanish dancers. Great care should be devoted to this feature.

It is customary to play a few chords before the regular melody is commenced, as shown in the Music Book (No. 124).

923. The dance is divided into four couplets, and the melody is played four times, ending with the coda.

The script of the first couplet is given upon the first line below the notes, the second on the next, and so on.

Each couplet contains four figures of sixteen measures each, for the third of which the music is the same as for the first.

924. It must not be forgotten that a number below the line of the floor indicates the advanced foot, and a period the foot which is behind; a comma below the period indicates a ball position, and a very small circle a toe or "point" position. A circle surrounding certain signs of the legs indicates that such positions are assumed during the execution of a *pirouette* or turn. The direction in which the turn is to be made is indicated by the direction of the circular sign, and the turning foot is shown by the sign of position. The thick end shows the starting, and the arrow-head the finishing point of the turn. If the beginning of the circle extends below the line of the floor it indicates a forward turn; if to the right, a right turn. The term "right" applies to the right side of the dancer, who is supposed always to face the spectator unless otherwise stated. The shaded line which is used to show the head represents the hair, and by it one may show the direction of the face, and even of the eyes.

925. In figures so small as those in the example it is difficult to draw them exactly, but the arm-positions can hardly fail to be understood. The 4th position of the feet is generally indicated by the number, and crossed positions of the legs by a little cross (×) above the line of the supporting leg (§ 105).

## Execution of the Cachucha

Prelude. Chords.

MEAS.

I

### FIRST COUPLET

**926. Figure I. Ziz-zag Forward (*Ballonné Progressif*). (Sixteen measures.)**

Enter from background at left, proceeding diagonally forward to the right, by
means of three *ballonnés dessous*, one *pirouette* and one *frappé dessus*, into 5th
position.   4

Repeat obliquely to the left.   4

Repeat obliquely to the right.   4

Repeat obliquely to the left to centre.   4

**927. Figure II. (*Pivoter.*) (Sixteen measures.)**

Turn slowly backward to the left upon the place by means of six *pas de ciseaux
dessous*, in 2d and 5th positions with the left arm raised, but without raising upon
the toe.   6

*Pirouette basque* to left.   2

Repetition to the right.   8

**928. Figure III. Zig-zag Backward (*Ballonné Rétrograde*). (Sixteen measures.)**

SYLL.

1-3   One *ballonné* to right, followed by raising into 5th point position and audible lowering of right heel, and carry left foot into 2d position balancing.   I

1   Put down left in 2d position.

2   Glide right into anterior 5th position, pointing toe strongly downward, and
audibly lowering the heel, immediately carrying the left into posterior
balancing position.

| SYLL. | | MEAS. |
|---|---|---|
| 3 | Carry left foot to 2d position and transfer. | 1 |
| | During this measure the right arm executes a large arm-circle (*grand rond de bras*), accompanied by bending the body to such a degree that the right hand nearly touches the floor, and then a corresponding movement of the left arm. | |
| 1 | Carry right foot to 2d position and transfer. | |
| 2–3 | Execute a *tour entier* upon right ball or point, carrying left foot first into 2d balancing, and thence into anterior 5th point position, and transfer. | 1 |
| 1 | Pound with whole sole of right foot into anterior 5th position, and transfer. | |
| 2 | Rest. | |
| 3 | Begin the *ballonné* as preparation for the repetition. | 1 |
| | *Ballonné rétrograde* to left. | 4 |
| | Repetition of entire *enchaînement.* | 8 |

929. **Figure IV.** (*Frappé Tortillé.*) In the background. (Sixteen measures.)

*Traversée* to right sidewise with one *frappé* and one *tortillé* repeated three times, and followed by one *coupé* and one *pas de basque latéral.*

| | | |
|---|---|---|
| 1 | One *frappé* with right into 2d position, and transfer. | |
| 2 | Turn left foot upon the heel until the toe comes to a point a little in advance of the right heel. | |
| 3 | Turn left into anterior 5th sole position. | 1 |
| | The second and third syllables constitute a *pas tortillé.* | |
| 1–3 | Repetition of first measure. | 1 |
| 1–3 | Repetition of second measure. | 1 |
| 1 | Execute *coupé dessous* with right foot into posterior 5th ball position. | |
| 2 | Put down left foot in 2d position, and transfer. | |
| 3 | Draw right foot into crossed anterior 4-5 position, and transfer. | 1 |

| SYLL. | | MEAS. |
|---|---|---|
| | The second and third syllables of the preceding measure constitute the *pas de basque espagnol*. | |
| | Repeat preceding four measures to left. | 4 |
| | Repeat preceding four measures to right. | 4 |
| | Two *frappés tortillés*. | 2 |
| | *Coupé pas de basque*. | 1 |
| 1 | *Frappé* on right foot into anterior 4th position, and transfer. | |
| 2 | Rest. | |
| 3 | Preparatory movement for succeeding *pas ballonné*. | 1 |

### SECOND COUPLET

**930. Figure I. The Inclined Rhombus Forward (*Le Rhombe en Descendant*).**

Obliquely forward to right to the middle line by one and a half *ballonnés*, two *pas élevés* forward into 4th position, one *demi-pas de basque* to left, one *tappé du talon gauche* (stamp with left heel), and one *frappé* with right into 2d position.      4

**931.** Divide figure into periods of several syllables. It is of advantage to both instructor and pupil to treat this figure as a verse-line divided into eleven syllables or counts, which may be designated as follows:

$$\breve{0}, \; \bar{1} \; \breve{2} \; \bar{3}, \; \bar{4} \; \breve{5} \; \bar{6}, \; \bar{7} \; \breve{8} \; \breve{9}, \; \text{and} \; \bar{10}.$$

**0** During the first part-measure, hop upon the left foot, carrying the right foot forward into balancing position and raising right arm to correspond, which is nearly to 5th position, and following the movement by lifting the eyes to the upstretched hand.

**1** Upon the first syllable of the first measure, put down right foot in 2d position, and transfer.

| SYLL. | | MEAS. |
|---|---|---|
| 2 | Draw left foot into posterior 3d heel position, and transfer. | |
| | These three syllables constitute a ball step, or *pas ballonné* [§ 527]. | |
| 3–4 | Repeat first two syllables of *pas ballonné*. | |
| 5–6 | Execute two high *pas élevés* upon line of direction. | |
| 7 | Carry left foot into 2d position, and transfer. | |
| 8 | Swing right foot into crossed anterior 4-5 position. | |
| | Syllables seven and eight constitute a half basque step or *demi-pas de basque*. | |

932. The name *demi-pas de basque* is entirely correct, for in executing it one steps half to the side and carries the other foot into crossed balancing position, but does not transfer the weight.

933. The step is called *pointe de pied* by many Spanish dancers, but that term is too indefinite, as it does not in any way explain the manner in which it should be done.

| | | |
|---|---|---|
| 9 | Raise left heel and lower it audibly, with weight still resting upon it. This movement is known as stamping or *taper* (§ 265). | |
| 10 | Stamp with right foot into 2d position and transfer, and rest during the second syllable of the fourth measure, again resuming the dance upon the third syllable thereof, by preparation for the succeeding step. | |

Most of the step-sentences of the *Cachucha* and other Spanish dances may be analyzed in the above manner.

The same *enchaînement* is repeated upon the next four measures with the other foot, and extends obliquely forward to the centre line of the stage. The accompanying arm-movements are clearly shown in the choregraphic description.      4

The same *enchaînement* is again performed upon the next four measures, commencing with the right foot and going backward obliquely to the left as far as the horizontal middle line of the stage. In doing this, it is necessary for the dancer to nearly turn her back to the spectators.      4

Still another repetition of this combination upon the remaining four measures brings the dancer once more to her place in the centre of the background, where, by means of the *demi-pas de basque*, she again faces the
spectators.

4

### Figure II.

This figure, which consists of sixteen *demi-pas de basque*, with *tapés de talon*,
brings the dancer to the front of the stage, as shown in the script.

16

### Figure III. The Inclined Rhombus Backward (*Le Rhombe en Montant*).

This figure is exactly similar to the first figure of the Couplet, except that
it is in counter-motion.

16

### 934. Figure IV. In the foreground.

*Demi-traversée à droite*, consisting of *coupé-tortillé, coupé-pas de basque, frappé-
ramassé* and *frappé-pirouette*.

4

The steps have already been explained in their respective places in this
Grammar; but the following repetition of the explanations is given that
the reader may more readily understand their application in this dance.
For that reason the *enchaînement* has been divided into twelve syllables,
in the same manner as previously employed.

1  *Coupé.* Put down left foot forcibly in posterior 5th position, and transfer.

2  *Tortillé.* Turn right foot inward upon the ball.

3  Turn right foot outward into anterior 5th position, and transfer.

4  *Coupé.* Put down left foot forcibly in posterior 5th ball position, and trans-
. fer, thus releasing right.

5  *Pas de basque.* Carry right to 2d position, and transfer.

Révérence au partèrre et sortie par des pas ballonnés

| SYLL. | | MEAS. |
|---|---|---|
| 6 | Carry left, by a circular movement, into anterior crossed 4-5 position, and transfer. | |
| 7 | *Frappé.* Stamp with right into 2d position, and transfer. | |
| 8 | *Ramassé.* Bend supporting right leg, and glide left foot into anterior 5th point position with corresponding bending of left leg, simultaneously bending the body and dipping the left arm to such a degree that it would be possible to pick up with the left hand a small object lying upon the floor. The movement receives its name from this bending, and the meaning of the word *ramasser* is to pick up. | |
| | The right arm is raised during this movement to a corresponding position in the opposite direction, and the eyes follow the movement of the left hand. | |
| 9 | Put down left and raise right heel, and straighten the body, commencing thereby the transfer of weight, which is completed upon syllable | |
| 10 | by a stamp in 2d position with the right foot. | |
| 11 | Raise right heel and execute a complete turn to right upon the toe, with left leg in three-quarters high flowing 2d position. | |
| 12 | Put down left foot in 2d position, and transfer. | |
| | *Retraversée* to left with same *enchaînement*, but in counter-motion. | 4 |
| | Repeat to right. | 4 |
| | Repeat to left to centre, but without *ramassé*. | 4 |

### THIRD COUPLET

**Figure I. Zig-Zag Backward (*Ballonné Rétrograde*).**

Same as third figure of first couplet.    16

**Figure II.** In the background upon the place.

Three *temps de ciseaux*, without hopping or turning, one *coupé* and one *pas de basque* to the right.    4

Repeat. — 4

*Pivoter* to left, with left arm raised and *pirouette basque* to left, as in the second figure of the first couplet. — 8

### Figure III.

Zig-Zag forward, with two successive *pirouettes*. *Enchaînement* of ten syllables.

| | |
|---|---|
| o | Hop preparatory to *pas ballonné*. |
| 1–4 | Move obliquely forward to the right half-way to centre, by one and a half *pas ballonnés*. |
| 5 | Complete turn upon right ball with left foot in balancing anterior 5th position with perpendicular sole. |
| 6 | Put down left into anterior 5th sole position, and transfer. |
| 7 | Stamp with right into 2d position, and transfer. |
| 8–9 | Repeat turning as in fifth and sixth syllables. |
| 10 | Stamp with right into 2d position, and transfer. |

Repeat *enchaînement* to left. — 4

Repeat figure. — 8

### 935. Figure IV. *Ramassé.* (Sixteen measures.)

Short zig-zag to rear with eight raising and picking up movements.

The phrase contains six syllables.

Execution :

Preparation : *Temps-levé* (this consists of a *fouetté* and a hop preparatory to the *pas ballonné*).

| | |
|---|---|
| 1 | Put down right foot in 2d position, and transfer. |
| 2 | *Ramassé* (already explained). |
| 3 | Put down left and raise right heel. |

| SYLL. | | MEAS. |
|---|---|---|
| 4 | Stamp with right into 2d position. | |
| 5 | *Temps fouetté-dessous.* Under crossed whip-syllable. (See § 487 *et seq.*) | |
| 6 | *Temps levé*, as used in the part-measure as preparation for *pas ballonné*. | |
| | This *enchainement* of six syllables is danced alternately eight times, and brings the dancer at its end into the centre of the background. | 16 |

### FOURTH COUPLET

**936.** Figure 1. *Grand Dégagé.*

Execution : Zig-zag forward to right and left, to a point slightly in front of the horizontal middle line of the stage.

The enchainment contains ten syllables.

| | | |
|---|---|---|
| 0 | Part-measure. Movement preparatory for *pas ballonné*. | |
| 1–4 | Move obliquely forward to right, half-way to centre, by means of one and a half *pas ballonnés*. | |
| 5–6 | Slowly execute one and a quarter turns upon the right toe, with left foot in high balancing 2d position. | |
| 7 | Put down left foot in anterior 4th position, raising the left arm and following its movement with the eyes. | |
| 8 | Transfer slowly and with dignity to left foot, at the same time bending the upper body, lowering the left and raising the right arm and bending the knees. | |
| 9 | Transfer, in like manner, to right foot. | |
| 10 | Raise again as in seventh syllable. | |
| | The dancer rests upon the eleventh syllable, and upon the twelfth executes again the movement preparatory to the repetition of the *enchainement* in the other direction. | 4 |

The music should be rendered *rallentando* from the fifth to the tenth syllable.   | MEAS.

These movements should all be executed in an easy, airy manner, with corresponding arm movements.

Repeat to the left forward to horizontal middle line.   4

Repeat to the right forward half way to front.   4

Repeat to left forward to a point slightly beyond the middle line of the front, kneeling slowly upon the left knee during the sixteenth measure, with right arm lowered and left arm raised, head slightly inclined forward, and eyes downcast.   4

### 937. Figure II. Transfer upon the Knees (*Dégagé à Genoux*).

During the first four measures, carry the right arm inside the right leg, by a *grand rond de bras*, which proceeds thence upward and through a raised position, returning again to a lowered attitude outside the right leg, accompanied by a similar but opposite movement of the left arm. During all this the eyes follow the movement of the right hand, while the head and body involuntarily coöperate.   4

During the fifth measure, carry the left arm into the crossed anterior horizontal position, and turn the upper body slightly to the left, following with the eyes the movement of the left hand, and rise slowly during the sixth measure, upon the right foot, at the same time continuing the raising of the body and the movements of the arms.

During the seventh measure, carry the right foot into 2d position, and transfer, and execute with the left a *jeté en tournant*, sinking in the eighth measure upon the right knee.   4

Repeat the entire *enchainement* in counter-motion to the eighth measure, in which the dancer, instead of kneeling as before, pauses during two syllables in anterior 5th position of right, once more executing upon the third syllable the movement preparatory to the *pas ballonné*.   8

### 938. Figure III. In the foreground.

One and a half *pas ballonnés* and two *pas élevés* to the right.   2

Deep curtesy to right, directed particularly to the occupants of the corresponding boxes, to whom the eyes are turned.   2

Repetition of *enchainement* to left.   4

Backward to centre by two and a half *pas ballonnés* in circular direction to right, followed by complete turn to right upon right toe, and low curtesy to centre to spectators.   8

CODA

The dancer concludes with one and a half *pas ballonnés* and several *pas élevés* to left. Exit left upon last syllable of music.

# Index

Unless marked "p." (signifying page) the numbers refer to the sections.

# Glossary

Most of the words in this Glossary are French; in cases where they belong to other languages they are indicated as follows: *Bo.*, Bohemian; *G.*, German; *It.*, Italian; *Lat.*, Latin; *Pol.*, Polish.

*à*, to, from, at, in.
*abaissé*, lowered.
*abaissement*, the act of lowering.
*abaisser*, to lower.
*accéléré*, accelerated, quickened.
*action*, action, motion.
*adagio* (It.), a slow movement of time.
*aile*, wing.
*air*, air.
*allée*, alley, passage.
*allegro* (It.), a rapid movement of time.
*aller*, to go, to walk.
*allonger*, to lengthen.
*alternatif, alternative*, alternate.
*alternativement*, alternately.
*ami*, friend.
*ancien*, ancient.
*anglaise*, English.
*aplomb*, self-command.
*approchent*, approach, draw near (plural).
*après*, after.
*arabesque*, an inclined attitude.
*arpeggio* (It.), the successive striking of the notes of a chord.
*arqué*, bowed, rounded, arched.
*arrière*, behind, backward.
*arrondi*, rounded.
*arsis*, up-beat in music.
*assemblé*, collected.
*assemblée*, assembly.
*assembler*, to collect, to bring together.
*attitude*, position, attitude.
*au*, to the.
*auf* (G.), up, at, in, by, for.

*autour*, around.
*autre*, other.
*aux*, to the.
*avançant*, advancing.
*avancer*, to advance, to go ahead, to move forward.
*avant*, forward.
*avec*, with.
*avoir*, to have.

*baissé*, put down, dropped.
*baisser*, to put down.
*balancé*, balanced, weighed; balance-step.
*balancer*, to balance, to weigh.
*balancez*, balance (imp.).
*ballonné*, inflated, swollen, distended.
*ballonner*, to inflate, to swell, to distend.
*balloté*, tossed.
*balloter*, to toss.
*basque*, Biscayan.
*battement*, beating.
*battre*, to beat or strike.
*battu, battue*, beaten.
*Begleitung* (G.), escort; accompaniment.
*bei* (G.), by, at, on, in, with.
*bestimmten* (G.), fixed, determined, settled.
*bipède*, bipedal, two-footed.
*boiteux*, limping, lame.
*bon*, good.
*bond*, bound, spring.
*bondir*, to bound, to spring.
*bondissant*, bounding, bouncing, springing.
*bottes*, boots.
*bourré*, stuffing.
*bourrée*, a stuffing step, a dance.

297

*bras*, arm.
*brisé*, broken.

*cæsura*, a strain, a portion of a melody.
*cadere* (Lat.), to fall.
*capriole*, a crossed jumping step.
*capriola* (It.), a prancing step.
*cavalier*, gentleman.
*ce, ces*, this, that, these, those.
*chaîne*, chain.
*changé*, changed, altered.
*changement*, the act of changing.
*chassé*, chasing step.
*chassent*, chase (plural).
*chasser*, to chase.
*chat*, cat.
*chevaux*, horses.
*chorégraphique*, choregraphic.
*chute*, an audible fall.
*cinq*, five.
*cinquième*, fifth.
*ciseaux*, scissors.
*classique*, classic.
*clausula*, a phrase.
*clef*, key, clef.
*clos*, closed.
*collo* (It.), neck.
*colonne*, column.
*comme*, as, like, how.
*commencée*, commenced, begun, started.
*commencement*, beginning, commencing.
*composée*, composite.
*conduire*, to conduct, to lead.
*contenant*, containing.
*continuer*, to continue.
*contraire*, contrary, opposite.
*contredanse*, contra-dance.
*contretemps*, contrary to time, unexpected.
*coquille*, shell.
*corps*, body.
*côté*, side.
*cou-de-pied*, the instep or ankle.
*coup*, a stroke or knock.
*coupé, coupée*, cut.
*couple*, two similar things.

*couplet*, a combination of figures.
*cour*, court.
*courant*, running.
*courante*, a dance.
*courbé*, curved, bent.
*course*, running.
*crevée*, split.
*crochet*, hook.
*croissé*, crossed, crossing.
*cuisse*, thigh.

*dactyl* (Lat.), a metric foot of two syllables.
*dame*, lady.
*danse*, dance.
*danser*, to dance.
*danseur*, male dancer.
*danseuse*, female dancer.
*de*, of, from, by, out of.
*des*, of the, from the (plural).
*dedans*, inward.
*dégagé*, disengaged.
*dégager*, to disengage, to transfer.
*dégagement*, disengagement, transfer.
*dehors*, outwards.
*del* (It.), of the.
*demi*, half.
*den* (G.), the, to the.
*der* (G.), the, that, which, who.
*descendant*, going down, descending.
*descendre*, to descend.
*desgleichen* (G.), the same.
*dessous*, behind, under.
*dessus*, in front, over.
*deux*, two.
*deuxième*, second.
*die* (G.), the, that, she, which.
*direction*, direction.
*dit*, said, called, named.
*dix*, ten.
*donnez*, give (imp.).
*dos-à-dos*, back to back.
*double*, double.
*droit*, right.

*écarté*, spread.

*échappé*, escaped.
*échapper*, to escape.
*Einleitung* (G.), introduction.
*élévation*, raising.
*élevé*, raised.
*élever*, to raise.
*emboîté*, fitted, boxed.
*en*, in, into, on, to, by, at.
*enchaînement*, step-combination.
*entier*, *entière*, entire, complete, whole.
*entièrement*, entirely, completely, wholly.
*entrechat*, a prancing step.
*envers*, reverse.
*épaules*, shoulders.
*épaulements*, shoulder-movements.
*équilibre*, equilibrium.
*espagnol*, Spanish.
*et*, and.
*étoile*, star.
*exercice*, exercise.

*fait*, makes.
*fausse*, false.
*fille*, daughter.
*fin*, end, conclusion.
*finale*, final.
*fixée*, fixed, determined.
*fleur*, flower, blossom.
*flore*, name of a mazurka-step.
*fois*, times.
*former*, to form.
*fouetté*, whipped.
*français*, French.
*frappé*, stamped, pounded.
*frapper*, to stamp, to pound.
*frotter*, to rub.
*führen* (G.), guide, conduct, lead.

*gauche*, left.
*générale*, general, usual, common.
*genoux*, knees.
*glissade*, gliding movement.
*glissant*, gliding.
*glissé*, glided.
*glissement*, gliding.

*glisser*, to glide.
*glissez*, glide (imp.).
*grâces*, graces.
*grand*, grand, large.
*grave*, grave, serious.
*guirlande*, garland, wreath.
*gyrus* (Lat.), a turn.

*hongroise*, Hungarian.
*huit*, eight.
*huitième*, eighth.

*iambi* (Lat.), metric feet of two syllables, one short and one long.
*il* (It.), the.
*immédiate*, immediate.
*inclinée*, inclined, tipped.
*intervalle*, interval.
*intrecciare* (It.), to weave or braid.
*intrecciata*, *intrecciate* (It.), woven or braided.
*introduction*, introduction.

*jambe*, leg.
*jarreté*, close-legged, knock-kneed.
*jet*, throw.
*jeté*, thrown.
*jeter*, to throw.
*jolie*, neat, pretty, nice, pleasing.
*jusque*, to, even, till, as far as.

*la*, the.
*latéral*, *latéreaux*, side, lateral
*latéralement*, sidewise.
*le*, the.
*legato*, connected, smooth.
*levé*, lifted.
*lever*, to lift.
*ligne*, line.
*links* (G.), left.
*lune*, moon.

*madame*, madam, a married woman.
*maestoso* (It.), majestic.
*main*, hand.
*mais*, but, why.

*mani* (It.), hands.
*manteau*, mantle, cloak.
*marche*, march.
*marquer*, to mark, to indicate, to trace.
*masur, masurek* (Pol.), Mazovian.
*matelot*, sailor.
*même*, same.
*menu*, small, neat, dainty.
*menuet*, minuet.
*mesure*, measure.
*milieu*, middle, centre.
*militaire*, military.
*minutus* (Lat.), small.
*moderne*, modern.
*monter*, to mount, to ascend, to go up.
*moulinet*, windlass.
*mouvement*, movement, motion.
*moyen*, medium, middle.

*oblique*, oblique, slanting, diagonal.
*opposée*, contrasting, opposing.
*ordinaire*, ordinary, common, usual.
*originale*, original, primitive, not copied.
*ou*, or, otherwise, else.
*ouvert*, open.
*ouvrez*, open (imp.).

*paire*, pair, two of a kind.
*par*, by, from, for, with, through, at.
*parade*, parade, show.
*parallèle*, parallel.
*parallèlement*, parallel.
*partie*, part.
*pas*, step.
*passage*, passage, going through.
*passant*, passing.
*passent*, pass (plural).
*petit*, small.
*phrase*, phrase.
*pied*, foot.
*piede* (It.), foot.
*pigeon*, pigeon, dove.
*piroetta* (It.), a turn upon one foot.
*pirouette*, a turn upon one foot.
*pistolet*, pigeon-wing step.

*place*, place.
*Platz* (G.), place.
*plié*, bended; bend of the knee.
*pliement*, bending.
*plier*, to bend.
*plus*, greater, more, also.
*pointe*, point, the tip of the foot.
*port*, carriage.
*porté*, carried.
*porter*, to carry.
*position*, position.
*pour*, for, in order to.
*poursuite*, pursuit.
*poussé*, pushed.
*précédentes*, preceding.
*prélude*, prelude, introduction.
*première*, first.
*presto* (It.), very quick.
*progressif*, advancing, progressing, going forward.
*promenade*, promenade.
*publique*, public.
*puis*, then, next, afterward, besides.

*quadrille*, quadrille, a square dance for four couples.
*quarré*, square, four-sided, quadrilateral.
*quart*, quarter, one-fourth.
*quatre*, four.
*quatrième*, fourth.
*queue*, tail.

*ramassé*, picking up.
*ramasser*, to pick up.
*rebours*, reverse, countermotion.
*rebroussale*, upward turned.
*rechts* (G.), to the right.
*reconduir*, reconduct, lead back.
*reculant*, retreating.
*redowatschka* (G.), redowaczka (Pol.).
*redresser*, to straighten.
*rejdovak* (Bo.), redowa.
*rejdovat* (Bo.), to push in zig-zag motion.
*relévation*, raising again.
*relevés*, reraised.
*renversée*, reversing.
*répété*, repeated.

*répétition*, repetition.
*reprise*, repetition, renewal.
*retour*, return.
*retourné*, returning.
*retraversée*, recrossing.
*rétrograde*, backward.
*révérence*, bow, courtesy.
*rhombe*, rhombus.
*rhythme*, rhythm.
*ritournelle*, signal, flourish, call.
*rivolta* (It.), turning again, an opposite turn.
*rôle*, character, part.
*ronde*, round, circle.
*roue*, wheel.
*rouette*, a small wheel.
*ruement*, kicking.
*ruer*, to kick.
*russe*, Russian.

*sa*, his, her, its.
*salle*, room, hall.
*salut*, salute.
*sauté*, jumped.
*sauter*, to jump.
*sauteuse*, jumping.
*sautillé*, hopped.
*sautillée*, a hop.
*sautiller*, to hop.
*Schluss* (G.), end, conclusion.
*Schlussbegleitung* (G.), conducting (one's partner) to seat at end of a dance.
*schräg* (G.), oblique, diagonal.
*Schrittsatz* (G.), step-sentence, enchainment.
*se*, himself, herself, itself.
*seconde*, second.
*semelle*, sole.
*séparée*, separated.
*sept*, seven.
*seul*, sole, only, alone, single.
*seize*, sixteen.
*signes*, signs, symbols.
*simple*, simple, single, pure.
*simultane*, simultaneous.
*sissonne*, a dance.
*six*, six.

*soldat*, soldier.
*solo* (It.), by or for one person.
*spalancare* (It.), to open wide.
*spondée*, a metric foot of two syllables.
*staccato*, short and distinct.
*suite*, succession, sequence.
*suive*, follows.
*sur*, upon.
*syncope*, syncopation.

*talon*, heel.
*tapé*, pounded, stamped.
*taper*, to stamp, to pound.
*tempi* (It.), time-syllables.
*tempo* (It.), time, speed.
*temps*, a dance-syllable.
*tenant*, holding.
*tendre*, to stretch.
*tendu*, stretched.
*tension*, stretching.
*tenu*, *tenue*, held, kept.
*termes*, terms, expressions.
*termine*, terminates, ends.
*terre-à-terre*, upon the ground.
*tête*, head.
*thésis*, down-beat in music.
*tire-bouchon*, cork-screw.
*tombé*, fallen.
*tomber*, to fall.
*ton*, tone, custom, style, taste.
*torse*, body, trunk.
*tortillé*, twisted.
*tortiller*, to twist.
*tournant*, turning.
*tourné*, turned.
*tourner*, to turn.
*tournure*, turn.
*tour*, turn, figure.
*tracer*, trace, mark, indicate.
*trait*, stroke, touch.
*traversé*, crossed.
*traversée*, crossing.
*tremblanté*, trembling, quivering, shaking.
*trillo* (It.), a quivering note.
*trio* (It.), the third part of a melody.

*triole*, a note divided into three parts.
*triple*, threefold.
*trois*, three.
*troisième*, third.
*tronc*, trunk.

*Uebergang* (G.), crossing over.
*um* (G.), in order to.
*un*, one.
*und* (G.), and.

*valse*, waltz.

*variation*, variation, difference.
*Verbeugungen* (G.), bows, reverences.
*vis-à-vis*, face to face, opposite.
*volta* (It.), turn.
*Vorspiel* (G.), prelude.
*vos*, your.
*votre*, your.

*wie* (G.), as, like.

*zéphire*, zephyr.
*zu* (G.), to, toward, at.

N